Chinese Criminal Trials

Ni He

Chinese Criminal Trials

A Comprehensive Empirical Inquiry

Springer

Ni He
School of Criminology and Criminal Justice
Northeastern University
Boston, MA
USA

ISBN 978-1-4939-4411-8 ISBN 978-1-4614-8205-5 (eBook)
DOI 10.1007/978-1-4614-8205-5
Springer New York Heidelberg Dordrecht London

Printed on acid-free paper

Springer is part of Springer Science+Business Media (www.springer.com)

For my loving family

Preface

Scholarly interests in Chinese law before the country's reopening to the world in the late 1970s have mostly focused on Imperial Chinese legal history (e.g., Bodde and Morris 1967; Ch'u 1961; Watt 1972) and the developing socialist legal system (e.g., Cohen 1968, 1970; Leng 1967). A burgeoning number of English writings with broader areas of focus have since emerged in the recent decades. Chinese legal tradition and legal system (e.g., Chen 2008, 1998; Clarke 2008; Head 2009; Hsu 2003; Jones 1994; Katz 2009; Liu 1998; Potter 2001, 2003; Woo and Gallagher 2011), criminal justice practice and reform (e.g., Biddulph 2007; Brown 1997; Hegel 2009, 2007; Leng 1985; Lo 1995; Lubman 1999; McConville 2012; Muhlhahn 2009; Shih 1999; Trevaskes 2007), human rights and rule of law (e.g., Diamant et al. 2005; Peerenboom 2002, 2010; Turner et al. 2000; Zou 2006) are some of the most popular themes.

These writings have successfully demonstrated the utility of historical, philosophical, and normative approaches to the study of Chinese law and legal practice. Cohen (1970) and Lubman (2003), two of the most respected legal scholars have well-articulated both the difficulties and rewards of studying Chinese law in action. Unfortunately (yet understandably), with the exceptions of McConville (2012) and Trevaskes (2007), very few recent studies have been able to place in-depth empirical investigations of the actual Chinese criminal justice practices at the center of attention. Access to the Chinese criminal justice field remains a major challenge, especially to non-native scholars. It seems that the discourse on the history, philosophy, and theory of criminal justice can be made more meaningful if it is combined with observations of the actual practices (see Clarke 2003). A key motivation for this study, therefore, is to build on the strength of the current field literature by taking a close look into Chinese criminal justice practices at the grassroots level with a particular focus on actual criminal trials. The original research which generated the bulk of empirical data used for this book is also an example of possible access to the Chinese criminal justice field.

Western impression of Chinese legal system in general and Chinese criminal justice practice in particular is marred by the socialist government's retarded progress in wholeheartedly endorsing the rule of law based on liberal-democratic principles. Reports by Western media on Chinese criminal trials tend to be selective, focusing mostly on highly sensitive cases where criminal defendants are often portrayed as victims of political witch-hunt. These Chinese criminal trials are seen (rightfully so) as an affront to the prevailing western model of due process and an embodiment of gross injustice. The Chinese government, on the other hand, defends its criminal justice practices by pointing to the positive progresses made and a seemingly effective legal system. There appears to be a miscommunication between the two sides due largely to the selective samples targeted for discussions. Western observers such as the media, the politicians, and the legal scholars alike, however, rarely had the exposure to the vast majority of the ordinary criminal trials in China.

This book seeks to fill this void by unveiling the mundane criminal cases tried by the lowest level courts in China. The choice of making criminal trials in grassroots courts, the focus of the study, is due mainly to the following considerations: first of all, the majority of all trials take place at grassroots level, in Basic People's Courts; second, the lower court's lack of visibility actually improves the feasibility for the completion of the study as designed[1]; and third, in China, the most significant innovations seem to come from lower courts (see Liebman 2007). Empirical data used in this study include unprecedented access to hundreds of criminal trial hearings, criminal case dossiers, and a comprehensive questionnaire survey of criminal justice practitioners from one large province located in China's southeast region. These data are also recent, collected from 2009 to 2011 with a generous research grant from the John D. and Catherine T. MacArthur Foundation.[2]

To advance our understanding of the routine criminal trials taking place in grassroots Chinese courts, we are deliberate in making our presentations contextual, relative, and relational. Although theory-testing is not the goal, Bourdieu's (1977, 1987) sociological concepts and perspective are used as the main catalyst to bridging the normative discussions with the actual Chinese criminal trial practices. We open the book with Part I which includes two chapters. Chapter 1 (*Chinese Legality*) and Chap. 2 (*Imperial Bureaucracy and Criminal Trials*) are introduced to provide a historical context to our current inquiry. Part II offers a socio-legal discourse on the contemporary *Chinese Criminal Trials*. Chapters 3 and 4 juxtapose tripartite rules (i.e., rule of man, rule by law and rule of law) to focus on the *modus operandi* of Chinese legal practice, connecting the present ideology with that of the past and comparing China's rule of law experience to that of the outside world.

[1] Cases tried at Basic People's Courts are by legal definition less serious and less sensitive. Obviously there is a trade-off in choosing between highly sensitive, well-publicized cases and less sensitive, little known local cases.

[2] The grant proposal submitted to the Foundation has legal representation and criminal processing as the main focus. Providing a benchmark for the current status of legal representation at grassroots level and potentially producing recommendations that would impact the most disadvantaged criminal defendants heavily influence the research design.

Part III includes four chapters. Chapter 5 describes the rationales, research design, and general observations of the MacArthur *Pilot Study* in China.[3] Chapter 6 explores the anatomy of Chinese criminal trials using court case dossier as a guide. The structures of the police, procuratorate, and court case dossiers and the inter-agency flow of case information reveal the internal logic of the Chinese criminal justice system. Chapter 7 begins with three cases studies to accentuate the relationship between law in the books and law in action. It goes on to illustrate why sentencing guidelines are needed and how they are actually applied in *Chinese Criminal Trials*. Chapter 7 closes with observations and reflections based on site visits to several Basic People's Courts, demonstrating the gap between the reality and the rhetoric of the rule of law. Chapter 8 attempts to make use of several Bourdieusian concepts in order to understand the contrasting perceptions of Chinese juridical practices held by three categories of survey respondents: the justice officials (a.k.a. the "iron triangle"-Judges, Procurators, and Police officers), Lawyers and other. Making sense of *Chinese Criminal Trials* is the goal for Chap. 9 which concludes the study.

This book is made more timely and comprehensive by incorporating other empirical evidences collected by native scholars in recent years. As a matter of fact, we make an effort to minimize the use of highly aggregated, government produced criminal justice data as much as possible.[4] We prioritize presentations of the first-hand data and, we focus more on explaining the current Chinese criminal trial process and less on speculating any determined future outcome. The rule of law dance is used as a metaphor to depict a delicate reality of the Chinese criminal justice system in a fast-changing and volatile social setting. Zooming in locally, *Chinese Criminal Trials* can be viewed as highlights of a rule of law dance that continues to transform into an uncertain future. Zooming out globally and historically, the Chinese legal system can be viewed as a real-time experiment putting to test the western-made rule of law "medicine" in a body of an ancient Chinese civilization inoculated with a heavy dose of socialist legality. The chapters that follow offer both the process and outcome evaluations (albeit limited in scope) of this experiment through a kaleidoscopic view of the grassroots *Chinese Criminal Trials* in action.

---

[3] Chapter 5 is based on an evaluative research design which was intended for targeted reforms and replication. The pilot is made necessarily modest and flexible in order to assure its successful implementation. The university-based international research cooperation could be considered a workable model in carrying out large-scale empirical research in the Chinese criminal justice field.

[4] He's (2014) book chapter on "The Politics of Numbers" provides justification for the skepticism and a cautious approach.

References

Biddulph, S. (2007). *Legal reform and administrative detention in China*. Cambridge: Cambridge University Press.

Bodde, D., & Morris, C. (1967). *Law in imperial China*. Cambridge, MA: Harvard University Press.

Bourdieu, P. (1977). *Outline of a theory of practice*. Cambridge, UK: Cambridge University Press.

Bourdieu, P. (1987). The force of law: Toward a sociology of the juridical field (translated by Richard Terdiman). *Hastings Law Journal, 38*, 805–853.

Brown, R. C. (1997). *Understanding chinese courts and legal process: Law with chinese characteristics*. Hague, The Netherlands: Kluwer Law International.

Chen, A. (1998). *An introduction to the legal system of the People's Republic of China*. Hong Kong, The Netherlands: Butterworths.

Chen, J. (2008). *Chinese law: Context and transformation*. Leiden: Martinus Nijhoff Publishers.

Ch'u, T. (1961). *Law and society in traditional China*. Paris: Mouton.

Clarke, D. (2003). Empirical research into the chinese judicial system. In E. Jensen & T. Heller (Eds.), *Beyond common knowledge: Empirical approaches to the rule of law*. Stanford: Stanford University Press.

Clarke, D. (Ed.). (2008). *China's legal system: New developments, new challenges*. (The China Quarterly Special Issues New Series 8). Cambridge, UK: Cambridge University Press.

Cohen, J. A. (1968). *The criminal process in the People's Republic of China, 1949–1963: An introduction*. Cambridge, MA: Harvard University Press.

Cohen, J. A. (Ed.). (1970). *Contemporary chinese law: Research problems and perspectives*. Cambridge, MA: Harvard University Press.

Diamant, N., Lubman, S. & O'Brien, K. (Eds.). (2005). *Engaging in law in China: State, society and possibilities of justice*. Stanford: Stanford University Press.

He, N. (2014). The politics of numbers: Crime statistics in China. Chapter 12. In L. Cao & I. Sun, & W. Hebenton, (Eds.), *The Routledge Handbook of Chinese Criminology* (pp. 147–159). New York: Routledge Publishers.

Head, J. W. (2009). *China's legal soul: The modern chinese legal identity in historical context*. Durham, NC: Carolina Academic Press.

Hegel, R. E., & Carlitz, K. (2007). *Writing and law in late imperial China: Crime, conflict, and judgment*. Seattle, WA: University of Washington Press.

Hegel, R. E. (2009). *True crimes in eighteenth-century China: Twenty case histories*. Seattle, WA: University of Washington Press.

Hsu, S. (2003). *Understanding China's legal system: Essays in honor of Jerome A. Cohen*. New York: New York University Press.

Jones, W. (1994). *The great qing code (trans.)*. New York: Oxford University Press.

Katz, P. R. (2009). *Divine justice: Religion and the development of chinese legal culture*. London and New York: Routledge.

Ladany, L. (1992). *Law and legality in China: The testament of a chinese-watcher*. Honolulu, Hawaii: University of Hawaii Press.

Leng, S.-C. (1967). *Justice in communist China*. Dobbs Ferry, NY: Oceana Books.

Leng, S. (1985). *Criminal justice in post-Mao China: Analysis and documents*. Albany: State University of New York Press.

Liang, B. (2008). *The changing chinese legal system, 1978–present: centralization of power and rationalization of the legal system*. New York: Routledge.

Liebman, B. L. (2007). China's courts: Restricted reform. *Columbia Journal of Asian Law, 21*, 2–44.

Liu, Y. (1998). *Origins of chinese law: Penal and administrative law in its early development*. Hong Kong: Oxford University Press.

Lo, C. W.-H. (1995). *China's legal awakening: Legal theory and criminal justice in Deng's era*. HK: Hong Kong University Press.

Lubman, S. B. (1999). *Bird in a cage: Legal reform in China after Mao*. Stanford, CA: Stanford University Press.

Lubman, S. (2003). The study of chinese law in the United States: Reflections on the past and concerns about the future. *Washington University Global Studies Law Review, 2*, 1–35.

McConville, M. (2012). *Criminal justice in China: An empirical inquiry*. Northampton: Edward Elgar Publishing Ltd.

Muhlhahn, K. (2009). *Criminal justice in China: A history*. Cambridge, MA: Harvard University Press.

Ocko, J. K. (1982). *Bureaucratic reform in provincial China: Ting Jih-chang in restoration Kiangsu, 1867–1870*. Cambridge, MA: Harvard University Press.

Peerenboom, R. (2002). *China's long march toward rule of law*. Cambridge, UK: Cambridge University Press.

Peerenboom, R. (Ed.). (2010). *Judicial independence in China: Lessons from global rule of law promotion*. Cambridge, UK: Cambridge University Press.

Potter, P. B. (2001). *The chinese legal system: Globalization and local legal culture*. London and New York: Routledge Curzon.

Potter, P.B. (2003). *From leninist discipline to socialist legalism: Peng Zhen on law and political authority in the PRC*. Stanford: Stanford University Press.

Shih, C.-Y. (1999). *Collective democracy: Political and legal reform in China*. Hong Kong: The Chinese University Press.

Trevaskes, S. (2007). *Courts and criminal justice in contemporary China*. Lanham, MD: Lexington Books.

Turner, K. G., Feinerman, J. V., & Guy, R. K. (Eds.). (2000). *The limits of the rule of law in China*. Settle, WA: University of Washington Press.

Watt, J. R. (1972). *The district magistrate in late imperial China*. New York: Columbia University Press.

Woo, M., & Gallagher, M. (Eds.). (2011). *Chinese justice: Civil dispute resolution in contemporary China*. New York: Cambridge University Press.

Zou, K. (2006). *China's legal reform: Towards the rule of law*. Leiden, The Netherlands: Martinus Nijhoff Publishers.

Acknowledgments

I am thankful to my colleagues in the School of Criminology and Criminal Justice (SCCJ) at Northeastern University for their continuous professional encouragement and support. Joining Northeastern faculty was the best career decision I have ever made. SCCJ Deans Jack Greene, Chester Britt, and Jack McDevitt showed remarkable foresight and provided critical support in the past decade, which resulted in a number of successful cross-national collaborations between SCCJ faculty and research partners from around the world. The empirical research presented in Chaps. 5–8 of this book is, in fact, based on the results of a 2-year U.S.-China joint pilot study funded by the John D. and Catherine T. MacArthur Foundation. This grant would not have been possible if not for the conducive research environment in the School and the collective efforts of a highly talented team: John Urban and Linda Powell (from Northeastern's Corporate and Foundation Advancement Office), Jack McDevitt and Lanying Li (Co-PIs of the pilot study), Matt White and Ronglan Hu (members of the U.S. research team) and numerous faculty and student research associates from team China. Mary Page and Barry Lowenkron at the MacArthur Foundation are truly a great joy to work with. I admire your decorated career achievements and inspiring visions. I treasure your warm personal encouragements. Needless to say, the opinions, findings, and conclusions expressed in this publication are those of the author's and do not necessarily reflect the views of the MacArthur Foundation.

I have always counted on the good cheers, friendship, and support from the following colleagues with Nebraska connections: Solomon Zhao, Ling Ren, Ineke Marshall, Finn Esbensen, and the late Denn Roncek. I would not be where I am now without your confidence and unyielding support. Peter Manning, a dear friend and delightful mentor at Northeastern, is my role-model as a scholar. Thank you for reading through the clumsy early draft of this book and for sharing your insightful, constructive comments. Thank you also for sharing with me the joy of conversation, reading, and writing. I could not possibly afford the tuition for what I have learned from you at a close distance.

Margaret Woo, Suzanne Ogden, Ira Belkin, Todd Foglesong, Chen Jie, Zuo Weimin, and Guo Zhiyuan, thank you for the stimulating conversations. I benefitted greatly from your expertise on Chinese culture, Chinese politics, and Chinese legal reforms. I am also very fortunate to have had the privilege to host several talented Chinese visiting scholars in the past 3 years: Zhang Xi, Yang Chunxi, Lu

Erqi, Fan Changchun, and Wang Jie. Thank you for taking the initiative to develop a Chinese Visiting Scholar Speaker Series at Northeastern. I have learned a great deal from your presentations.

Northeastern University Office of the Provost provided the sabbatical support which coincided with the last leg of the MacArthur grant project. This valuable time away from teaching has been crucial in not only completing the grant project but also jump-starting the book writing project. Last but not least, I wish to express my gratitude to Katie Chabalko, my editor. Thank you for your patience and understanding. It has been such a pleasure to work with you and the team from Springer.

Contents

Part I
Historical Context

Chapter 1
Chinese Legality

1.1 Introduction

There is no denial that "legality" can be a contested term. We operationalize the word *legality* in this book to embody law's rationale, spirit, and authority. In our view, law's rationale is minimally a philosophy about why law is made and, how law relates to other definitions of conduct norms. The spirit of the law necessarily reflects the essence of both the letters and the practices of law. Likewise, the authority of law is not only a display but also a perception. We explore the contents and genealogy of Chinese legality in order to better understand the realities and dilemmas confronting contemporary Chinese legal world. A discourse on legality placed in a fluid sociohistorical context is also a prerequisite to understand the evolution of the Chinese conception of justice and law in general and criminal justice in particular. The longevity of the so-called 'Chinese despotism' has enticed countless exercises from legal historians, philosophers, and other scholars. A widely accepted truism is that, for more than two millenniums, the Chinese imperial courts have stubbornly held on to a peculiar governing position juxtaposing the rule of *man* and the rule *by* law in maintaining social order. This is a legacy, although often taken for granted by the Chinese natives, which continues to bewilder and intrigue outside observers.

There is quite a lesson that could be learned from the evolution of Chinese legality. This exercise is particularly relevant today in light of China's rapid ascent to the ranks of powerful nations where democratic values unfamiliar to the Chinese hold sway. A fuller understanding will only emerge when this lesson is learned through both the Chinese and the non-Chinese perspectives. As one of the oldest surviving civilizations in the world, the Chinese are able to lay claims to many indigenous inventions; however, the concept of rule *of* law may not be one of them. As the twenty-first century unfolds, the native Chinese rule by law mentality and rule of man actuality and, the imported Western rule of law ideal leave colorful traces on an aging canvas that portrays both the spirit of the Chinese civilization and a renewed image of Chinese legality.

N. He, *Chinese Criminal Trials*, DOI: 10.1007/978-1-4614-8205-5_1,

This chapter provides a condensed sociohistorical context necessary for a better understanding of the contemporary legal practices in China. Sections that follow focus on China's long and winding journey toward modernization, the spirit of the Chinese in the light of Chinese civilization, the legacy of Chinese legality, the tradition of despotism, the multiple turning points in modern China, and the development of a socialist legality with Chinese characteristics.

1.2 From Antiquity to Modernity

Many influential Western thinkers have written about China from afar since the seventeenth century. Their writings have had a lasting impact on the outsiders conceptions (or misconceptions) of the Chinese way of life writ large. Although these earlier writers have used raw materials from the reports of the Jesuits missionaries traversing the ancient land of Middle Kingdom since the mid-sixteenth century, their impressions of China are interestingly polarized. At one end of the continuum, a reader could find Leibniz's glowing admiration of the rational social order of China (during the Kangxi reign from 1661 to 1722), the respect for law, the social stability, and the moral system (Cook and Rosemont 1994; Lach 1945). Voltaire (1759) compares the Chinese emperor (Qianlong) to a "philosopher-king," that elusive figure in Plato's utopia. Quesnay's (1767) infatuation for Chinese culture bestowed him the title—"Confucius of Europe." (Rothbard 2006) On the other side of the continuum, however, Montesquieu (1748) sees Asia the natural milieu of despotism and China a society best described as repressive, despotic, and superficial (Ladany 1992). Poet Tennyson, in *Locksley Hall*, a poem he wrote in 1835, pens the famous line "Better fifty years of Europe than a cycle of Cathay." In addition, Weber (1915/1951) ponders why capitalism did not develop in China through investigation of the Chinese religion and bureaucratic labyrinth.

Modernity stands out as a puzzling concept that the Chinese continue to grapple with today, as much as they did centuries earlier. Hegel (1820) once commented that China had stagnated in the eighteenth–nineteenth century because the Chinese were never interested in the kind of abstract knowledge (e.g., scientific theory and logic) passionately pursued by their Western contemporaries. It is a historical fact that China, although a "mature feudal system par excellence" since the Tang and Song dynasties, did not see the first trace of capitalism until the late Ming dynasty, almost two centuries later than the coastal cities of Italy, the Netherlands, and England (Fang 2000). There is no "rational depersonalization of business" and no legal forms and social foundations for capitalist enterprise comparable to its counterparts in Europe (Weber 1915/1951). Tennyson is not to be blamed for his rendition of Cathay that seems to be frozen in time. China indeed fell asleep while the Western world raced to modernity.

The Chinese Empire was finally awakened by its humiliating defeats in the Opium Wars (1839–1842) with the British and in the Sino-Japanese Wars (1884–1895). Modernity, "the holy grail of Chinese nation builder for well over a century," remains elusive to the most Chinese (Steinfeld 2010: p. 61). China's single-minded drive to pursue wealth and power in the twenty-first century necessitates a revisit of the key qualities (e.g., rational understanding of nature, individualism, human rights, democracy, and free market economy) that supposedly propelled the Western nations to the apex of power. The Western notion of rule of law embodies a modern legality, a part of the modernity that the Chinese fail to understand conceptually but are eager to embrace. There is no doubt that the ideas from the West have played an undeniable role in challenging and weakening traditional social orientations in countries like China. The Western liberal capitalism including its associated rule of law values are brought to non-European parts of the world by example (e.g., Japan which is never colonized) and by conquest (e.g., semi-colonized China and colonized India). The Chinese have always been known as more practical than theoretical. Learning from the West to ultimately defeat the West seemed to be a prevailing sentiment among the revolutionists at the turn of the twentieth century. A century has passed; however, one could still wonder whether the exact sentiment exists for the same reason among the Chinese reformers today.[1] The People's Republic of China has ushered in its 5th generation of Communist leadership (led by Xi Jinping) in the beginning of the second decade of the twenty-first century. The current rhetoric of restoring the country to the zenith of its most glorious past makes a fitting time to revisit the spirit of the Chinese.

1.3 The Spirit of the Chinese

The spirit of the Chinese is often an emotion arousing topic. Depending on the context and the role of the protagonist, this discussion invokes pride, nostalgia, contempt, ignominy, and bewilderment, sometimes all of them at once. The self-introspection on the spirit of the Chinese and the future of the nation assumes greater exigency among the patriots in the dying years of China's last imperial Dynasty. Young pupils in Chinese grade schools today are taught that the second half of the nineteenth century marked a time of darkness in Chinese history when their country was at the complete mercy of Western industrial-military aggressions, commercial exploits, and cultural invasion. They are told that the inept late Qing Government knew no better than to negotiate on its knees with the 'foreign devils,' signing one after another humiliating treaties, relinquishing both Chinese territories and national dignity. China's debilitating defeats in the hands of the Western powers have sparked a passionate national debate which continues to this day. The different perceptions of the true spirit of the Chinese as a people, a nation,

[1] This sentiment coexists with the perceived tendency of western scholars (particularly North American scholars) who find in China an "unfinished, failed or incomplete" modernity (see Jones 2011).

and a civilization are captured in three political currents: conservatism, radicalism, or a moderate third alternative.

To the nostalgic traditionalists, the spirit of the Chinese is the essence of the Chinese civilization, or "the Chinese type of humanity." Gu Hongming[2] (Gu 1915/1956) sees the spirit as the "inexpressible gentleness" in the mind, temper, and sentiment of the Chinese people that are distinctive from those of modern Europe and America. According to Gu, the Chinese spirit is "a spirit of perpetual youth," the spirit of "national immortality," and the secret of this immortality is the "happy union of soul with intellect." Gu views Confucianism China's "social religion" or "state religion." He argues that Confucianism has a universal "religious" appeal, to both the mass of the whole Chinese nation and to the learned. In contrast, he posits that philosophies from Plato, Aristotle, and Spencer are for the learned only. Moreover, Gu clarifies that a religion in the European sense of the word (e.g., Christianity, Buddhism, etc.) teaches man to be a good man but Confucianism teaches a man to be a dutiful son and a good citizen. Gu (1915/1956) grants the Confucius *Spring and Autumn Annals* the status of "*Magna Carta* of the Chinese nation" with the divine duty of loyalty as its prime principle. In his eyes, China qualifies as a civilized nation because it has a spiritual asset, that is, the realized Confucian ideals.[3]

Gu's nostalgic, ultra conservative view stands in sharp contrast to the impulse of his revolutionary contemporaries. To his critics, the image of the late Qing China is a body weakened by opium and a mind numbed by cultural values that cease to fit for the time. In Lu Xun's (1921) satirical and piercing "True Story of Ah Q" and "A Madman's Diary", the author sets out to expose cannibalism under the veneer of the virtue and morality extolled by the Confucian ethics. Ah Q, the fictitious simple-minded Chinese peasant who gets joked about, kicked around, and humiliated in every way possible (including condemnation to death by mistake), manages to be content with his own fateful demise. The Confucian values celebrated by Gu are deemed inappropriate, inadequate, if not the ultimate culprit of China's descent as a powerful nation. It appears that all but the relics like Gu understand the inevitable reality for China to reform in order to survive as a nation.

[2] Gu Hongming was born in Malaysia to a rubber plantation superintendent father and his Portuguese wife. Gu has received extensive Western educational training since the tender age of ten. He eventually earned multiple degrees, including a graduate degree in literature from the University of Edinburgh and a diploma in Civil Engineering from the University of Leipzig. He also studied law in Paris. Gu returned to China and served as an advisor for ranking officials in the late Qing imperial court for 20 years. His spirited defense of the Chinese traditional culture at the dawn of the twentieth century was intriguing given his western background and at a time of substantial change in Chinese history.

[3] Gu (1921) made what could be taken as a condescending comment in a New York Times article titled "Uncivilized United States" that at that time (ca. 1920s), the only real spiritual things which the Americans as a nation have done…, are "the work of Poe's *Annabel Lee*" and "the music of the plantation songs of the negroes in America." He views civilization as a state of mind and heart—a spiritual life. He would go on to end the article by calling America, Russia, and China the three great future empires of the world.

Gu's defense of an idealistic Chinese way of life neither reflects the reality at the time nor offers a viable solution for national salvation. Is Gu simply naïve or in denial? Is he Don Quixote reincarnated? Or, is everyone else simply wrong by abandoning the Confucius moral high ground that has stood the test of time to embrace an alien Western civilization with its maddening materialistic pursuits?[4] These are the questions that could still be asked and answered a century later.

Liang Qichao is among the earliest advocates for a nationalistic morality revolution.[5] Liang's (1902) major work (*Xin Min Shuo*, or *Discourse on the New Citizen*) draws both from the Darwinian law of the survival of the fittest (Pusey 1981) and from the "gladiatorial virtues" repudiated by Huxley's evolutionary ethics (Pusey 1983). Like Gu, Liang is proud of being a Chinese but torn between bitter condemnation of China's traditional system and deep love of his country (Ladny 1992). By writing his book (and editing a new journal), Liang is to offer a treatise on Chinese new citizenship and nation-rebuilding. The stance he took was contrarian and the languages he used appear to be contradictory in certain aspects. Liang (1902) urges the Chinese to not be "slaves of the ancients (*Confucian values*)" yet he wants them to be "slaves of their group (*Chinese new citizen/nation*)." He justifies that "if they are not slaves to their own group, they will assuredly become slaves to some other (*foreign powers*)."[6] (italics added) Liang also speaks of "freedom" and "slavery," and "democracy" and "enlightened dictatorship" in the same breath. Clearly, his mind is set in the context of China's humiliating defeats in the hands of the Western powers in the second half of the nineteenth century.

Liang is a nationalist and his solutions call for transcending Chinese culture from the individually focused "Little I" (Xiao Wo) to a group focused, altruistic "Great I" (Da Wo). Liang's revolutionary virtues are the antithesis of the spirit of the Chinese described by Gu. More specifically, struggle and self-assertion form

---

[4] The Chinese history could certainly attest to the resilience of Confucianism as a state religion —the source of ethics embraced by the state and enforced upon the Chinese people. This is true not only under Han emperors in large, unified empires such as Han, Tang, and Ming; it is also true in Yuan, Qing, and other dynasties under the alien rulers.

[5] Liang was to be remembered as a patriotic revolutionary of his time, while Gu was portrayed as the epitome of an ultraconservative. Gu would later become a English professor at Peking University. The queue and late Qing attire he wore to his lectures provided ample inspiration for the comics. Gu was fluent in English, German, French, and Chinese. Gu's writings in English were read broadly outside the country particularly in the first half of the twentieth century. Substantial domestic interest in Gu's work and in reevaluating his patriotism would reemerge in the first decade of the twenty-first century when the spirit of the Chinese becomes once again a highly relevant subject.

[6] By placing national dignity above individual dignity, Liang's philosophy for national salvation contradicts some of the prevailing Western assumptions on human rights, human dignity, and justice. For example, a life-defining group affiliation is seen as an "existential surrender" of individuality and individual rights, not an enlargement of the self (see Kateb 2011). And, rights and privileges obtained by the group do not necessarily trickle down to the individuals in the group (however, large or small that group is). This exemplifies why human rights should be contextualized and culturally relative (Sharma 2006).

the twin pillars of Liang's public morality. On private morality, Liang wants to convert the virtue of self-restraint (for the self) to that of self-sacrifice for the group and for the nation. Struggle runs contrary to the pacifist gentlemen's ethic advocated by the Confucians. Revolution, as understood by Liang, is to seek progress via destruction of the past. Such revolution is pointed directly at the heart of two Confucian values, i.e., loyalty and filial piety which are the very foundation of autocracy as defended by Gu. Liang's political view takes its own evolutional turns. After the collapse of the Qing Dynasty, Liang would renounce his prior support for a constitutional monarchy to become a founder of the Progressive Party, advocating nationalism with strong government and liberty through the rule of law (Tang 1996). Liang Qichao's early twentieth century morality revolution is replaced by Marxist revolutionary morality as a guiding principle in the ensuing communist movement that would fundamentally alter the course of Chinese history in the remainder of the twentieth century.

In addition to the boiling debates between revolutionists represented by Liang and traditionalists represented by Gu, a third alternative is gaining traction in the early 1920s. A group of Western-trained Chinese intellectuals begins to spread modern Western values and turn their attention to educate their compatriots to build China into a democratic nation modeled after the United States. This group quickly draws a loyal following among their own college students and the reform-minded citizens from major cities within the reach of their newspaper publications. While on sabbatical leave from his teaching post at Columbia University, John Dewey receives an invitation from his former students (some of them are among the most influential educators at the time, serving in positions such as college President or Provost) to visit China and give lectures. He would eventually spend much longer time in China than he had planned. Dewey has traveled widely across China from 1919 to 1921. His key lectures are transcribed by a former student-Hu Shi and published in Chinese with much fanfare. Dewey becomes a well-known and much respected public figure in China. He personifies the image of "Mr. Science" and "Mr. Democracy", slogans popular among liberal reformers at the time and as popular a century later.

Dewey's reform recipe for China includes three major ingredients: modern science, democracy, and education. Dewey and his students see schools and education as the foundation for rebuilding China (see Keenan 1977). They believe in the power of education in delivering the longest lasting social impact. Dewey preaches the same philosophies of pragmatism and experimentalism in China as he did in the U.S. He promotes democratic values, but advises the Chinese to try them out in education sector and in private industry first before applying them in politics and law. Dewey insists that pursuing science is essentially doing democracy. He argues that science unleashes human power to seek truth and to reduce ignorance. He urges the Chinese to utilize all the best elements of the industrialized West and adapt them to their native environment.

Like John Dewey, Bertrand Russell is also invited to lecture in China at around the same time (1920-1921). Unlike the American Professor who does not make explicit statement on the character of the Chinese, the British philosopher offers unusual observations on the subject in his book titled *The Problem of China* (i.e., Russell 1922). Describing this ancient foreign land upon his arrival, Russell sees a place full of "obvious evils: the beggars, the terrible poverty, the prevalence of disease, the anarchy and corruption in politics." He expresses tremendous amount of respect for the Western-educated Chinese elites such as Hu Shi whom he frequents. However, Russell reluctantly puts in writing that the shortcomings of the ordinary Chinese can be summarized in three words: "avarice, cowardice and callousness." He observes a strange phenomenon in China that "the spectacle of suffering does not of itself rouse any sympathetic pain in the average Chinaman; in fact, he seems to find it mildly agreeable."[7] In other words, Russell's observation correlates with the same quality described in Lu Xun's story of Ah Q.[8] Nevertheless, Russell is amazed by the Chinese "capacity for civilized enjoyment, for leisure and laughter, for pleasure in sunshine and philosophical discourses" as compensation to the prevailing social evils he just described. Interestingly Gu (1915/1956) who has made comments on the Chinese "insensibility to the physical discomforts" explains that "the real Chinaman lives so much a life of soul that he may be said sometimes to neglect more than he ought to do."

An interesting coincidence of time for Gu's (1915/1956) work on the *Spirit of the Chinese People* was the publication of Weber's (1915/1951) seminal work on *The Religion of China: Confucianism and Taoism*. Weber's work offers a systematic study of China's complex social structure and ethical value system. Weber explores in his book why China has failed to develop a rational bourgeois capitalism like those in the West. He finds that the Chinese lack a particular kind of religious ethic similar to the Protestant ethic found in Europe and North America as a much needed motivating force. According to Weber (1915/1951), "Confucian rationalism meant rational *adjustment* to the world; Puritan rationalism meant rational *mastery* of the world." (italics added) This is Weber's fundamental position in accounting for the failure of the Confucian ethic to initiate any drastic change of the socioeconomic order toward capitalism. It would be impossible to gauge how Gu and Liang would react to Weber's insight on the impact of Chinese non-theistic religion on modern capitalist development in China. What remained true is the fact that the profound industrial revolution occurred in Europe had propelled the Western civilization to "the summit of world power, wealth, and prestige." (Yang 1951: xiv) Yet, capitalism has remained embryonic in China for centuries.

Gu (1915/1956) and Weber (1915/1951) are certainly in no dispute on one point that Confucianism is an ethical doctrine, not a theistic religion. To answer his main research question on the impact of Chinese religion on capitalism, Weber delves

[7] Scholars suggest that the attitude of indifference toward violence is closely related to one's own experience (e.g., Evans 1996). In his book on Chinese criminal justice, Muhlhahn (2009) suggests that long-term exposure to war and revolution makes people more insensitive to the suffering of the others.

[8] Ah Q is unsympathetic to his own suffering and the pains of the others. The numbed, stupefied state of mind among the Chinese is what Lu Xun wants to awaken.

deeper into other Chinese cultural institutions and values. As a result, Weber is able to offer a good dose of sociological perspective linking Confucian ethos to the creation and operation of a powerful Chinese bureaucracy based on a unique Chinese conceptualization of legality.

1.4 The Legacy of Chinese Legality

The rationale, spirit, and authority of Chinese law (i.e., the Chinese legality) deserve a closer examination. As stated earlier, China has one of the world's longest lasting civilizations. When, why, and how law emerges in China, how it is enforced by the ruling class and how it is perceived and observed by the ruled are some of the most interesting and challenging questions. The path of the Chinese legality from antiquity to modernity cannot be understood unless one is willing to venture beyond a Eurocentric conceptualization of law, rule of law, and the legal system.[9] In addition, a comprehensive and historical review of the China legal tradition provides a benchmark for assessing the current legal reforms with both adoptions and adaptations of models inherited from China's own past and/or imported from the outside world. Some scholars suggest that the Chinese social norms in the half millennium prior to the long imperial period (since Qin Dynasty) can be best characterized as open and pluralistic. It is argued that this observation "liberates the theorists of today from the limiting ideologies of empire: fear of chaos, suppression of regional and individual difference and reliance on harsh top down control mechanisms," and "China now needs this kind of liberation." (Weld 2003).

History tells us that traditional social order in China has been maintained through various norms, including the positive (man-made) law (or *fa*). This set of pluralistic norms includes *dao* (the Way), *de* (moral precepts), *li* (rites), *fa* (law), and *xisu* (custom). Although different priorities are given to these norms throughout dynasties, most Chinese rulers have allowed the coexistence of these norms.[10] The classic Confucian view places these norms in a preferred hierarchy, with *dao* at the top, *fa* at the very bottom, and the other norms in between. The official acceptance of the Confucian hierarchy would also mean the acceptance of

---

[9] For example, Lubman (1999) refers only to "the Chinese legal institutions" but not "the Chinese legal system" throughout his book. The major causes of concern for him are the politicized nature of Chinese legal institutions and China's lack of unified concept of law. Lubman's "startling claim" (see Peerenboom 2002) that China does not even have a legal system is subtly criticized in Peerenboom's concluding chapter as Eurocentric and self-contradictory (i. e., Lubman advocates not to measure China using liberal democratic rule of law standards on the one hand, yet determines himself that China does not have a legal system with the implicit application of western standards).

[10] The exceptions are when the *Daoists* or the *Legalists* are in control of the imperial courts. They would advocate making either *dao* or *fa* as the sole norm.

the principle in resolving conflicts between the norms. In the event when a lower norm such as *fa* could not be clearly interpreted, higher norms such as *dao*, *de*, *li*, or *xisu* may all be applied to supplement the lower norm. A higher norm would always prevail (Chang 2000).

In the Confucian world, positive law is made by design less authoritative and less independent. A key Confucian argument is that *fa* (law) cannot be counted on to restrain its own creator without the other norms. The Confucians also find fault in the argument for the uniformity in the enforcement of law. The Confucians believe a uniform legal result is neither possible nor necessary. Judgment on any human acts (including criminal acts) requires far more criteria than those specified in the letter of law. Dispensing justice and maintaining social order thus demand the *rule of* (wise) *man* which embodies the true spirits of *dao*, *de*, *li*, *xisu*, and lastly, *fa*. In an idealistic Confucian world, pluralistic norms would coexist; the hierarchical order of these norms is clearly observed; and the society is ruled only by the selective group of highly educated gentlemen whose wisdom and integrity in absorbing and applying all the norms are never in doubt. The Confucians do not necessarily hold the letter of law in contempt, but the failure of all the higher norms in preventing crime and unethical behaviors that leads to the unfortunate use of law as a last resort.

Legalists who uphold a philosophy that emphasizes strict obedience to the law strongly object the Confucian premise based on the rule of (wise) man. Their opposition begins with a negative assumption of human nature that men are naturally evil and laws have to be made and administered to prevent evil. The Legalists' ideal government is ruled *by* laws that are applied equally to all but the Emperor. Legalists such as Shang Yang (390–338 BC) and Han Fei (280–233BC) advocate harsh punishment on light offenses and a sophisticated rule of the

Photo 1.1 Legalists

Photo 1.2 Babylonian

Photo 1.3 RomanLaw

government officials.[11] Only one dynasty (Qin) in Chinese history has made *Legalism* the sole norm of rule. It not only stroke a reign of terror against the

[11] Portraits of Shang Yang and Han Fei are carved in the stone wall of a Basic People's Court in J Province (see Photo 1.1). Images of Babylonian law and Roman law are also found (see Photos 1.2 and 1.3). The design idea came from the young court President whom the researchers met on a court visit trip (see Chap. 7 for other observations of his court). The Chinese legalists are placed on the east side wall, while the western legal inspirations are placed on the west side.

Confucianists who were buried alive en masse, but also ended a period of time in Chinese history that was most tolerant of different political philosophies. The succeeding Han dynasty (206BC–AD220), especially under the guidance of philosopher Dong Zhongshu (179–104BC), sees the formal installation of the so-called "Confucianization of law" which laid the foundation for the theoretical harmonization of Confucianism and Legalism throughout the remainder of the China's imperial history.

Chinese legal system under the imperial rule deserves a unique place in world history. It is clear that Confucianism has played the most significant role in the conception and development of the Chinese legality. The law's empire in China is designed to be limited. Its dependence on the other sociocultural norms is to be expected. The Confucian aversion of law's premise and the brutal rule *by* law campaigns waged by the Legalists in China's first imperial dynasty (Qin) creates a legacy that leaves a genuine distaste and fear of law in the hearts and minds of the Chinese people for more than 2,000 years.

Although in general the Confucians and the Legalists are able to coexist peacefully with each other for a millennium, the dominance of the classic Confucianism is to be challenged as a singular, uniformed orthodoxy. The neo-Confucian idealist represented by Zhu Xi would face off with a fierce utilitarian opponent represented by Chen Liang. The debate between them symbolizes what Tillman (1982) calls the two dominant trends within Chinese thoughts: "ethics of absolute ends or personal virtue" and "ethics of social orientations or end results." The context for the debate between the two is particularly important since history tends to repeat itself. Barely half a century earlier at the time, China was experiencing a renaissance of Confucian studies, yet the revival of classics would quickly fade away at the beginning of the twelfth century. The foreign military invasion and the humiliation of the Song dynasty (960–1279) suffered in the hands of the Jurchen (or 女真族) "barbarians" put the whole Chinese nation in crisis.[12] Fueled by the indignation of the lost territory and national pride, Chen Liang faults the stagnant, dogmatic, and inflexible teaching of the classic Confucians. In Zhu Xi's view, Chen is dangerously deviating from the timeless integrity and absolute values of Confucianism. Chen's relativism in values and standards is deemed utilitarian, materialistic, and nationalistic. This is because Chen would want nothing less than the permanent expulsion of all foreign barbarians from China. He would want the ruling class to adopt any political values, ethics, and rules, as long as the end goal can be achieved, that is, to keep the Chinese blood and culture pure from alien contamination (Tillman 1982). To his opponent, Chen's utilitarian rhetoric is a simple-minded reaction to events bound by one time and one place in history. To Zhu Xi, the loss of the metaphysical idealism embodied in the Confucian pursuit of the ethics of absolute ends or personal virtue is a loss of greater

[12] Pye (1968/1992: pp. 50–66) gives an intriguing discussion on the so-called "Middle Kingdom complex" which could explain the thin line between national pride and racial arrogance. Chinese Emperors consider all foreigners as barbarians.

magnitude.[13] Whether the ruling class embraces Confucian dogmatism or pragmatism is largely influenced by one man on the top—the Emperor. A brief overview of Chinese despotism and despots is in order.

1.5 Despotism and Despots

One of the first Western impressions of the Chinese empire is that of *despotism*. Although Oriental despotism as an original concept is used as early as Aristotle's time, no evidence suggests that the Chinese civilization is referred to at the time.[14] Nonetheless, some of Aristotle's arguments do resonate with the observations of the Chinese society. For example, Aristotle argues that the rule of oriental despotism relies on consent, not on force. This is a point not inconsistent with the teaching of the Confucius. Despotism is not always a negative term. Francois Quesnay's (1767) book on *The Despotism of China* presents a rather positive example of Oriental despotism. He suggests that it is possible that a well-ordered government could be run by a strong central authority headed by the Emperor (the despot) who embodies the image of *virtuous despotism* (Minuti 2012).

Recall earlier discussion on Gu (1915/1956) who makes a passionate plea for the revival of Confucian's ethics. Gu cites in his writing a passage from Thomas Carlyle (1841) that "in kings and in all human authorities and relations that men god created can form among each other, there is verily either a divine right or else a diabolic wrong." Gu goes on to argue that the teachings of Confucius may be summed up in one word: the law of gentlemen. The Confucius gentlemen are the best complement of a sage ruler—the "philosopher-king" Plato dreamed about and the real example found by Voltaire in Emperor Qianlong. The rule of gentlemen also fits nicely as an ingredient in Quesnay's *virtuous despotism*. Gu, however, leaves out an important passage from the same writing by Carlyle which states that, "there is no act more moral between men than that of rule and obedience. Woe to him that claims obedience when it is not due; woe to him that refuses it when it is."

Gu's faithful interpretation of the Confucian ethics makes the divine duty of loyalty to the despot a Code of Honor. The Confucius teachings bind the whole of Chinese and their nation to be *absolutely* loyal to the Emperor, whether or not this despot is virtuous or evil, and whether or not such obedience is due (emphasis added).[15] The cult of "hero" (be it Confucius or a Chinese despot) worship would

[13] A similar contrast has been drawn between the communist ideal (where all laws shall cease to exist) and the (bourgeois) rule of law (where law is omnipresent) immediately after the establishment of former Soviet Union and the People's Republic of China in the twentieth century.

[14] Aristotle's "oriental despotism" and the "peoples of Asia" are likely to be limited to the reference of Persia which was conquered by his student Alexander the Great.

[15] According to the writings of Mencius, a key Confucian figure after Confucius, deposing an evil ruler (in which case a mere villain) is justified on the ground of upholding the *dao*. In other

surely come in direct conflict with Aristotle's ideal that the will of law must be above the will of any man. The Chinese Legalists would come close to endorse the Aristotle's conception of law as the supreme rule. It would be a serious mistake, however, if one confuses Chinese rule *by* law with the Western notion of rule *of* law.[16] The Chinese Legalists have never gone as far as subjecting the Chinese despot to the law he creates himself. Contemporary legal scholars (e.g., Turner 2000) use "political realism" to describe the Chinese legalists, in contrast to "humanism" associated with the Confucians. A middle ground between the two is perhaps a better description of the reality of Chinese imperial rule. Paradigms of Chinese law and legality would continue to shift in modern time. The post-imperial Chinese society faces an onslaught of ideologies old and new, domestic and foreign. The trajectory of Chinese legality would prove to be the most tumultuous in the twentieth century.

1.6 Turning Points in Modern China

Chinese law is in a league of its own, judging by its longevity, stability, and effectiveness. Legal scholars have long argued that stability is the character of the Chinese legal system in the imperial period, from Qin (221–206 BC) to Qing (1644–1912) dynasties. The legacy of Chinese traditional law can be summarized in major aspects that: law is used as a political tool to maintain social order and social stability; law is administered through administrative bureaucracy; and law is a secondary tool for regulating state affair, after the guidance of Confucianism as the state orthodoxy (Chen 2008). The modern period that covers from the turn of the twentieth century to the current time can be characterized as "fluid" (Head 2009) and deserves closer examination. The major ideological turning points in modern Chinese legal history are highlighted below.

Constitutional democracy is a novel idea to a traditional Confucian society that places authority over liberty, kinship responsibilities over individual rights, and hierarchy over equality. Some (e.g., Keenan 1971) argue that *only* Western cultures (particularly those of the northwestern Europe) provide a suitable setting for developing constitutional democracy. In contrast to the *Oriental despotism*, either in the form of Confucianism or Islam, Western civilization is said to be most distinguishable with two traditions: Renaissance and Reformation. Renaissance lays the foundation for the modern concept of universal human right. Reformation gives birth to Western constitutional democracy, a fruit of labor from the struggles for toleration of political dissent. Western constitutionalism represented especially

(Footnote 15 continued)
words, a ruler is to be obeyed as long as he remains a benevolent leader who attends to the needs of the ruled.

[16] The two concepts (rule by law, *fazhi* and rule of law, also *fazhi*), although written differently, are pronounced identically in Chinese pinyin.

by the so-called "constitutional constellation" of Britain, France, and (to a lesser degree) the United States espouse liberal constitutional democracy, the rule of law, and recognition of individual rights throughout the world (Billias 2009). The wave of "Europeanization of the World" (Headley 2007) would eventually reach China.

In 1912, the Republic of China, the post-Qing Government headed by Sun Yat-sen, made the first attempt to implement a Provisional Constitution inspired by the American model (Billias 2009).[17] Lincoln's words come alive in Sun's *Three Principles of the People*: China shall be a democratic republic *of* the people, (to be governed) *by* the people and *for* the people. For the first time in history, the Chinese government proclaims popular sovereignty as a hallmark of its legitimacy (Clarke 2003), putting to an end of its multimillennium tradition of despotism.

The Westernization of Chinese law has already begun in the final years of Qing. Japan has been regarded as the most suitable model for China to emulate. The Japanese legal system has borrowed heavily from the Continental Europe, especially from Germany. After the overthrow of the Qing Dynasty, the Republican government continued the use of the Qing laws until what known to be the "Six Codes" (i.e., Constitution, Criminal Law, Criminal Procedure Law, Civil Law, Civil Procedure Law, and Administrative Law) of the Republic were established (under the authoritarian rule of Nationalist Party, or KMT). It is understood that although the Chinese government borrows languages from the foreign legal codes, it does not necessarily share the underlying values of these law. Chinese law treats family, clan, and society as basic units of its legal protection (Chen 2008). In other words, individual rights are protected vicariously through the protection of the safety and stability of the society. This is a culture heritage consistent with the traditional Confucian values, an advantage rather than a disadvantage in the eyes of Chinese legislators.

There is a complicated history featuring paralleled development of multiple legal systems in China from the early 1920s to 1949, before the People's Republic of China under the Communist rule was formally established. Discussions on the pre-1949 communist revolution and communist justice are particularly important in order for us to understand the socialist legality we face today. At the turn of the twentieth century, Chinese intellectuals are influenced simultaneously by ideologies featuring both the Russian communist revolution and the Western liberalism. The two major political parties in Chinese, the Nationalist and the Communist, formed a united front in 1923–1927 under the rubric of Leninist ideology. After the breakup of the united front, the Chinese Communist Party would establish in Jiangxi Province a Chinese Soviet Republic and marks the beginning of revolutionary justice featuring ruthless violence and terror against the counter-revolutionaries.

[17] Billias's (2009) conceptualization of *American Constitutionalism* is much broader than that of the other scholars. He includes not only the U.S. Constitution, but also the Declaration of Independence, the first state constitutions, the Articles of Confederation, the Federalist, and the Bill of rights.

Japanese invasion in 1937 would force the second united front between the Communist and the Nationalist. This time, the KMT government laws are adopted in the Shan-Gan-Ning Border Area controlled by the Communist.[18] Greater protection of private property, human rights, and political freedom were afforded to all people who opposed the Japanese invasion. The united front would break up again after the victory over the Japanese. The so-called "people's justice" would become the norm ruling all areas under the Communist's control. People's justice is politicized justice based on Marxist concept of law as an instrument of people's dictatorship. People's justice is also popularized justice following a "mass line".[19] It is dispensed following a class line separating the people and the enemy. Public trials are held for both public education and indoctrination purposes. Extralegal measures and extra-juridical organizations are routinely used. People's justice is revolutionary justice that bears no resemblance from Western liberal legal doctrine or Chinese historical legal tradition.

Shortly after the establishment of the People's Republic of China, the KMT legal system and its Six Codes were completely abolished, creating a legal (but not a social) vacuum that would not be filled until several years later.[20] Even after the adoption of the Soviet inspired 1954 Constitution, the Chinese Communist legality did not change substantially from the spirit of revolutionary justice seen in the earlier years. After 1957, Mao's theory of uninterrupted revolution was expressed as 'politics takes command' and that negated the value of law. Eventually, he came to declare: law is useless. Such legal nihilism emphasized struggle and conflict instead of cooperation and harmony (Lo 1995). During the Cultural Revolution (1966–1976), the fledging Chinese legal system and all laws would be destroyed completely. Personal pronouncements and party policies replaced law. It is fair to say that there was no law or legal system under Mao's leadership from 1949–1976 (Chen 2008). The next turning point in Chinese legal history did not arrive until 1978 when Deng Xiaoping took leadership.

1.7 Socialist Legality with Chinese Characteristics

The originality of Socialist law lies in its revolutionary nature, in which a socialist order and collectivized economic structure are expected to be formed under the guidance of the Communist Party (David and Brierley 1985). A few key characteristics stand in stark contrast to the Western liberal democracy-based legality. First, the division of labor within a socialist legal system is based on the so-called

---

[18] Shan-Gan-Ning Border Area with Yan'an as its capital resulted from the Second United Front between the CCP and the KMT in 1937. It is carved out of three adjacent provinces: Shaanxi, Gansu, and Ningxia in north-central China.

[19] Party cadres and their work should come "From the People; Back to the People" (or).

[20] It can be argued that in everyday life Confucian ethics remained as the basis for social order.

'democratic centralism," which means that all administrative, judicial, and procuratorial agencies are created by and responsible for the People's Congress at a corresponding level. The People's Congress is the legislative body which is tightly controlled by the Communist Party. Second, State ownership of land is another major element of socialist law. In other words, individuals can lease and transfer the usage but not the ownership of the land.[21] Third, socialist law places far greater emphasis on achieving a collective society and upholding socialist morality than on protecting individual rights. Fourth, the guardianship of socialist legality rests with the People's Procuratorate which serves both the prosecution function and the function of an Ombudsman's office. The supervisory function of the People's Procuratorate is most visible in the field of criminal justice (which we will elaborate in later chapters). Finally, major law-making in a socialist country generally begins with the ruling Party's inner circle, with laws proposed and approved by the Party leadership first before being subject to symbolic scrutiny and approval by the legislative body-the People's Congress. Unlike the typical constitutional design based on the concept of separation of power in the liberal West, there is no de facto, constitutionally stipulated constraint of the ruling Communist Party.

Within the discussion about socialist legality, Chinese politicians and scholars have also begun to publish views on the meaning of the term rule by law. In the West, democracy is often linked to the rule of law; but the Chinese government always refers to democracy in association with rule by law. However, since the 1990s, Chinese scholars have shown a growing interest in discussing the meaning of the rule of law (Shih 1999).

The socialist legality with the Chinese character literature is found to have focused on three central themes. The first of which is ideological in nature that, law is seen as the reification of class willpower and it reflects the dominance of the ruling class over the ruled. This is to be accomplished via both dictatorship and democracy, i.e., dictatorship is used to strike the bourgeois enemy; democracy is to be used to resolve internal contradictions among the people. The second theme of discussion focuses on the practical nature of the socialist legality, which is to use law to release the maximum creativity and power of productive force. The third theme, which takes greater importance in the recent decades, is the definition of China's current socialist status as being in the "primary stage".[22] The dilemma lies in the ruling Party's attempt to balancing the need to emancipate the socialist productive force on the one hand, while being keenly mindful of the international

---

[21] In Amendment one to the Chinese Constitution approved on April 12, 1998 (at the 1st Session of the 7th NPC meeting), the sentence which states "The right to the use of land may be transferred according to law" was added to the fourth paragraph of Article 10 of the Constitution.

[22] Approved at the 1st Session of the 8th NPC meeting on March 29, 1993, specific revisions (in italics) were made in the seventh paragraph of the Preamble of the Constitution: 1) "*China is at the primary stage of socialism*" was added to the beginning of the paragraph; and 2) two new words were added so the conclusion of this paragraph reads "…step by step to turn China into a socialist country with *prosperity and power*, democracy and culture".

antagonistic forces to subvert the Chinese socialist system on the other.[23] Stability and flexibility are two key terms in concept and in practice. The twin purposes are expected to be achieved through the combination of rule by law and rule of man—the millennial and battle-tested formula.

Deng Xiaoping's attitude toward law is pragmatic. Having suffered bitterly himself under the despotic rule of Mao, Deng understands the necessity of incorporating certain amount of democracy into his conception of law. Deng insists on finding a Chinese path in the development of Chinese socialist legality. Four Cardinal Principles, namely the socialist road, the dictatorship of the proletariat, the leadership of the Party, and Marxism–Leninism and Mao Zedong Thought crystallize this thinking and were adopted in 1979 (Lo 1995). In 2004, the Fourth Amendment of Chinese Constitution was added to incorporate additional principles laid out by post-Mao Chinese leaders. It reads "...along the road of Chinese-style socialism..." and "...under the guidance of Marxism-Leninism, Mao Zedong Thought, Deng Xiaoping Theory and the important thought of Three Represents."[24]

With the tattered image of the country from the lawless decade of Culture Revolution still lingers in the rear view mirror, the Post-Mao Chinese Communist Party leadership waged a political campaign aimed at achieving a society ruled by law. As stated earlier, the linguistic confusion between rule by law and rule of law remains unnoticed and unclarified until later. Rule by law campaign was widely accepted by the Chinese populace, including the intellectuals as at least a step forward in the opposite direction of anarchical period of the Culture Revolution (1966–1976). The campaign is to serve three major goals: to shift from class struggle to economic development[25]; to translate the Party policy in the form of legal language for uniform implementation nationwide; and to create an orderly society to assure economic modernization. Lichtenstein (2003) observes that legal reform and economic reform in China are mutually dependent, intertwined strands,

---

[23] Constitutional Amendment two approved on March 29, 1993 includes the following sentence "The state has put into practice a socialist market economy. The State strengthens formulating economic laws, improves macro adjustment and control and forbids according to law any units or individuals from interfering with the social economic order." This Constitutional Amendment sets the tone for the strict enforcement of Chap. 3, Part II of the Chinese Criminal Law with specific regard to punishing Crimes of Disrupting the Order of Socialist Market Economy." We will elaborate on the practice with criminal case examples in later chapters.

[24] "Three represents": the CCP should be representative to advanced social productive forces, advanced culture, and the interests of the overwhelming majority. They are credited to CCP General Secretary Jiang Zemin and they have become the guiding ideology of the Party since its 16th Party Congress in 2002.

[25] The word "counter-revolutionary activities" originally included in Article 28 of the Chinese Constitution was dropped with the adoption of the Third Amendment on March 15 at the 9th NPC meeting. Article 28 now reads "The State maintains public order and suppresses treasonable and *other criminal activities that endanger State security*; it penalizes actions that endanger public security and disrupt the socialist economy and other criminal activities, and punishes and reforms criminals." (replacement language in italics).

not parallel, independent tracks. Law has played an important role in China's recent economic development and vice versa. The unusual modalities used to reform the legal framework for State enterprises show how creatively China has adapted legal substance and process to the needs of economic reform. Not only have China's economic reforms made rule of law a necessity; in a symbiotic relationship, economic reform is essential to make rule of law a reality. However, there is no genuine desire from the Party to promote the true Western rule of law values, i.e., to use law to restraint government power and ensure procedural justice. In fact, all attempts to advance democracy and legalism to limit the power of CCP are met with swift and brutal force from the central government (Shen 2000).

China's reluctance in embracing the Western style of legality is due both to the nature of socialist ideology and the indigenous legal tradition. Because Party policy is the soul of the socialist law and law is viewed a mere instrument for political goals, lower-ranking officials in China have no respect for the law. They are more policy brokers than law enforcers (Shen 2000). Just like any despot in the Imperial China, the CCP, the reincarnated modern version of a despot, remains above the law. The despot's domination depends on charisma. He does so by making an appearance through (the rule by) law that would actually advance his own authority more so than the interest of the general public he rules. Once again, the public's interest is expressed collectively, achievable only vicariously through a collective stable social order. This "patrimonial" political structure rule has been discussed by Weber (1915/1951) in his work on Chinese religion. A verdict has long been reached that under such patrimonial rule, law will be unable to achieve its formal rationality because the real (and only) goal for the law is to advance the charismatic authority of the ruler, the despot. The despotic rule has stubbornly survived through all the glorious and inglorious episodes in Chinese history. Whenever foreign ideas are introduced, the Chinese has appeared to be more willing to accept the provisions and concepts of the foreign imports than their values and underlying principles (Head 2009).[26] Other China specialists also noticed that legal reform in China today has been complicated by issues of political reform and by ambivalence about the introduction of ideals of governance associated with the West (Potter 2001).

Optimistic observers (e.g., Lo 1995) suggest that China has entered an age characterized by the rule of law. A highly institutionalized legal system has been built up which functions on the basis of socialist legality. The Communist regime has undergone a legal awakening in which both Party leadership and popular masses have seen that the rule of law is a sound alternative to the former disastrous rule of man. To explore more fully the socialist legality with Chinese characteristics, researchers focus on four key themes. One of them relates to the continuity of the Chinese legal tradition. The second theme revolves around the reaction of

[26] For example, given the mounting international and domestic pressure, the Fourth Amendment of Chinese Constitution was adopted at the 10th National People's Congress meeting (March 14, 2004) with a symbolic, declarative sentence added to the third paragraph in Article 33, stating that "The State respects and preserves human rights".

China to foreign legal influences. The third concerns rule of law in China. The fourth involves in the examination of the modern Chinese legal identity. In his conclusion, Head (2009) suggests that the modern Chinese legal identity revolves around a materialist-oriented, legitimate, extroverted, China-appropriate, restorative progressivism. This characterization seems to be a far cry from an integrated system of legal ideology rooted in Confucianism.

Chinese scholars seem to be more skeptical of true foreign influences on Chinese legality. They argue that neither the democratic revolution of 1911 (which established the Republic of China) nor the communist revolution of 1949 (which established the People's Republic of China) has seriously challenged the modality of Chinese traditional rule of governance. The Chinese government today continues to place great emphasis on Confucian principles of moral order, collective responsibility, and harmonious society (e.g., Chang 1984; Lin 1998). While it is possible that the government's rhetoric may appear to have been influenced by foreign ideologies (Marxist or non-Marxist), some argue that the essence of social behavior remains traditional and Confucian (see Hall 1995). Furthermore, research that focuses on the interplays of foreign legal norms and local legal culture in China suggests that the Chinese legal institutions reflect much about the process of selective adaptation and that "the notion of popular sovereignty that informs liberal legal institutions and the accompanying norms restraining state action is largely absent in Chinese tradition." (Potter 2001: 2) Chinese legal culture has always drawn upon a reservoir of tradition derived from Confucianism and its assumptions of authority and hierarchy in social organization.

For example, Mao's theory of revolution and law was based on a philosophy of struggle deeply affected by Marx's and Lenin's revolutionary theory. The state apparatus, which includes the army, the police, and the courts, is the instrument by which one class oppresses another. It is an instrument for the oppression of antagonistic classes; it is violence and not "benevolence". If western rule of law is described as to emphasize on the power-balancing mechanism and the prevention of violence, the socialist rule of law is more appropriately expressed as stressing on harmony and consultation (Shih 1999).

In sum, the fundamental doctrine-the socialist legality or the socialist rule of law with Chinese characteristics-which is officially advocated, is not equivalent to the Western concept of the rule of law, but simply implies broad adherence to the law while being able to act beyond the formal and detailed legislative provisions (Potter 1994). Critics (e.g., Yin and Duff 2010) argue that socialist legality is likely to prevail in a foreseeable future in the field of criminal procedure and elsewhere in the Chinese legal system as long as it continues to be deemed necessary by the political authority.

1.8 Conclusion

With criminal trial practices in the lowest level Chinese court the main focus of this book, we set out in this chapter to first introduce the key elements of Chinese legality, which we define as the rationale, spirit, and authority of the Chinese law. China's multimillennial history of despotic rule and China's rude-awakening exposure to the values underwriting the rise of Western powers in modern history concocted a strange mix of Chinese sentiment toward political and legal reforms. It is under this context that we initiated discussions on China's legality with rule by man mentality, rule by law actuality, and rule of law inspiration (and to some, illusion). These discussions are further complicated by the historical fact that China chose to deviate both from its authentic cultural heritage dominated by Confucian and neo-Confucian values and from the prevailing liberal democratic values exemplified by the Western powers at the turn of the twentieth century.

China's radical socialist revolution based on a Marxist ideology with a unique Chinese interpretation, aims to bring ruins to both the feudal (i.e., to bury the decadent Confucian ethics which was blamed for China's stagnation and defeat in modern time) and the bourgeois (i.e., to crush the imperialistic-colonial aggression and to unclothe the liberal-capitalist hypocrisy which brought indignation to the Chinese nation). The Marxist revolution thus delivers a utopia that promises to end decades of warfare and countless human tragedies that would constitute the national image of much of the tumultuous century.

The evolving and contextualized Chinese legality illustrated in this chapter, we hope, would delineate the character of Chinese legal system and enliven the spirit of Chinese legal practices. The next chapter exemplifies the imperial Chinese criminal trial practices in a uniquely Chinese administrative-judicial bureaucracy. Bringing together the legacies of Chinese legality and the imperial bureaucracy demystifies the lineage of contemporary legal practices to be discussed throughout this book.

References

Billias, G. A. (2009). *American Constitutionalism Heard Round the World, 1776–1989: A global perspective*. New York: New York University Press.

Carlyle, T. (1841). Hero-worship, and the heroic in history. London: James Fraser, Regent Street.

Chang, D. W. (1984). Government and crime control in China: Its relevance to U.S criminal justice. *Police Studies,7*, 94–111.

Chang, W. (2000). Foreword (pp. vii-xii), in Turner, K, Feinerman, J. V. & Guy, R. K. (eds.). *The limits of the Rule of Law in China*. Seattle: University of Washington Press.

Chen, J. (2008). *Chinese Law: Context and transformation*. Leiden: Martinus Nijhoff Publishers.

Clarke, D. c. (2003). Puzzling observations in chinese law: When is a riddle just a mistake? (pp. 93–121), chapter 3. In S. Hsu (Eds.), Understanding china's legal system: Essays in honor of Jerome A. Cohen. New York: New York University Press.

Clarke, D. C. (Ed.). (2008). *China's legal system: New developments, new challenges. The China Quarterly special issues new series, no. 8*. Cambridge: Cambridge University Press.

Cook, D. J., & Rosemont, H. (1994). *Writings on China*. Chicago: Open Court.

David, R., & Brierley, J. (1985). *Major legal systems in the world today: An introduction to the comparative study of law* (3rd ed.). London: Stevens & Sons.

Evans, R. J. (1996). Rituals of Retribution: Capital punishment in germany 1600–1987. Oxford: Oxford University Press.

Fang, X. (2000). *Conclusions*. Part v. In X. Dixin and W. Chenguing (eds.), (pp. 375–428) Chinese capitalism, 1522–1840. New York: St. Martin's Press.

Gu, H. (1915/1956). The spirit of the Chinese people: With an essay on "The war and the way out." Taipei: Committee for publication of Dr. Ku Hung-ming's works.

Gu, H. (1921). Uncivilized United States. The New York Times (June 12, 1921).

Hall, D. L. (1995). *Anticipating China: Thinking through the Narratives of Chinese and western culture*. Albany: State University of New York Press.

Head, J. W. (2009). *China's legal soul: The modern Chinese legal identity in historical context*. Durham: Carolina Academic Press.

Headley, J. M. (2007). *The Europeanization of the world: On the origins of human rights and democracy*. Princeton: Princeton University Press.

Hegel, G. W. F. (1820/1899). *Philosophy of History* (translated by J. Sibree). New York: The Colonial Press.

Jones, A. F. (2011). *Development fairy tales: Evolutionary thinking and modern Chinese culture*. Cambridge: Harvard University Press.

Kateb, G. (2011). *Human dignity*. Cambridge: Harvard University Press.

Keenan, B. (1977). *The dewey experiment in China: Educational reform and political power in the early republic council on East Asian studies*. Cambridge: Harvard University.

Lach, D. F. (1945). Leibniz and China. *Journal of the History of Ideas,6*, 436–455.

Ladany, L. (1992). *Law and legality in China: The testament of a Chinese-watcher*. Honolulu: University of Hawaii Press.

Liang, Q. (1902/1936). *On New People*. Shanghai: Zhonghua Shuju.

Lichtonstein, N. G. (2003). *Law in china's legal system: Essay in honor of Jerome A*. Cohen. New York: NYU Press.

Lin, M. M. (1998). A modern Chinese journey of enculturation. *International Review of Mission,87*, 9–24.

Lo, C. W. (1995). *China's legal awakening: Legal theory and criminal justice in Deng's Era*. Hong Kong: Hong Kong University Press.

Lu, X. (1921). *Selected stories of Lu Xun*. Peking: Foreign Language Press.

Lubman, S. B. (1999). *Bird in a cage: Legal reform in china after Mao*. Stanford, CA: Stanford University Press.

Lubman, S. (1999). *Bird in a cage: Legal reform in China after Mao*. Stanford: Stanford University Press.

Minuti, R. (2012). *Oriental despotism, in european history online* (EGO), published by the Leibniz Institute of European History (IEG). Mainz Retrieved May 13, 2012, URL: http://www-ieg-ego.eu/minutir-2012-en URN: urn:nbn:de:0159-2012050313.

Montesquieu, C. (1748/2001). *The Spirit of Law*. Translated by T. Negent. Kitchener, ON: Batoche Books.

Muhlhahn, K. (2009). *Criminal justic in china: A histroy*. Cambridge, MA: Harvard University Press.

Quesnay, F. (1767/1946). Le Despotosme de la Chine, translated by Lewis A Maverick in China: *A model for Europe*.

Peerenboom, R. (2002). *China's long march toward rule of law*. Cambridge, U.K.: Cambridge University Press.

Potter, P. B. (1994). *Riding the tiger: Legitimacy and legal culture in Post-Mao china*. The china Quarterly, *138*: 325–358.

Potter, P. B. (2001). *The Chinese legal system: Globalization and local legal culture*. London and New York: Routledge Curzon.
Pusey, J. R. (1983). *China and charles Darwin*. Cambridge, MA: Harvard University Press.
Pusey, J. R. (1981). On Liang Qichao's Darwinian Morality Revolution, Mao Zedong's Revolutionary Morality and China's Moral Development, in Wilson, R., Greenblatt, S. L. & Wilson, A. A. (eds., 1981). *Moral Behavior in Chinese Society*. Praeger.
Pye, L. W. (1968/1992). *The spirit of Chinese politics*. Cambridge: Harvard University Press.
Rothbard, M. N. (2006). *Economic thought before Adam Smith*. Ludwig von Mises Institute.
Russell, B. (1922). *The problem of china*. London: George Allen and Unwin.
Sharma, A. (2006). *Are human rights western? A contribution to the dialogue of civilizations*. New York: Oxford University Press.
Shen, Y. (2000). Conceptions and receptions of legality: Understanding the Complexity of Law Reform in Modern China (Ch. 1, pp. 20–44), in Turner, K, Feinerman, J. V. & Guy, R. K. (eds.). *The Limits of the Rule of Law in China*. Seattle, Washington: University of Washington Press.
Shih, C. (1999). *Collective Democracy: Political and Legal Reform in China*. Hong Kong: The Chinese University Press.
Steinfeld, E. (2010). *Playing our game: Why China's rise doesn't threaten the west*. New York: Oxford University Press.
Tang, X. (1996). *Global space and the nationalist discourse of modernity: The historical thinking of Liang Qichao*. Stanford: Stanford University Press.
Tillman, H. C. (1982). *Utilitarian confucianism: Ch'en Liang's challenge to Chu Hsi council on East Asian studies*. Cambridge: Harvard University.
Turner, K. G., Feinerman, J. V., & Guy, R. K. (Eds.). (2000). *The limits of the rule of law in China*. Settle, WA: University of Washington Press.
Voltaire, F. (1759). *An Essay on Universal History, the Manners, and Spirit of Nations from the Reign of Charlmaign to the Age of Louis XIV*. London: J. Nourse.
Weber, M. (1915/1951). *The religion of China: Confucianism and taoism* (translated and edited by Hans H. G.). New York: The Free Press.
Weld, S. (2003). Grave matters: Warring states law and philosophy, pp. 122–179, in Hsu, S. *Studies in Chinese law: Essays in honor of professor Jerome A. Cohen*. New York: New York University Press.
Yang, C. K. (1951). Introduction. In Weber, M. (1951). *The Religion of China: Confucianism and taoism* (translated and edited by Hans H. G.), pp: xiii–xliii. New York: The Free Press.
Yin, B., & Duff, P. (2010). Criminal procedure in contemporary China: Socialist, civilian or traditional? *International and Comparative Law Quarterly,59*, 1099–1127.

Chapter 2
Imperial Bureaucracy and Criminal Trials

2.1 Introduction

This chapter attempts to shed lights on the millennial bureaucratic tradition of magistrate's court, the indigenous notion of justice and the conduct of imperial criminal trials. Law in ancient China is developed completely free of Western influences (Jones 2003). In the long history of imperial China from 221 BC to 1911 AD, the public image of law is mostly that of penal law and fearful sanctions. There is almost no exception that threat of physical punishment is attached to any normal criminal trial. Legitimized judicial torture is a permanent feature in reality as well as in the literary and dramatic depiction of Chinese imperial criminal trials. On the one hand, torture can be used indiscriminately to those entangled in a criminal case—the petitioners, the accused, and the witnesses.[1] The magistrate has the sole discretion. His decisions are also unchecked and uncontestable during the court trial, since no legal representation on behalf of any parties would be allowed. On the other hand, at least in theory, magistrates who conduct these criminal trials are subject to strict imperial administrative regulations for official misconduct (Ch'u 1962; Hegel 2009; van Gulik 1956 /1997). For example, failing to solve a criminal case expeditiously, failing to conclude a criminal trial within 4 month (Watt 1972), improper or excessive use of torture, and ultimately misjudgment resulting in wrongful convictions (especially death) could all lead to disciplinary actions against an otherwise competent magistrate. Reduction in pay, demotion, flogging, and dismissal from the current post or permanent banishment from official posts are possible outcomes for these magistrates. For an imperial magistrate operating under the Confucian state orthodoxy, the volume of criminal trials could be used as a measure of his ability to maintain a jurisdiction free of gross disharmony (e.g., Ocko 1982) and blatant criminal transgressions. Disputable

[1] Ear-twisting and kneeling on chains are "mild" forms of torture reserved for officials. Commoners are subject to harsher forms of tortures (e.g., use of finger-squeezers for female offenders, ankle-squeezing blocks for male offenders, in addition to the usual slapping, beating techniques). Hegel's (2009) work with compilation and translation of 20 cases from the eighteenth century China is a fascinating read in this regard.

N. He, *Chinese Criminal Trials*, DOI: 10.1007/978-1-4614-8205-5_2,

criminal trial outcomes could trigger a free fall of a magistrate from his official post if an incessant amount of appeals is sent to his superior. Chinese history is replete with examples of injustice that are tied to the actions that transpired inside the magistrate's courts. The authentic Chinese experience from the long imperial period in the history lays the foundation for the modern conceptions of criminal law and criminal trials.

This chapter includes three interrelated themes. We begin with an introduction of the Chinese imperial administrative-legal system with a focus on the mundane operation of the local magistrate's office (or *yamen*), including the working relationships between yamen employees and their interactions with the public. This is followed by the illustration of a popular play depicting Dou E's story which exemplifies the Chinese conception of justice. Relatedly, a brief discussion on legitimized judicial torture both contextualizes the trial of Dou E and accentuates the indignity and injustice suffered by all Chinese who were ill-fortuned to be entangled with the imperial Chinese criminal trials.

2.2 Chinese Bureaucratic Labyrinth

Imperial bureaucracy entrusts both administrative and legal responsibilities to a single official—the magistrate.[2] It is estimated that, by the mid-1700s, fewer than two thousand district magistrates were responsible to govern a vast Chinese empire of 350 million (Edwards 2003). The official to population ratio worsens in late Qing Dynasty with the expanding population but without increased official posts (Watt 1972).[3] The Emperor rules through a highly centralized bureaucracy with the appointments of the magistrates selected based on competitive national examinations. In his seminal work on Chinese religions and capitalist development, Weber (1915/1951) devotes a great deal of attention to untangle the Chinese bureaucratic-legal labyrinth. He labels China as a patrimonial state where the "typical ramifications of administration and judiciary created a realm of unshakable sacred tradition alongside a realm of prerogative and favoritism". The centrally appointed officials often found it difficult to penetrate the tight control by the local elites. In the city, the influence of sib (or guild) was equivalent to the prerogatives of the overlord. In the villages, the temples had jurisdiction over matters of all sorts. Returning to his main focus, Weber believes that industrial capitalism failed to develop in imperial China due to the lack of rational and calculable administration and law enforcement.

[2] "Mandarin" is an alternative name used for "magistrate" in English publications.

[3] A similar argument is made by many Chinese basic courts today that the number of judges did not grow proportionality with the local population, including the rapid increases of transient population in urban districts.

Figure 2.1 depicts an elaborative Chinese Imperial criminal justice bureaucracy structure. At the very bottom of officialdom is the local Magistrate who manages complex relationships with the constituency within his jurisdiction and with superiors above him in the Imperial bureaucracy. For majority of the minor criminal cases, the local Magistrate usually makes the final decision. However, death sentence always needed to be approved all the way at the top, by the Emperor. The local Magistrate conducts preliminary investigation and sends his findings, the criminal, and the witnesses to the Prefect. The Prefect then holds an official trial and renders his own judgment. After sending most of the witnesses home at the conclusion of his trial, the Prefect expedites the records, the criminal (and his accomplices, if applicable) to the provincial Judicial Commissioner who verifies the records and hear the case again if needed (most often not) before preparing a memorial intended to be sent to the Emperor. The provincial Governor, although not directly involved in the trial or review of the case, needs to acknowledge that he supports such a report to be sent out by his Judicial Commissioner. The "Three Judicial Authorities" (the Board of Punishment, the Censorate, and the Court of Judicial Review) conduct the final review on behalf of the Emperor. The Emperor, upon the unanimous recommendation of the Three Judicial Authorities, orders the final execution decision by instructing on the outside fold of the Board's memorial (Meijer 1984).

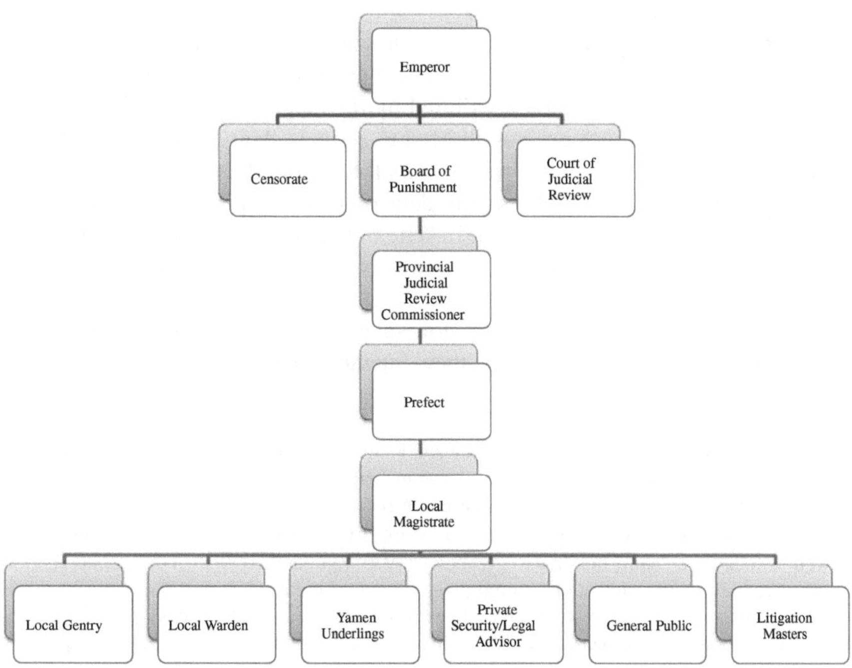

Fig. 2.1 Imperial chinese criminal justice hierarchies

2.2.1 Yamen

By design, a local magistrate is an "Emperor in little". (Jones 2003) His office is called *yamen*. Thomas Meadows, a British official serving in China in the mid-nineteenth century provides perhaps one of the most vivid first-person observations of the Chinese *yamen* in any English documentation.[4] The physical structure of the place, the key players inside the *yamen,* and their interactions with both the local elites and ordinary residents offer a fascinating account of social life in the yesteryears.[5]

Meadows (1970) attributes the remarkable durability and continuity of the Chinese imperial dynasties to three powerful factors. The first two are based on the Confucian conception that, a government should be ruled by virtue of its moral prerogatives rather than by exercise of physical force and, the rule of gentlemen should be the norm, i.e., the best place for the wisest men should be in government. These two factors are the essential elements of the rule *of* man advocated by Confucius. The third factor is based on Mencius' teaching that popular rebellion is an acceptable response to oppressive and tyrannical rulers. This can be seen as an ultimate remedy for the breach of the rule of man ideal. The spirit of Mencius' teaching is applicable both to the Emperor at the very top and to the local magistrates.

The *yamen*, exclusive of the magistrate and his family, includes the following inhabitants divided into four classes: *shi ye* (judicial advisers and private secretaries of the magistrate), *yemun* (followers of the magistrate who are negotiators of special bribes), and *purse* (like *shi ye* but without fixed pay), are all private employees of the magistrate. *shu pan* (clerks) and *chai yu* (the police runners and prison guards) are public employees hired by the magistrate's office.[6]

The district magistrates are not allowed to serve in their home province. They are relocated to different posts every 3 years throughout their careers. This design is aimed to prevent political elites from developing permanent local interests with the economic elites at the local level. In spite of the preventive measures, *yamen* is prone to corruption and, abuse of its power is almost guaranteed with the absoluteness of its dominance in local affairs.

The magistrates are paid on a fixed, low salary rate in comparison with the level of wealth held by the local elites they interact with. The magistrates are, in

---

[4] Weber (1915/1951) never set foot in China and admitted that his materials were largely based on the literature of missionaries. This is also true to Leibniz, another influential Western scholar who has written extensively about China based on secondary materials. .

[5] The physical structure of *yamen* is virtually identical throughout the country in ancient China as well as today (i.e., court buildings). Meadows (1970) reports that 90 % of the *yamen* in Qing China were built on the same architectural plan. All *yamen* are south facing. Contemporary *feng shui* specialists in China have often advised new home builders to select sites a few degrees *off* south facing to avoid a perfect alignment with *yamen*, a place that generates negative qi.

[6] According to Meadows (1970), the size of *yamen* can be quite substantial, ranging from 300 to 500 people who live and work there.

essence, "obliged to gain their incomes by means of extortion, bribery, and illegal fees" levied by their underlings (Meadows 1970). The magistrate's undivided power in ruling over all aspects of life in his jurisdiction makes them an all important figure, a mini-despot mirroring that of the Emperor. They are the lowest level officials in the imperial hierarchy of administrative ranks. However, they are also the highest officials who are the closest to ordinary people's lives at local level. The magistrates are the local officials whose role combined both authority and power (Watt 1972).

It seems that no one has ever challenged the generous assumption that the magistrates who are well-educated Confucian scholars and who are intelligent and righteous represent the majestic imperial power that is incorruptible.[7] This is anything but true in reality. A clean government is almost humanly impossible given this structure. On the one hand, the magistrates are entrusted with all-encompassing responsibilities that range from collecting tax, regulating labor services, investigating crime, administering lawsuits, promoting education, and culture to controlling custom all in one. On the other hand, these magistrates are only generalists selected from literary exams. They are forced to relegate specialized tasks to clerical staff, both his private employees and those paid by his office.

The private employees paid for by the magistrate become the negotiators of all the special bribes, and the channels through which the other illegal gains of a magistrate are conveyed. Locally recruited and publically paid clerks and runners are not supposed to serve for more than 5 years, yet they creatively manage to either stay on forever (by changing their names every 5 years) or sell the position to the highest bidder. Those who are in charge of catching the criminals form strong connections with the criminal gangs to offer protection, to frame the innocent or to delay the cases. The most unfortunate outcome of this unchecked local power is illustrated in the observation that a good magistrate makes people pay for justice; the bad magistrate sells injustice to the highest bidder (Meadows 1970).

Meadows' (1970) description of the lawyer-like professionals called *tai shu* in imperial time is also worth noting. *Tai shu* are attached to a yamen and are those who passed the specialized examination administered by the magistrate to be permitted for local practice. Their business is mainly confined to putting into a proper form his client's accusation or defense in writing. To no one's surprise, Meadows suggests that *tai shu* as a group is known to invent stories for their clients when the cases are weak. Their incomes are generated by the fees they

---

[7] Although the corruption and miscarriage of justice at the hands of local magistrates are often taken for granted by the public, the Chinese tradition has consistently proved true that people continue to have faith in the imperial justice from the Emperor in the capital city (Li 1981). The legal system as a whole always leaves a channel open so people can appeal their grievances directly to the very top officials. This can be seen even today in the forms of letters and petitions submitted to the central government offices after a case has been adjudicated, appealed, and supposedly closed.

charge their clients for the written documents that are accepted by the magistrate. Without an impression of a *tai shu*'s stamp, no accusations or petitions are formally received at the yamen.[8] Litigations in general and criminal trials in particular are actively discouraged by imperial Chinese government. There is a Chinese Proverb that says "it is better to die of starvation than to become a thief; it is better to be vexed to death than to bring a lawsuit" (Li 1981).[9] The works performed by the litigation specialists who assist others in creating unwanted lawsuits and potential risk for the magistrate's career are met with both disrespect and disgust.[10]

The rule of the magistrate, at least according to the Confucian ethics, depends on both the diligence and benevolence of those who rule and the sense of duties and responsibilities from those who are ruled. Reciprocity is a key to the success of this Confucius logic. The enlightened leadership built on the rule of gentlemen and the self-regulating populace did not materialize in reality.[11] The magistrate's court, supposedly a place to dissolve discord and contention, often ended up as the place that generates more contempt, contention, and fear from the public.

At one end of the continuum, the corruptive and horrid actions of the magistrate's underlings against the poor, uneducated, and sometimes unruly locals present a risk to the fate of the magistrate. At the other end, the relationship between the magistrate and the local gentry proves to be another challenge of a completely different nature. With the gentry, the magistrate relies on them to fulfill imperial tax quotas, to obtain information on local customs and problems, and to finance public works. To the gentry, the magistrate represents the imperial authority that can provide them connections with higher level officials in the province. The office of the magistrate and the local gentry keep a symbiotic relationship. Their mutual demise or mutual benefit rests largely on a delicate balance in power (Watt 1972). A similar local dynamic with intertwined administrative, legal, and economic powers can be found today.

---

8 "Litigation master" is a more generic, easily identifiable term that we use in Figure 2.1. A rare study on litigation masters in later Imperial China was conducted by Macauley (1999) who pointed out that the practices of these litigation masters are an integral part of the systemic order of formal dispute resolution, especially for women (particularly widows) who were not allowed to act in court without a male proxy.

9 There are other interpretations of the same saying. For example, Ocko (1983) quotes it simply "rather to die of indignation than to be involved in litigation" to show how the Chinese have been socialized to avoid lawsuit and *yamen* at all cost.

10 Weber(1915/1951) describes in his writing that the educated "sib members" or "low brow consultant" have functioned as "lawyers" in preparing written documents for clients. Lawyering has never been a respectful career for the Chinese in history. This observation may remain largely true today.

11 Weber(1915/1951) suggests that the type of self-control advocated by the Confucians is of an "aesthetic and essentially negative nature." Comparing Confucianism to Puritan ethics, Weber argues that the constant and vigilant self-control is demanded by the former to maintain the dignity of the universally accomplished man of the (this) world, while the latter demands self-control in order to concentrate man's attitude on God's will.

2.2.2 *Interface of Vertical and Horizontal Bureaucratic Norms*

In much of the imperial time, Chinese local government is ruled by a comprehensive administrative code with keen focuses on conformity and uniformity. This highly centralized system has created multiple problems. The imperial administrative code is too rigid to allow local magistrates to exercise their own personal judgment and to allow adjustment according to special conditions in a locality (Ch'u 1962). It seems avoidance of punishment has become the ultimate *modus operandi* of the local officials.

To the officials above him, the local magistrates serve as agents of the central government in collecting taxes according to a set quota. The magistrate's office, however, does not receive central funding to meet the expenditure needs of the local administration. This gives rise to the various fees imposed by the local government. From the fiscal management point of view, there is also no distinction between yamen expenses and the personal expenses of the magistrate. Added to the complexity of running a local office, there are two sets of distinctive relationships that connect a magistrate to his employees. With his personal secretary and servants, the magistrate forms an informal and personal relationship. The private employees of the magistrate had no local ties to begin with, but they are the closest to the magistrate who has both power and authority. They are loyal to the magistrate more than anyone else. The clerks and runners who are recruited from the locals develop a formal and impersonal relationship with the magistrate. These are the people who have strong incentives to forge a workable relationship with both the magistrate and the local elites. The existence of these two types of relationships gives a unique flavor to the Chinese bureaucratic practice. The private and public employees of the magistrate keep each other in check. They also work closely with each other in extracting the maximum benefit from the common people based on their alliance. Because of the multiplicity of magistrate's roles and his lack of specialized training to handle all his charges, ample room of discretion is created which renders commission of all kinds of injustice by his underlings "easy and safe." (Meadows 1970) In spite of the dissatisfaction of the local people against the "teeth and claws" of the magistrate, the *status quo* in the social and political order is largely preferred. Unless such dissatisfaction accumulates to a degree that triggers open revolt, Chinese imperial bureaucracy was able to enjoy stability throughout much of the imperial time.

Little is known or discussed about the vertical bureaucratic relationship between a district magistrate and his superiors at the provincial level. The most obvious aspect of their relationship lies in the appeal of civil or criminal cases handled by the district magistrate as judge of the court of first instance. The layers of review needed depend on the severity of the cases and possible penalties. For example, convictions of capital crimes are approved by the Board of Punishments in the imperial capital. In reality, however, the district magistrate has the final word in deciding most of the cases (Watt 1972). The magistrate's first preference is to discourage a lawsuit. However, if a case is accepted for trial, the magistrate would want it to be tried and concluded quickly. A crowded docket can be seen by his superior as a failure to maintain social harmony (Ocko 1982).

2.3 Justice and Imperial Criminal Trial

The imperial criminal trial is a raw nerve of the Chinese legal history. Judging and punishing encapsulate the final phases of a social drama that delivers both pain and fear to the public (Muhlhahn 2009). Quite often the magistrate's court in imperial China is portrayed as a place haunted by ghosts who are still searching for justice. *The Injustice to Dou E* is a popular play written by Guan Hanqin (1241–1320), a notable playwright and poet from Yuan Dynasty (1271–1368). Perhaps, no other play in Chinese history is better known or more frequently replayed than this story of epic injustice that befalls a young widow-Dou E. Every Chinese must have known some of the key episodes in Dou E's story:

> Dou E lost her mother at the age of seven. Her father, Dou Tianzhang, a diligent but unsuccessful Confucian scholar had borrowed a substantial amount of loans from Cai Popo, a local widow, to partake in exams to be eligible for an official post. He fails the exams repeatedly and gets deeper in debt. Before he leaves for yet another exam, Dou Tianzhang goes to Cai Popo, asking for one last loan to finance his long journey to the capital. To offset his debt, he leaves behind Dou E, his 10 year old daughter, to be the child-bride for Cai Popo's son.
>
> Dou Tianzhang then disappears from the story until the very last play. Cai Popo's son dies barely two years into his marriage with Dou E. On an ill-fated trip to visit one of her debtors, Cai Popo was nearly strangled to death by an enraged debtor if not for the sudden appearance of two strangers at the door. The son (Donkey Zhang) and father who had "rescued" Cai Popo would soon find out that this "wealthy" widow lives with the young and beautiful Dou E, a new widow. They would offer to move in with the widows and be their "protectors." Feeling indebted to the life-saving encounter with the Zhangs, Cai Popo almost yields to the pressure. Dou E, however, vehemently rejects the Zhang's indecent proposal. Dou E pleads with her mother-in-law to preserve her (their) virtue as widows.
>
> With Cai Popo watching over Dou E closely, Donkey Zhang plots to rid Cai Popo in order to seize Dou E for his pleasure. As fate would have it, the poisoned lamb intestine stew Donkey Zhang prepared for Cai Popo is accidently consumed by his father. To cover up his own tracks, Donkey Zhang goes to the magistrate's court and frames Dou E as the murderer. The magistrate who had been bribed by Donkey Zhang authorizes torture to induce Dou E's confession. Dou E endures the worst torture without admitting to the charge. Cai Popo who is old and frail is summoned to serve as a witness, and the magistrate threatens to apply the same torture to her. Dou E finally relents in order to spare her mother-in-law from the unbearable ordeal. By confessing to the murder charge, Dou E is promptly sentenced to death.
>
> At the public execution, the indignant Dou E pleads to the heaven and earth to witness the injustice she has suffered. She cries "let earth be moved and let heaven quake!" She makes three pledges: not a single drop of her blood would touch the ground but to stain the white

> silk banner flying above the execution ground; snow would fall in June; and there will be three years of drought in the region. All her pledges are realized exactly.
>
> Dou Tianzhang (Dou E's long lost father who is now a high-ranking imperial emissary) reenters the play. As a ghost, Dou E confides her plight to her father and pleads for justice and retribution. Justice would finally prevail with the dismissal of the corrupt magistrate and the execution of Donkey Zhang.

Although the plot of this Yuan drama is set in an imperial dynasty many centuries ago, criminal trials conducted by magistrates remain largely unchanged until the end of the nineteenth century. Works based on first-hand or second-hand materials by various scholars have provided us great insights on the local magistrate's dual administrative and judicial functions, especially from the Qing dynasty. Many writers cite the supernatural phenomena illustrated in the drama of Dou E as reflecting the Chinese conception of cosmic harmony. A notion mostly accepted states that it is not necessarily crime itself but the injustice perpetrated by the corrupted officials (for example, magistrates, and their underlings) that causes cosmic disruption (Li 1981). Unlike Western detective stories, a Chinese drama usually leaves no suspense about who is the culprit of the crime. The crime scene is often introduced earlier in the play. A Chinese drama writer is compelled to end the story with a symbolic triumph of justice to compensate for its absence in reality. In fact, Dou E's story that has been continually replayed centuries later attests to its lasting value as a cultural icon. It symbolizes a longing for true justice that remains elusive in Chinese reality since antiquity.

2.4 Legitimized Judicial Torture

An eyewitness account of the operations inside a Qing Dynasty *yamen* is as rare as unforgettable.

> The almost unceasing flail-like sounds of beating with the bamboo, either as a punishment for ascertained guilt, or to extort confessions and evidence; the cries of the sufferers; the voices of the examining mandarins questioning, bullying, and wheedling; and the frequent appearance of criminals and witnesses being escorted to and from the prisons and rooms for examination, are sounds and sights that bewilder and agitate those who have not been accustomed to them, and serve to heighten that dread which all private Chinese entertain of entering a yamen (Meadows 1970: 115).

Two questions can be immediately asked: is this description an anomaly? If not, for what purposes does imperial China legitimize judicial torture? The answer to the first question appears to be easier. As seen in Dou E's story, judicial torture and coerced confession have been portrayed as a routine practice in China many centuries earlier. Chinese law dates back to more than two millennia. However, a clearly documented and codified legal tradition has only existed since the seventh century (Jones 2003).[12] There is little dispute that the Chinese imperial law has a long tradition of strong focus on penal sanctions. Outside the artistic rendition of the dark social reality such as the Yuan Dynasty play depicting Dou E's story, there is very little well-documented court dossiers for the scholarly investigation until the last two dynasties in Ming and Qing. Despite thc limited empirical evidence, the very public display of judicial tortures in plays and folk stories is more than enough to leave an indelible impression of judicial torture, not only of its existence but also of its absolute tyranny. The evolution of criminal interrogation rules in China is the focus of Wu and Vander Beken's (2011) recent study. Their ambitious paper presents a thorough historical analysis that covers from the pre-Han to the post-Mao reform era.

Confucian moral standards (*li*) and its penal attribute could be found in the well-preserved Tang (Penal) Code. The first clue on why judicial torture is tolerated starts with the obsession on finding truth and seeking substantive justice.[13] Recall earlier discussion (Chap. 1) on the Confucian hierarchy of norms which places law at the very bottom. Likewise, the Tang Code's treats law as an unfortunate but necessary remedial measure to restore the imbalance between man and nature caused by a disruptive criminal action. Whenever a crime occurs, finding truth and allocating factual guilt are of paramount importance. In particular, an offender's confession (either voluntary or coerced admission of guilt) and repentance of the crime are two of the most important elements for concluding the criminal case in front of a magistrate. Despite the horrors of the practice of coerced confession, it is a system that has worked for the Chinese (Jones 2003).[14]

The differentiation of confession by persuasion and confession by judicial torture offers additional depth to our understanding of the subject. Wu and Vander Beken (2011) argue that through the interplay between Confucian moral standards and legalist's bureaucracy, the persuasive interrogation model of the Tang Code offers a norm that has remained stable until the early twentieth century. On the other hand, there is a hardened view that law should be unsympathetic as it is a necessary evil in order to restore the broken social order. The heavy reliance on informal social control per Confucian moral principles makes a criminal trial an outlier of social action: an accusation is more than enough to indicate a moral failure. Therefore, seeking confession by judicial torture during a criminal trial is

[12] Jones is likely referring to the Tang Code which was first created in 624 AD at the request of Emperor (Tang) Gaozu. The Tang Code contained 500 Articles separated in 12 large Sections.

[13] It is difficult to ascertain the credibility of a cultural characteristic observed by Meadows (1970: 216) who wrote: "nationally considered, the Chinese are most unscrupulous liars." Native Chinese may not agree with his assessment. The Chinese are known to be more reserved in their dealings with the foreigners. Many Chinese would probably not consider withholding their true thoughts to a stranger as lying. It is simply a preventive, self-protective measure. Truthfulness and forthcoming mentality are not taught as a part of the Confucian ethics. Coerced confession used in the magistrate's court could be based on such an unflattering assumption of the ordinary Chinese.

[14] It remains at the same time a persistent human rights and criminal due process violation problem facing Chinese criminal justice today (see Belkin 2011).

intended to serve a multitude of utilitarian purposes. It symbolizes the power of the magistrate representing the state in addition to proclaiming the weakness of the punished and the bystanders who are made to witness the ordeal (Muhlhahn 2009). Although by design judicial investigation conducted in front of the public is to teach, humble, and extract repentance from the wrongdoers, in reality, however, judicial torture is widely used by the magistrates as a short cut to end cases quickly (Zu 2008) and to deter future lawsuits.

2.5 Conclusion

In sum, the Chinese imperial criminal justice is the unfortunate last resort in reaction to the breaches in the personal and social conduct norms accorded in the Confucian ethics. Law's lowly place in the hierarchy of norms dooms the prospect of benefit to be gained by pursuing a legal resolution for a criminal matter. Punishment and pain, not rights and procedural justice, would symbolize the Chinese criminal process as a whole. This realization is deeply ingrained in a Chinese psyche and culture that was true in the imperial time and may be still true today. Chinese criminal justice has always been a subject more relevant to those who rule than to those who are ruled. The Chinese preoccupation of substantive justice while ignoring procedural justice is motivated by the government's need to enhance its own legitimacy than to redress the injuries of the victims.[15] According to some scholars (e.g., Kahn 2009) justice and legitimacy have long captured the legal imagination in the West. However, in imperial China, legitimacy absorbs justice in that when a political order is perceived as legitimate (i.e., Emperor is the son of the heaven, thus his legitimacy and mandates are unquestionable), people can be quite tolerant of substantial failure of justice (e.g., coerced confession, judicial torture, and other procedural breaches). The belief in a fair and just Heaven (with its own principles of justice) by the common man is one of the key rationales that legitimize the Chinese legal system with all its imperfections (Li 1981). Reconciliation of the heavenly principle of justice and fairness with the humble human sentiment and imperfections is a Chinese dilemma that remains unsolved for thousands of years.

Responsible for much of the failure in delivering justice by the imperial magistrates is a Chinese bureaucratic system that relies too heavily upon the generous assumption of the virtue of rule of man. A local office with a single official who is responsible for all matters administrative and legal is simply too ambitious and leaves too much room for the abuse of his absolute power. To some, the stability of millennial imperial bureaucracy attests not to the superiority of the imperial organizational design, but to the success of systematic suppression of

[15] "Substantive justice" is used in a Weberian sense depicting the ideals of justice, in contrast to legal formalism or procedural justice.

individual rights in favor of social order and collective gains. The next chapter offers more in-depth, relative, and relational discussions on the tripartite rules: rule of man, rule by law and rule of law.

References

Belkin, I. (2011). China's tortuous path toward ending torture in criminal investigations. *Columbia Journal of Asian Law,24*, 273–301.

Ch'u, T. (1961). *Law and society in traditional china*. Paris: Mouton.

Edwards, R. R. (2003). *The role of case nprecedent in the Qing judicial process as reflected in appellate rulings*. In S. Hsu (Ed.), Understanding china's legal system: Essay in honor of Jerome A. Cohen. New York: NYU Press.

Ch'u, T. (1962). *Local government in china under the ch'ing*. Cambridge: Harvard University.

Hegel, R. E. (2009). *True crimes in 18th-century china: 20 case histories*. Seattle: University of Washington Press.

Jones, W. C. (2003). Trying to understand the current chinese legal system. In Hsu, S.(Ed.), *Understanding chinese legal system: essays in honor of professor Jerome A. Cohen*. New York: New York University Press, 7–45.

Jones, W. C. (1994). *The Great Qing Code*. New York: Oxford University Press.

Kahn, P. W. (2009). Justice or legitimacy: A response to ocko and gilmartin. *Journal of Asian Studies,68*, 106–111.

Li, P. (1981). In search of justice: Law and morality in three chinese dramas. In: Wilson, R., Greenblatt, S. L. & Wilson, A. A. (Eds.), *Moral Behavior in Chinese Society*. New York: Praeger Publishers, 104–125.

Macauley, M. (1999). *Social power and legal culture: Litigation masters in late imperial china*. Stanford: Stanford University Press.

Meadows, T. T. (1970). *Desultory notes on the government and people of china and on the chinese language*. New York: Praeger Publishers.

Meijer, M. T. (1984). Autumn assizes in ch'ing law. *T'oung Pao, Second Series,70*, 1–17.

Muhlhahn, K. (2009). *Criminal justice in china: A history*. Cambridge: Harvard University.

Ocko, J. K. (1982). *Bureaucratic reform in provincial china: Ting jih-chang in restoration kiangsu, 1867–1870*. Cambridge: Harvard University Press.

van Gulik, R. (1956, 1997). *The chinese maze murders: A Judge Dee Mystery*. Chicago: University of Chicago Press.

Watt, J. R. (1972). *The district magistrate in late Imperial china*. New York: Columbia University Press.

Weber, M. (1915/1951). *The religion of china*: Confucianism and Taoism (translated and edited by Hans H. Gerth). New York: The Free Press.

Wu, W. & Vander Beken, T. (2010). Police torture in china and its causes: A review of literature. The Australian and New Zealand Journal of Criminology 43(93), 557–579.

Wu, W., & Vander Beken, T. (2011). The evolution of criminal interrogation rules in china. *International Journal of Law, Crime and Justice,40*(4), 1–25.

Zu, W. (2008). Primary rules on criminal evidence in ancient china and its theoretical basis (zhongguo gudai jugongdingzui xingshizhengju shouyaoguize ji lilunjiexi). Law and Social Development 79(1), 42–62.

Part II
Socio-legal Context

Chapter 3
Tripartite Rules: Rule of Man, Rule by Law and Rule of Law

3.1 Introduction

Three types of rules are often associated with the discourse of governance and legal practice: rule of man, rule by law, and rule of law. In the Chinese context, the first two are deeply rooted in history and culture experience (see Chaps. 1 and 2). They are the taken-for-granted twin norms of Chinese legal practice and principles of governance writ large. The Western notion of Rule of Law is a relatively new concept to the Chinese. Its strong focus on protecting individual rights and restraining governmental power runs contrary to the traditional Confucian rule of gentlemen orthodoxy, the Legalist's instrumentalist rule by law dogma, and the Marxist class-based rule of people's dictatorship. In spite of the historical origins and the contradictions in the preferred modalities of governance characterized by the rule of man, rule by law, and rule of law, it is undeniable that elements from all three coexist today in China. Revealing the interconnectedness of these tripartite rules is a prerequisite to a better understanding of the criminal trials that take place in contemporary Chinese court.

Rule of law, more so than rule of man and rule by law, remains a contested concept in the West (Peerenboom 2004). It is not surprising that different definitions of "rule of law" are adopted by scholars (e.g., philosophers, legal scholars, linguists, sociologists, and anthropologists), social activists, public media, general public, and politicians alike. The eclectic nature of the rule of law definition is both its strength and its weakness. The words "Rule of Law" is simple enough for easy conversation and propaganda. These words, however, are also confusing at the same time, especially when they are used without definitional and/or cultural context. The linguistic simplicity fails to convey fully its substantive and symbolic meanings. Rule of law has had a long and difficult journey in Chinese history and it is now made more indispensable than ever.

This chapter traces the general chronological sequence laid out in Fig. 3.1. It offers a terse survey of the evolution of China's rule of law experiences. We begin with a discussion of the key characteristics of imperial China's blended rule of man and rule by law traditions (Sect. 3.2). Using rule of law as a nation-building

N. He, *Chinese Criminal Trials*, DOI: 10.1007/978-1-4614-8205-5_3,

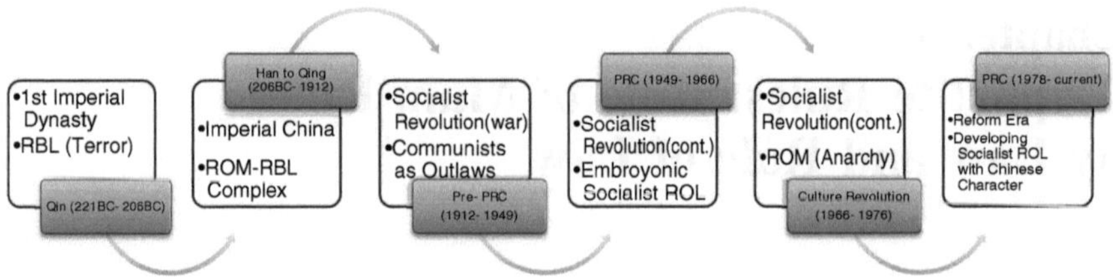

Fig. 3.1 *RBL* rule by law; *ROM* rule of man; and *ROL* rule of law emphases in ideal types as applied chronologically

instrument for the transition, either from Qing Dynasty to the Republic of China or from the capitalist Republic of China to the socialist People's Republic of China, is a common theme in Sects. 3.3 and 3.4.

3.2 The Imperial Rule of Man and Rule by Law Complex

In the Chinese imperial history, the Emperor is the undisputed despot, the son of the heaven whose rule shall be legitimate and absolute. Qin, the first Chinese imperial dynasty, is characterized as a brutal Legalistic rule by law regime. Rule by law, according to Shang Yan (the key statesman and reformer in Qin whom we briefly referred to in Chap. 1), is aimed to eliminate the discretions of the lower officials due to distrust of their integrity (Watt 1972). In addition, rule by law unites all politics under one powerful ruler-the Emperor. Qin is the only dynasty in Chinese history that has acted aggressively to curtail the coexistence of other conduct norms. If Confucianism breeds disdain of law as a model of social control, Legalism brings the fear of law into public conscience.

After Qin dynasty, Confucianism is widely adopted as the state orthodoxy precisely due to its perfect alignment with the concept of rule of man. The Emperor at the very top is destined to carry out his heavenly mandates. Officials employed by the highly centralized government are selected only from Confucian scholars based on regular national exams. The Emperor rules the country through the rule of the local magistrates. The local magistrates are bound both by the Confucian rule of gentlemen and by the extensive imperial administrative code. In theory, both the Emperor and his officials are held to a high standard prescribed by the Confucian ethics. Their rules are expected to be virtuous. The public shall have complete trust in their personal and professional competence and integrity in ruling the country. High degree of group identification or "sociocentricism" in the culture is a remarkable force in shaping a conformist mentality among the ordinary Chinese. The Confucian moral virtuousness expressed in the form of loyalty and filial piety extends naturally from one's own family to the district magistrates and higher level officials, the true *parens patriae*, representing the best interest of the state. The Chinese culture can be said to rely heavily on situational cues, especially those that are related to rules and the dictates of custom and to the pronouncement of authority figures (Metzger 1981). However, the symbiotic relationships between the magistrates and the local elites, between the magistrates and their provincial superiors, between themselves and their underlings, and between the collective behavior of the magistrate's office and the general public attest to the complexity and unpredictability of the rule of man.

3.3 Rule of Law as Instrument for Sovereignty

The late Qing China confronts two debilitating dilemmas: the decline of the empire as a world power and the erosion of public confidence in the model of governance based on Confucian rule of man ethics. The former is realized by China's humiliating military defeats in the hands of the British (Opium War), the Japanese (Sino-Japanese War), and the commercial exploitation imposed at will by other Western powers. Once the Western powers set foot in Chinese territories, they find Chinese law barbarous. Correspondingly, self-governing foreign enclaves are established in major Chinese coastal cities where foreign laws and legal systems are applicable (i.e., extraterritoriality). Getting rid of extraterritoriality becomes one of the major motives to promote rule of law by adopting Western legal system (Hsu 2003). The latter is a constant reminder of the fragile conceptual foundation that places the legitimacy of the government in the hands of lower officials (the magistrates) as moral exemplars. The stagnant economy, rampant official corruption, and inept central government in the face of foreign invasion give rise to the need for rule of law for the first time in Chinese history. Unlike in the West, the late Qing rule of law discourse is intended for nation-building, i.e., to construct a "modern sovereignty" (Ocko and Gilmartin 2009) modeled after the West yet without its core contents in assuring individual human rights.[1] The legacy of the late Qing Westernized reform demonstrates the difficulty of true value immersion across culture lines.

Different from the political parties in the West which are developed after the establishment of a modern state to rationalize its political process, the two Chinese ruling political parties in the twentieth century play a drastically different role. Both the Nationalist Party (KMT) and the Chinese Communist Party (CCP) are established for the purpose of state building. The Republic of China and the People's Republic of China claim the same DNA of Chinese history. In spite of the civil war that resulted in two separate Chinese governments after 1949, the essential rule of government modality is quite similar between them. Both the

---

[1] Chinese intelligentsia who were exposed to the Western rule of law values opted for the more instrumentalist use of "rights" as a means for nation-building rather than treating it as an intrinsic value to individuals, as originally intended by the Western liberal philosophers such as Kant and Locke. In fact, the notion of "rights" as a word and concept was not known in China until the mid-1800s (Cao 2004).

mainland and the Taiwan governments have tried to maintain one-party rule for as long as it can. Taiwan has now a more mature rule of law tradition that the mainland could find helpful. In many aspects, the mainland society is following the same social development pathway treaded by the Taiwanese decades earlier, albeit on a much larger scale.

Taiwan's upward trend toward embracing the rule of law values is accelerated after the substantial growth in economy resulting in a burgeoning middle class. The social protest activities in the forms of citizen petitions for civil rights and welfare, civil disobedience, and riots against authoritarian government seen in the 1980s Taiwan is replaying in mainland China two decades later. The Taiwanese social movement has engaged the public in reevaluating traditional authoritarian rule with the rule of man (KMT Party personified) juxtaposed with rule by law, the legacy of imperial China. The unique outcome for Taiwan is that a two-tiered legal system has been created from its rule of law struggle. There is a high standard of the rule of law at the highest court (i.e., the Constitutional Court). At the lower level, however, there is neither sufficient government support for legal access, especially for the poor, nor sufficient public demand due to traditional distrust of the judicial system. In other words, the rule of law realized at the governmental level in Taiwan has not "trickled down into the popular mind" (Chen 2003).

Compared to Taiwan, the Mainland China's trajectory toward rule of law is complicated further by its decades of experience with the strictly enforced socialist ideology aimed to smash both the feudal (Imperial/Confucian) and capitalist (Western/liberal) legal traditions. Because the rule of law is "alien and unknown throughout thousands of years of authoritarian rule" in China, some Western observers are cautiously pessimistic of China's potential in developing genuine rule of law (e.g., Lubman 1999). Other Chinese specialists are more generous with their assessments of the rule of law tradition in China. For example, Ocko and Gilmartin (2009) argues that "rule of moral men" remains a powerful ideal throughout the Qing and well into the twentieth century, but the Qing government also abides the Legalist teaching to "keep two handles of reward and punishment in the hands of the emperor and to constrain lesser officials by *rule of law*" (Italics added).[2]

Li (2010) suggests that the Chinese rule of law is a "*sui generis* case for Western ontology." He argues that the Confucian rule of man and the Legalist rule by law approaches present alternative ways of compromise between "law as reason" and law as "human fiat." Li made it clear that a few major principles of Chinese jurisprudence are misunderstood or neglected by the Western legal scholars. For example, the Chinese applies case law but in a different way. Their appreciation for the precedential value of the history is reflected in following the

---

[2] More than half of the provisions of the Qing Code are what would be concerned as administrative rules that regulate the conduct of governmental officials (Jones 1994). From the point of argument that the rule of law has a lot to do with constraining governmental power, Qing as well as earlier Chinese dynasties do have a tradition of limited rule of law. This remains a contestable argument.

"general intent" rather than the specific adjudicated outcomes of the cases.[3] In addition, the Chinese division of power is more practical than philosophical. The mechanism of checks and balances used in the West grants "partial trust" to the officials while the Chinese system gives "whole trust" then "verifies its proper use." Both the Chinese and the Western rule of law models are based on the supremacy of the will of the people.[4] In a nutshell, Li's (2010) conclusion can be seen as to contradict Lubman's (1999) assertion that the rule of law is unknown to the Chinese in its ancient history. Interestingly, Li is certainly not alone in breaking the taken-for-granted norm of definitions endorsed by the Western scholars. In an earlier publication, De Bary (2000) calls the joint enterprise consisted of Confucianism and Legalism "Chinese Constitutionalism." More recently, Tsai (2007) finds additional value of Chinese traditional cultural practices that would not qualify under standard Western definitions of democracy and would not be included in the conversation of rule of law. Her book, which draws on extensive empirical research on Chinese village governance, suggests that informality and informal institutions can provide "accountability without democracy." The rule of man, the rule of charismatic village officials, delivers services, and justice that are functional equivalent of democratic institutions.

3.4 Socialist Rule of Law with Chinese Characteristics

According to some scholars (e.g., Soltan 1987), a common ground in the shared vision of the desirable society and the goals for reform and revolution can be found between two drastically conceptualized social theories. In each of its extreme form, a typical social contract based "liberal utopia" (e.g., Kant, Locke, and Rawls) envisions a society based on a voluntary, equal, and fair arrangement where the state does not interfere with the activities of the citizens. A typical Marxist "liberal socialist utopia," on the other hand, sees a society without a state and where valuable resources are generated "from each according to abilities" and distributed "to each according to needs." Although there is a greater realization of the former (i.e., liberal democracy) than the latter (i.e., the Marxist social revolution) in reality, the ideological divide still remains. China's continued pursuit of a socialist revolution with an increasingly more adaptive and pragmatic mindset makes the discussion of socialist rule of law necessary. Socialist rule of law has a psychological advantage in China which coincides with the most salient

[3] Li's (2010) argument can find support in Edwards' (2003) work which suggests widespread use of case precedents in the Qing judicial process especially at appellate level. Edwards does warn that officials in the provinces and in the capital city (Board of Punishment) apply case precedents not as a matter of legal principle but for mainly practicality reasons.

[4] Certainly, this remains a provocative argument made by Li (2010). The prevailing impression has been that China never had a true rule of law model that reflects "the supremacy of the will of the people."

characteristics of the Chinese traditional culture, i.e., group identification, conformity to group expectations, and loyalty to group leaders. The triadic nature of the socialist rule of law (i.e., its relative, relational, and contextual contents) warrants further explanation.

Socialist revolution has gone through three major phases in the post-imperial China. The first phase is bookended by the introduction of the Marxist ideology in the early twentieth century and the establishment of the People's Republic of China in 1949. The communist regime existed in the shadow of the Republic of China ruled by the Nationalist Party. Power struggles between warlords, the Japanese invasion and the bitter civil war fought between the Communist and the Nationalist armies capture much of the social realities during this time. There are quick installments of Western-inspired key systems of law (i.e., the Six Codes: Constitution, Criminal Law, Criminal Procedure Law, Civil Law, Civil Procedure Law, and Administrative Law) during the first few decade after the demise of the Qing Empire. Rule of law under the Republic of China government has been in existence more as a structure rather than a value system. National survival simply took precedent over anything else including a genuine rule of law development.

The embryonic socialist rule of law began to develop shortly after the establishment of PRC. The process is exceedingly slow not only because of the perceived need to continue struggle against the remnant class enemies but also due to the lack of legal expertise in crafting new laws. Determined to differentiate itself from the legal system used by the Nationalist Party and to sever the ties with the imperial legal tradition, the Communist government abolishes the Six Codes, and incapacitates the judicial apparatus built by the Nationalists. The 1950s and the first half of the 1960s are a trials and errors period of socialist construction. This description also applies to the legal development. Although the PRC's first Constitution was enacted in 1954 (modeled after that of the former Soviet Union), socialist rule of law remains only symbolic and only in written language. Criminal justice during the first decade and half of the new PRC follows a functionalist and differential system. It is best characterized as being designed to strike against the class enemies with violent excesses (Muhlhahn 2009).

The decade long "Great Culture Revolution" (1966–1976) brings a lawless rule of terror that rivals the brutal rule by law campaign waged by the first Chinese Emperor more than 2,000 years ago.[5] The Maoist political movement is a continuation of the socialist revolution that features fierce struggles against class enemies that created chaos and disorder. Law is used purely as a brutal instrument, a weapon in the hands of the omnipresent public security force which has since been granted the complete functions of the criminal justice system, substituting the

[5] By the government's own admission (SPC 2009), 400,000 antirevolutionary criminal cases have been processed during the period from 1966 to 1976. Majority of these cases are incidences of miscarriage of justice against innocent Chinese citizens.

courts, the prosecution offices, and the correctional facilities (prison, jail, and reeducation through labor camps).[6]

The goal for reform after 1978 is to move away from the unmediated revolutionary popular justice during the culture revolution and to resuscitate the earlier attempt (in the 1950s) to institutionalize the socialist rule of law. During much of the 1980s and the early 1990s, the Chinese legal reform relies heavily on "rhetorical and symbolic display of reformist governance" in order to promote political legitimacy and authority of law (Trevaskes 2007). Legal institutions are used to reshape and reflect the society's new norms and values (Muhlhahn 2009). The performative Chinese criminal justice operations in the last three decades continue to evolve today. Socialist rule of law with Chinese characteristics is gaining increased recognition as well as facing greater public discontent in the first decade of the twenty-first century.

3.5 Conclusion

This chapter fast-rewinds the mainland Chinese legal history that begins with Qin dynasty's brutal but short-lived rule by law regime, followed by the millennial imperial justice with infused rule of man and rule by law principles, and the tumultuous journey undertaken by the communist regime in search of a socialist rule of law model with Chinese characteristics in the last century. The true story is that of a resilient civilization which has learned through harsh lessons to adapt to any changing conditions.[7] Chinese culture and law, in spite of being shaped and reshaped in history, have managed to retain much of the same ancient ingredients. The Chinese are the ultimate pragmatic people. The socialist rule of law with Chinese characteristics is their newest but incomplete invention. This tripartite domain of mixed rules we see today serves a great utilitarian purpose that, it not only lays claim to the reliability of imperial China's bimodal (rule of man and rule by law) practices, but also cashes in on the rule of law's legitimacy and global currency. Different from any time in history, the Chinese government's bag of tricks now has all three ingredients. Mixing these ingredients in the making and application of law is likely to be conditioned on the CCP's constant assessment of China's local and global realities. In the next chapter, we offer a glimpse of the prevailing social milieu in China and explore the public's sentiment toward rule of

[6] The destruction of the legal apparatus is a devastating blow to the fledging socialist rule of law movement that sees incremental development in the decade before the Culture Revolution. The disbandment of virtually all law schools and the smashed court and prosecution services create a legal vacuum for the post-Mao China. Building a culture of rule of law from the ashes of the Culture Revolution and the millennial rule of man and rule by law traditions is a daunting task.

[7] Pye (1992: ix) famously commented about China's unique political culture that "as a collectivity, China is not just a normal nation-state; it is a civilization trying to squeeze itself into the format of a modern state."

law development at the current time. Additionally, Chap. 4 compares and contrasts the current condition of Chinese rule of law with that of the other nations based on a recent international survey.

References

Cao, D. (2004). *Chinese law: A language perspective*. Burlington: Ashgate Publishing Company.

Chen, T-F. (2003). The rule of law in Taiwan: Culture, ideology, and social change. In S. Hsu (Ed.), *Understanding China's legal system: Essays in honor of Jerome A. Cohen*. New York: New York University Press.

De Bary, W. T. (2000). *Asian values and human rights: A confucian communitarian perspective*. Cambridge: Harvard University Press.

Edwards, R. R. (2003). The role of case precedent in the Qing judicial process as reflected in appellate rulings. In S. Hsu (Ed.), *Understanding China's legal system: Essays in honor of Jerome A. Cohen*. New York: New York University Press.

Hsu, S. (2003). *Understanding China's legal system: Essays in honor of Jerome A. Cohen*. New York: New York University Press.

Jones, W. (1994). *The great qing code*. New York: Oxford University Press.

Li, J. (2010). China: A sui generis case for the western rule-of-law model. *Georgetown Journal of International Law,41*, 711–748.

Lubman, S. B. (1999). *Bird in a cage: Legal reform in China after Mao*. Stanford: Stanford University Press.

Metzger, T. A. (1981). Foreword. In Wilson, R. W., Greenblatt, S. L., & Wilson, A. A. (Eds.), *Moral behavior in Chinese society*. New York: Praeger Publishers.

Muhlhahn, K. (2009). *Criminal justice in China: A history*. Cambridge: Harvard University.

Ocko, J. K., & Gilmartin, D. (2009). State, sovereignty, and the people: A comparison of the "rule of law" in China and India. *The Journal of Asian Studies,68*, 55–133.

Peerenboom, R. (2004). Varieties of rule of law: An introduction and provisional conclusion. In R. P. Peerenboom (Ed.), *Asian discourses of rule of law: Theories and implementation of rule of law in twelve Asian countries* (pp. 1–55). London: RoutledgeCurzon.

Pye, L. W. (1992). *The spirit of Chinese politics*. Cambridge: Harvard University Press.

Sołtan, K. E. (1987). *The causal theory of justice*. Berkeley: University of California Press.

The Supreme People's Court of China. (2009). Criminal trials: steady progress. http:\\www.chinacourt.org/article/detail/2009/10/id/377239.shtml

Trevaskes, S. (2007). *Courts and criminal justice in contemporary China*. Lanham: Lexington Books.

Tsai, L. L. (2007). *Accountability without democracy: Solidary groups and public goods provision in rural China*. New York: Cambridge University Press.

Watt, J. R. (1972). *The district magistrate in late imperial China*. New York: Columbia University Press.

Chapter 4
Rule of Law in China: Social Milieu and Global Survey

4.1 Introduction

This chapter provides an empirically based assessment of the prevailing public sentiment toward social problems, social harmony, and social control in China at the current time. It gauges the level of willingness and readiness of the Chinese public toward supporting rule of law. It serves to bridge the understanding of mainland China's current contentious social experience in the event of fast economic development with that of Taiwan from a few decades earlier (as mentioned in Chap. 3). It also compares and contrasts China's rule of law performance with that of the other countries. In particular, this exercise draws comparisons between China and other large, emerging economic-political powerhouses (i.e., the so-called BRIC countries); between China and mature democracies such as the US and Japan; and, between China and the culturally similar Eastern Asian countries (e.g., Japan, Singapore, and Korea). The empirical assessment of China's current socio-political context and the cross-national comparison exemplify a learning process that is relative, relational, and contextual. In this sense, contemporary Chinese criminal trials which we cover at length in Part III (Chap. 5–8) can be viewed as both the product of and the raw materials for this fluid and cultured experience.

4.2 Current Socio-Cultural Context for the Rule of Law in China

Scholars and China observers have produced a great deal of recent work centered on the topics of China's miraculous economic growth, drastic social changes, intensified social conflicts, and stagnated institutional reforms. The tenfold increase in the number of the collective contention incidents from 8,700 in 1993 to a high of 90,000 in 2006 gives a particular reason for the heightened national and

N. He, *Chinese Criminal Trials*, DOI: 10.1007/978-1-4614-8205-5_4,

international attention.[1] Chen (2009) summarizes the major social groups and primary issues involved in Chinese public protests from the mid-1990s to the mid-2000s in the following seven categories: (1) laid-off State-owned enterprise workers protesting for unpaid (or underpaid) payments; (2) peasants protesting the large urban–rural discrepancies in access to income, healthcare, and educational opportunities; (3) city/rural dwellers protesting over the terms and inadequate compensation offered for their requisitioned homes/land for redevelopment; (4) occupational groups (e.g., taxi drivers, teachers, and merchants) struggling for their respective work rights; (5) migrant workers protesting against anomalies in their wage remuneration and work environment; and (6) Falun Gong members and other political dissidents confronting the Communist Party's monopoly of power.

The popular discontents that underline the outburst of large-scale collective incidents are extremely worrisome to the Chinese leadership. Chinese leaders have witnessed how large-scale nationalist mobilization has led to quick collapse of the once mighty Soviet State (Beissinger 2002). The resolutions of the 6th Plenum of the 16th Central Committee of the Chinese Communist Party (2006) include a list of so-called "disharmonious features." It is now widely acknowledged that a successful transition from economic construction to social harmony building is a key element in maintaining both the political leadership of the Chinese Communist Party and China's rising world power (Bergsten et al. 2008; Lee et al. 2009). Not surprisingly, due to its sensitive nature, the official police statistics on *collective incidents* is treated as a state secret and disappeared from the public after 2006. On the other hand, the Chinese government has since made maintenance of social stability a top priority with special namesake offices (*weiwenban*) set up at all levels of governments nationwide. In some jurisdictions, a cash reward card system is set up to allow citizens to redeem points collected for reporting, preventing, and solving minor public incidents that could lead to major disorder. The evaluation and promotion of local government officials are now closely tied to the success of maintaining stability in their jurisdictions. This is a significant shift from the single-minded focus on GDP growth in the recent past. There have been reports of astronomical costs associated with local government's efforts in maintaining stability.

China's transition from a socialist planned economy with a relatively egalitarian income distribution to a market economy with ever widening income differentials is a case-in-point for the timeliness of a discussion of the rule of law. A parallel hypothesis can be tested that China is facing a similar means-ends disjuncture as described in Merton's (1938, 1957) theory of social structure and anomie. The Chinese Dream[2] may look a lot like the American Dream in that

[1] Collective contention incidents are defined by the Chinese government as public protests or disturbances that involve more than five persons.

[2] China's new leader Xi Jinping also uses the term "Chinese dream" in a recent public speech (spring 2013). His coinage of the term is meant to be nationalistic, used in a similar vein as the rhetoric uttered by the CCP pioneers at the early twentieth century. Chinese dream is the collective dream for the Chinese State and the Chinese civilization, unlike the largely individualistic "American dreams" made known to every new immigrant to the United States.

unabashed pursuit of economic success is not only justified but universal; and just like in the American society (and perhaps many other industrialized societies), the norms governing individuals' strive for economic success may become weakened in China, producing anomie. In turn, this anomic condition produces strain which demands adjustment or adaptation by individuals. Merton (1938) offers five such "logically possible" adaptations: conformity, innovation, rebellion, retreatism and ritualism. Given the current Chinese context, Merton would probably approve that someone who takes his/her (financial or other rights related) grievance to the street with a crowd would qualify as an innovator, i.e., someone who strives to achieve accepted cultural goals while using novel or unaccepted methods.

Parsons (1966) views evolutionary social change as a change in cultural values. He disagrees with the assumption of an antithesis between traditional values and economic modernization. Inglehart's (1997) World Value Surveys across 43 nations attest to Parsons' argument that traditional cultural values could sometime be more helpful to the development of a modern economy rather than being obstacles to it. For example, Ingelhart (1997) concludes that the bureaucratic authority developed within the Confucian system in China probably helped to facilitate its rapid economic growth in recent decades. Tong (1991), when discussing why social change failed to spur the significant level of collective violence predicted by the theory in Ming dynasty, credits the cultural integration manifested in the elaborate system of Confucian indoctrination in schools and the official commendation of Confucian virtues. Both works seem to have arrived at the same conclusion which lends good explanation to Chinese government's renewed effort in promoting harmony, a core of Confucian (and Taoist) values. On the other hand, however, researchers have found significant intergenerational differences in cultural values. The younger generations of Chinese who are brought up in conditions of relative stability and prosperity are more individualistic (e.g., Inglehart 1997; Wang et al. 2011). They constitute a major force that is changing the social balance in China in support of democratization and the rule of law (e.g., Inglehart 1997; Wang 2005).

How traditional Chinese cultural values and prevailing ideological teachings affect individual adaptation to strain and proclivity for participation in collective contentions deserve further elaboration. But first, how does one measure an abstract concept such as Chinese traditional culture values? There isn't any established battery of measurement of individual values in China such as the eighteen-item terminal values instrumented by Milton Rokeach (1973). However, inspiration can be drawn from one of the most unique and creative studies conducted by Cao (2004) in her linguistic approach to the study of Chinese law. She states that "Chinese culture and language are hereditary, and the influence and effects of cultural values and traditional notions manifest themselves in contemporary life, and they are most visible in the Chinese language if one is willing to see them." (p. vii) Cao sees both language and law as semiotic systems that they are "interactive, relational, referential and evolutionary" (p. 2). She suggests that "even a cursory glance at the Analects reveals that many words and expressions as well as the ideas of Confucius are used in everyday Chinese. Chinese culture and

Confucian values are transmitted through living as a Chinese and being a Chinese." (p. 3).

Cao (2004) takes one step further by examining examples of applications of Austin's (1962) and Searle's (1969) speech act theories and Habermas's (1987) communicative action through languages used in Chinese law. If Cao's (2004) assessments are true, one could infer from her study that Chinese cultural values could be readily captured through people's identification of some of the most commonly used languages, such as idioms and popular slogans. This certainly looks like an inviting adventure. It is perhaps hard to argue against a caution that, even the most modest attempt at gathering the Chinese cultural values developed in the pre-Imperial and Imperial China would require the inclusion of the core teachings from the Confucians, the Legalists, and the Daoists.

As stated in earlier chapters, revolutions that have occurred in China since the beginning years of the last (twentieth) century have brought waves of attack on these traditional Chinese values. Ironically, a reversal of this trend also becomes evident in the twenty-first century. Liang Qichao's "Darwinian morality revolution" and Mao Zedong's "revolutionary morality" are well illustrated in the fascinating work done by James Pusey (1981). Some of Liang's and Mao's moral languages stand in stark contrast to those based on the Confucius teaching particularly. The familiar revolutionary vocabularies used by Liang include, for example, "zaofan you li" (its' justified to rebel), "gong de" (public morality) including "zheng" (struggle or contention), "si de" (private morality). Mao used some of the same languages as used by Liang but extended for more. For example, Mao's writings are littered with communicative languages such as change, struggle, rebellion, self-assertion for the people, self-restraint, self-sacrifice, and liberation. Mao's legacy also includes his definition of 'the people' as "all classes, strata, and social groups that support and take part in Socialist construction"; he defines all others as enemies of the people (Mao 1960).

In the post-Mao era, the Chinese Communist Party's core ideology has shifted from that of class struggle to one of economic development. This major shift has gone through three phases in the recent decades, from Deng Xiaoping's 'get-rich-first' to Jiang Zemin's 'economism and three represents' to Hu (Jintao)-Wen (Jiabao)'s 'harmonious society' and 'people-centered' policies. Each phase of these ideological shifts has its own focus yet each moves another step away from its "puritan Maoist roots." (Zheng 2009) Accompanying these ideological shifts are massive propaganda campaigns nationwide. Ideologies were turned into slogans, and slogans became daily languages. It seems that an onslaught of culture value transformation has already taken place. Yet, cultural values of the old, new, and foreign origins coexist in China. There are many interesting questions worthy of investigation. Which value(s) ordinary Chinese citizens draw to cope with individual strain? How well does the collectivist Chinese culture survive the impact of rising individualism? How conscious are people in acting together and inserting group pressure? After all, Bentley (1949) did argue long ago that group pressures would always triumph, whether there was dictatorship, constitutional monarchy, oligarchy, or democracy.

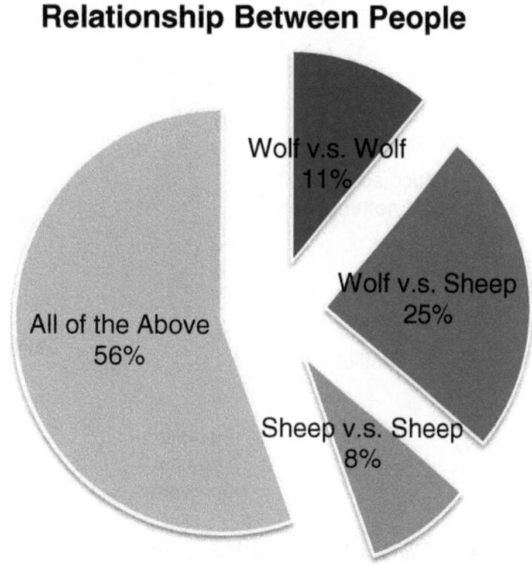

Fig. 4.1 Views of the nature of the basic relationships between people

Data from an empirical study (He and Pi 2011; Wang 2011) of social harmony, social hostility, and conflict resolutions mechanisms (including both formal and informal) in China has been made available recently. Although the survey is based on a convenience sample, it covers 28 provinces, autonomous regions, and province-equivalent large cities. A total of 1,279 completed survey questionnaires are collected from 322 different zip codes nation-wide.[3] Selective results are presented below to provide a critical domestic social context for the contemporary rule of law reform.

Figure 4.1 reports on the public assessment of the aggressiveness expressed in the prevailing human relationship in China. An analogy with four response categories is used: "wolf vs. wolf" (predator- predator relationship), "wolf vs. sheep" (predator–prey relationship), "sheep vs. sheep" (prey–prey relationship, at peace with each other but equally vulnerable to predators) and a catch-all "All of the above" (a complicated network of social relationships). Not surprisingly, we find that the majority of the respondents chose the catch-all category (56 %), in addition to the three standalone categories: "wolf vs. sheep" (25 %), "wolf vs. wolf" (11 %), and "sheep vs. sheep" (8 %). To decipher the broader social context underlying these response patterns, let's look at a few additional questions asked in the same survey.

Figure 4.2 presents the outcome of a question asking the major causes for the increasing number of collective incidents in China. Among the six categories included, "unequal distribution of wealth" (90.8 %, 钱和利益分配不均) is by far the most selected response. The second highest response is the "government-business coalition detrimental to the general public" (64.8 %, 官商纠结侵犯民众权). "Lawlessness (51.1 %, 法律名存实亡), "rebellion against government oppression" (40.9 %, 官逼民反), and "social values in conflict" (34.2 %, 价值标

[3] Respondents who are 16 years old or older are eligible. Unfortunately, no data was available from three provinces/autonomous regions: Guangxi, Ningxia, and Hainan.

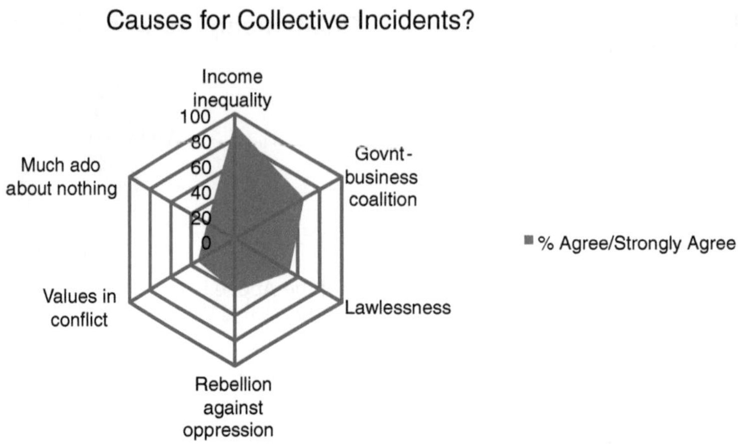

Fig. 4.2 Causes for collective incidents

准混乱) constitute the other major responses. About 26 % of the respondents do not feel sympathetic to the participants of collective incidents, agreeing that their activities are "much ado about nothing." (部分人吃饱了没事干瞎起哄)

Respondents of the survey are asked to rank order the seriousness of a list of eleven social problems. As a result, Fig. 4.3 documents the percentages of response categories that have received a top three ranking. "Corruption" (59 %) and "public official power abuse" (55.6 %) are two of the most agreed upon and most serious social problems on the list. Varying percentages are recorded for other major social problems such as "public order" (35.7 %), "income inequality" (29.0 %), "education" (25 %), and "political reform" (24.7 %). The relative concentration of problematic areas on corruption and public official power abuse necessitates a closer look

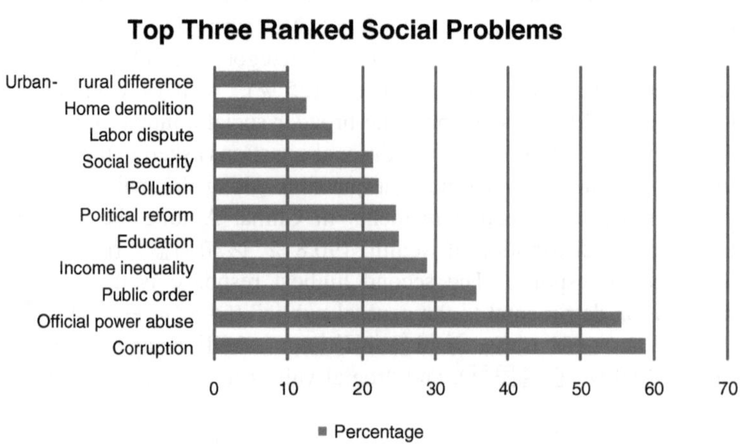

Fig. 4.3 Top three ranked social problems

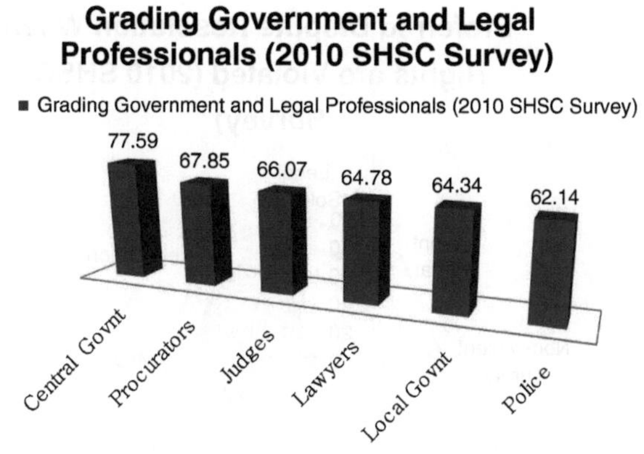

Fig. 4.4 Grading government and legal professionals (2010 SHSC survey)

at the public assessment of trust in government (both central and local) and the legal practitioners (i.e., the police, judges, prosecutors, and lawyers).

In the case of China, many scholars have demonstrated empirically that both interpersonal trust and system-based trust are comparatively high (Inglehart, 1997; Shi, 2001; Tang and Parish, 2000). Figure 4.4 suggests that the survey respondents place far more trust in the Chinese national government (77.59 %) than in their local government (64.34 %). This central-local observation may be a remnant of a historical legacy. A C plus ranking for an authoritarian regime that rules one of the largest landmass and the most populous country in the world is itself an indication of both the resiliency of the ruling Party (CCP) and the strength of culture identification of a strong central government. With regard to the public trust in the legal practitioners, we find that public prosecutors rank the highest (67.85 %), followed by court judges (66.07), lawyers (64.78 %) and lastly, the police (62.14 %).

With the generally lower than expected public trust in the Chinese judiciary in mind, we take a closer look at the preferred dispute resolution mechanisms reported by the survey respondents (see Fig. 4.5). When asked pointedly a question "What would you resort to when your rights are seriously violated, e.g., unable to collect pay for your work?" we find that, the overwhelming majority of the respondents would resort to "legal solution" (91.4 %) more than any other non-legal options. This is a strong indication that legal reforms in China in the past three decades may have begun to occupy the public conscience and that the public support for the expansion of the rule of law has been vastly improved. This observation, however, does not mean that other battle-tested and culturally relevant dispute resolution mechanisms are disappearing anytime soon. We find that the respondents continue to rely heavily on, for example, "negotiation between the parties" (84.9 %), "newspaper, TV, and Internet" (75.5 %),[4] "petition to higher level government agencies" (62.0 %), and the

[4] The effectiveness of venting through public media varies and is largely under government control. The Economist (2013) issued a recent special report on China and the internet. It states that "Chinese internet resembles a fenced-off playground with paternalistic guards," and that "the internet requires the party center to be more efficient at being authoritarian."

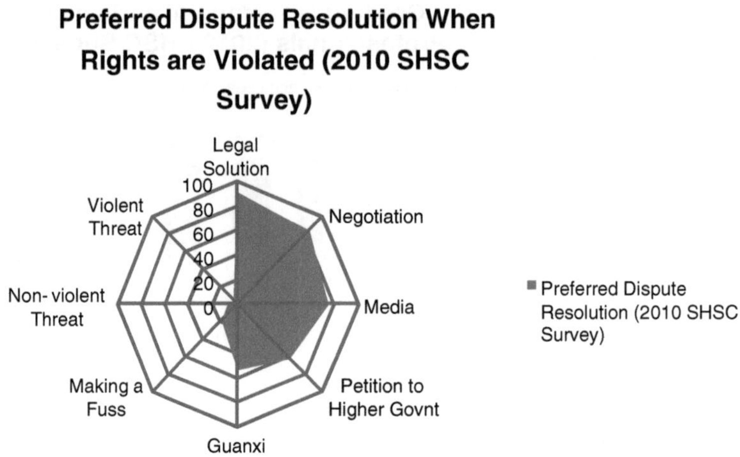

Fig. 4.5 Preferred dispute resolution when rights are violated (2010 SHSC survey)

old-fashioned use of "Guanxi network" (52.9 %).[5] Far less prevalent but still applicable solutions include the use of "the bigger the fuss, the better the solution" (18.2 %), "non-violent threat" (8.1 %) and "violent threat" (4.5 %). Having surveyed the landscape of China's present-day social context, we place in the next section a comparative assessment of China's rule of law based on a recent report released by the World Justice Project (see Agrast et al. 2012).

4.3 Cross-National Rule of Law Discourse

One of the most persistent and prolific scholars on the subject of rule of law in China is Randall Peerenboom. He combines theoretical rigor with practicality in his writings to offer a sensible understanding of China's rule of law potential. Peerenboom (2004a) suggests that the mainland China would likely fall into one of several rule of law varieties, that is, a rule of law in a "soft authoritarian, non-democratic or limited democratic state." Countries such as Singapore and Malaysia belong to this category. Chinese Hong Kong with its blended Chinese and Western cultural-legal heritages is also such an example. The idealized rule of law model is the mature Western liberal democracy and legal systems exemplified by countries like the US, Japan, and France. There are a large host of countries that would fall between these two categories. These nations subscribe to the rule of law ideal but are in transitional stage of their democracy, constitutionalism, and legal

[5] Guanxi is a term that is similar to the English translations of "relationship" and "connection" but it is much more, given China's rule of man culture heritage. A good read of the dynamics in the personalized Chinese networks of influence can be found in Gold et al's. (2002) work.

development. Peerenboom (2004b) draws an interesting conclusion that the Western "liberal democratic form of rule of law" is not without shortcomings and it can benefit from the "communitarian strands of rule of law" illustrated by (for example) some East Asian countries. This is a welcomed extension to his main theoretical thesis that distinguishes "thin" and "thick" rule of law visualized as components in a concentric circle where the inner most circle contains the core elements of a thin rule of law.

Rule of law is treated as both a means for political and economic reforms and an end to itself in China. Scholars seem to have agreed on two important concerns: first, aspects of a true rule of law are possible in a non-democratic state, albeit limited in the quantity of its contents (i.e., thin rather than thick rule of law); second, different types of rule of law are also possible (e.g., liberal democratic vs. communitarian categories of rule of law). Accordingly, those promoting rule of law based on a liberal democratic ideal need to be mindful of a foreign country's socio-political context and to interject a good dose of "humility." (e.g., Carothers 1999; Alford 2003)

Rule of law promotion in China has gained enormous momentum since the late 1970s when the country began to open its doors to the outside world. The rhetoric on rule of law is heightened by the high profile Presidential summit meeting between President Jiang Zeming and President Bill Clinton in 1997. By the year 2000, more than a thousand foreign funding organizations (e.g., single or multilateral governmental offices, faith-based charitable organizations, NGOs, foundation offices, etc.) are operating in China. Together, they give more than $100 million each year to support various rule of law projects and civil society programs (Yuan 2003).

As stated by Kahn (1999), "the rule of law is a product of the imagination before it is a product of legislation or judicial acts." The early promoters of the rule of law in China were strongly motivated by China's economic potential. The most rudimentary rule of law needs to be established to ensure a stable environment for the foreign investors. The programmatic approaches under the rubric of rule of law necessarily target the followings: (1) legal education reform through curricular and pedagogical designs and exchange of scholars and students[6]; (2) capacity-building aimed at improving the functions and capabilities of the Chinese legal system with a particular focus on the professionalism of the actors (i.e., judges, prosecutors, police officers, lawyers, paralegals)[7]; (3) structural reform to promote

[6] Increasing number of Chinese universities have signed MOU agreements with their counterparts from foreign (mostly Western and English-speaking) countries for faculty and student exchanges and joint research. Each year a healthy number of Chinese law school faculty, criminal justice practitioners, and doctor of law candidates are sponsored by the Chinese government (e.g., Chinese Scholarship Council) to spend a semester or a year as a visiting scholar.

[7] For example, a comparative moot court pilot project funded by the US State Department was carried out jointly in 2001–2002. It involved the Massachusetts Judges Conference, the Supreme People's Court of China, Tsinghua University School of Law, Xiamen University School of Law, Sichuan Judges Conference, and the High Court of Jiangsu Province. The moot court used a civil case under the US rules to introduce key participants to aspects of American judicial procedures and to demonstrate the rule of evidence and the principles of due process (CPDD 2013).

transparency, accountability and technical competence of the legal apparatus[8]; and (4) establish a legal culture through enhancing rights awareness and joint foreign-Chinese research projects.[9]Today, no one would deny that China has made substantial improvement in many aspects of the rule of law in the last three decades.

The World Justice Project which produces the rule of law index is an independent, non-profit organization founded in 2006 as a presidential initiative of the American Bar Association. The Index makes a unique attempt to measure the abstract concept of the rule of law in four operationalized areas: (1) whether the government and its official are accountable under the law; (2) whether the laws protecting fundamental rights are clear, publicized, stable, and fair; (3) whether the process by which the laws are enacted, administered, and enforced is accessible, efficient, and fair; and (4) whether justice is delivered by competent, ethical, and independent representatives.[10]

The Rule of Law Index (Agrast et al. 2012) offers a set of quantitative measures based on nine global factors and 48 subfactors. The nine global factors include: limited government powers, absence of corruption, order and security, fundamental rights, open government, regulatory enforcement, civil justice, criminal justice, and informal justice.[11] The score of each global factor is based on the normalized average scores of subfactors. For example, the score for the global factor-"criminal justice" is calculated using the average scores from the following eight subfactors: effective criminal investigation, timely adjudication, effective correctional system, impartiality of the criminal justice system as a whole, free of corruption, free of government interference, and protection of due process rights for the accused.

Table 4.1 places China in the context of a comparison with the United States, Japan, and Hong Kong on the key global measures of the rule of law. This comparison is meaningful for several reasons. The US constitutionalism and Japan's early Westernization have been regarded as models by the Chinese intelligentsia at the beginning of the twentieth century. Hong Kong (SAR) which has been under British rule for a century is touted as a success story of rule of law's triumph. The US, China and Japan are also the three largest economies in the

---

[8] American Bar Association (ABA) developed a Prosecutorial Reform Index (PRI) under its Rule of Law Initiative. The PRI Index draws criteria from the ABA standards for criminal justice (prosecution function), the UN Guidelines on the role of prosecutors, the Council of Europe recommendations on the role of public prosecution in the criminal justice system, and the International Association of Prosecutors Standards of Professional Responsibilities and Statement of the Essential Duties and Rights of Prosecutors (Greer 2007).

[9] Empirical legal research funded by the Ford Foundation has generated great interest in the Chinese legal community. There is strong indication that outcomes of these studies are playing an increasingly important role in guiding policy making and revising legal statutes.

[10] Detailed methodology used for the survey is described on the organization's website at http://worldjusticeproject.org/methodology.

[11] Country scores for "informal justice" are not reported by the organization.

Table 4.1 Rule of law index: comparisons of China, USA, Japan and Chinese Hong Kong[a]

Global Factors/Country	Score				Global ranking ($N = 97$)				Income group ranking			
	USA	China (PRC)	Japan	HK (SAR)	USA	China (PRC)	Japan	HK (SAR)	USA	China (PRC)	Japan	HK (SAR)
Limited government powers	0.77	*0.36*	0.80	0.73	17	*86*	10	22	17/29	*26/30*	10/29	20/29
Absence of corruption	0.78	*0.52*	0.84	0.89	18	*40*	10	9	17/29	*10/30*	10/29	9/29
Order and security	0.83	*0.78*	0.89	0.93	22	*32*	7	2	19/29	*4/30*	7/29	2/29
Fundamental rights	0.73	*0.35*	0.78	0.71	25	*94*	17	31	22/29	*29/30*	17/29	27/29
Open government	0.77	*0.42*	0.82	0.82	13	*69*	9	10	13/29	*23/30*	9/29	10/29
Regulatory enforcement	0.70	*0.41*	0.87	0.75	19	*80*	2	14	17/29	*28/30*	2/29	14/29
Civil Justice	0.65	*0.43*	0.77	0.71	22	*82*	8	17	19/29	*27/30*	8/29	16/29
Criminal Justice	0.65	*0.54*	0.68	0.76	26	*39*	23	8	24/29	*8/30*	22/29	8/29

[a] *Data Source* The World Justice Project 2012–2013 Survey Results. China-Upper Middle Income Group ($N = 30$); USA, Japan and HK (SAR)-High Income Group ($N = 29$)

Table 4.2 Rule of law index-criminal justice sub-factors[a]

Criminal Justice sub-factors/country	BRIC/East Asian countries								
	USA	Brazil	Russia	India	China (PRC)	Japan	Singapore	Korea (ROK)	HK (SAR)
Effective criminal Investigation	0.78	0.49	0.57	0.45	*0.77*	0.63	0.93	0.57	0.88
Timely/effective adjudication	0.76	0.42	0.42	0.40	*0.59*	0.58	0.90	0.80	0.81
Effective correction system	0.46	0.23	0.29	0.39	*0.63*	0.60	0.95	0.80	0.71
Impartiality (CJ system)	0.38	0.37	0.37	0.35	*0.65*	0.65	0.82	0.78	0.75
Free of corruption	0.77	0.61	0.39	0.43	*0.59*	0.84	0.88	0.79	0.85
Free of government interference	0.80	0.84	0.41	0.67	*0.09*	0.77	0.72	0.74	0.55
Due process rights/ accused	0.62	0.44	0.32	0.39	*0.49*	0.69	0.85	0.80	0.78

[a] *Data source* the world justice project 2012–2013 survey results

world today. In addition, China's status as an emerging world power necessarily makes its rule of law reality and commitment an inescapable topic.

China does not look impressive at all on the Rule of Law global measurement. China ranks close to the very bottom of all nations participated in the survey ($N = 97$) on the protection of fundamental rights (94/97), limited government powers (86/97), civil justice (82/97), regulatory enforcement (80/97) and open government (69/94). The US, Japan, and Hong Kong (SAR) share strong similarities with their consistent top third ranking in all these measures among the participating countries. Japan (and Hong Kong to some extent), in particular, also outrank the US on these measures within the High Income Country group ($N = 29$). A reasonably strong argument can be made based on this comparison that, the Western based rule of law values are not necessarily incompatible with the Confucian influenced values endorsed by East Asian countries. The two could co-exist to great effect as evident in the high rule of law rankings of Japan and Chinese Hong Kong.

With regard to subfactors measuring realization of rule of law in the criminal justice field, a revealing image emerges. Table 4.2 compares China's ranking with the US, the other BRIC countries (i.e., Brazil, Russia, and India),[12] and the other East Asian countries with shared Confucian traditions. The most visible anomalies are the exceptionally low score of China on the factor of "free of government interference" (0.09) and the lower scores of the US on two items "effective

[12] The acronym of "BRIC" countries are first used by Jim O'Neill, a global economist at Goldman Sachs. The four BRIC countries combine for a quarter of the world landmass and forty percent of the world population. They are predicted to become among the most dominating economies by the year 2050.

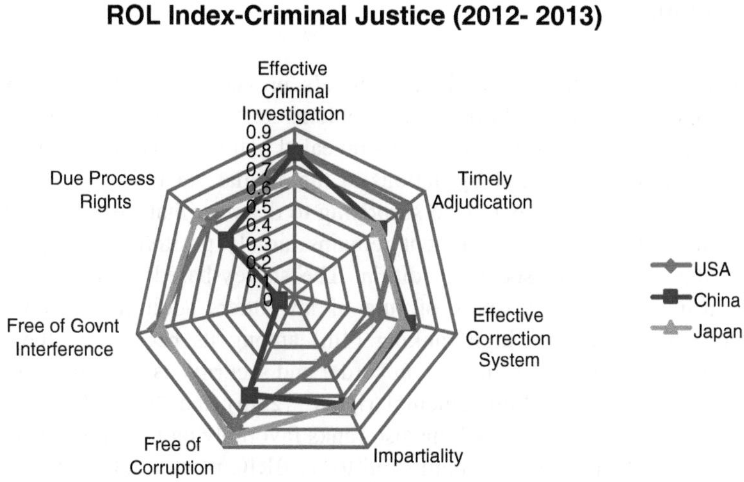

Fig. 4.6 ROL Index-criminal justice (2012–2013): comparison of USA, China and Japan

correctional system" (0.46 for the US vs. 0.63 for China) and "impartiality" (0.38 for the US vs. 0.65 for China) than the corresponding scores for China.

With the exception of a low score on government interference, China's scores on criminal justice related rule of law subfactors do compare favorably to those of its peers in the BRIC country cluster. The BRIC countries are among the most populous and fast developing economies in the world. To some extent, China is in the same position as the rest of this group that it has to balance its new found economic prosperity with a need to deepen political reform to sustain the development momentum. China and Russia also share the socialist revolution past and both are confronted with international pressure to ease off government interference on all aspect of social lives. However, China presents one example in contrast to its BRIC peers that substantial government interference is not necessarily detrimental to the *effectiveness* of its criminal justice system overall. This observation is also an example consistent with the Chinese tradition of emphasizing substantive rather than procedural justice.

Figure 4.6 offers a visual comparison of China, the US, and Japan on various aspect of ROL Index with regard to criminal justice practice. The most apparent difference lies in the measurement of "free of government interference" where the finding on China is in sharp contrast with those on the US and Japan. The differences are far less prominent in other measures, particular those concerning criminal justice "effectiveness" (e.g., effective criminal investigation, timely adjudication, and effective correction system).

4.4 Conclusion

It is perhaps no surprise to find that China's prevailing social milieu is both complex and contentious. Major social problems such as income inequality, corruption, and abuse of government powers revealed in this chapter (see Fig. 4.3) are not unlike those experienced by nations at the similar stage of socio-economic development. However, it is indeed surprising to discover that the Chinese public perception of the central government remains largely positive (see Fig. 4.4) in spite of the challenging social condition. The survey-based international comparison using nuanced measures of rule of law offers additional insights. For example, China's relative high ranking (4th) among its peers (i.e., the Upper Middle Income group of 30 nations) on "order and security" is accompanied by its glaring low rankings on "fundamental rights" (29th) and "limited government power." (26th) (see Table 4.1) China also ranks favorably on multiple measures of criminal justice "effectiveness" compared to its BRIC peers (and even to mature democracies such as the US and Japan). However, the Chinese advantage in "effectiveness" comes at the price of overwhelming interference of criminal justice due process exerted by the government (see Table 4.2). In sum, these empirical findings reflect a pair of paradoxes: the legitimacy of the central government remains intact while corruption and abuse of governmental power at local level are wreaking havoc; the government is effective (at collective level in achieving order and security) but intrusive (at individual level in trumping individual rights) in the administration of criminal justice. How long does the Chinese government could safely live with such paradoxes is an open question.

Some observers (e.g., Jones 2003) express a concern that the future of Chinese legal system is hard to foresee. Others (e.g., Peerenboom 2004) are somewhat more optimistic, arguing that the Chinese ruling regime is likely to keep its own power in check to boost legitimacy and remain in power. They argue that a communitarian rule of law model is possible in which social harmony and solidarity can go hand-in-hand with more individual rights (e.g., Peerenboom 2002). Researchers urge a better understanding of the argument of "cultural particularism" made, for example, by the East Asian countries that cultural factors can affect the prioritizing of rights, the justification of rights, and the moral foundations for distinctive political practices and institutions (Bell 2005). There is no doubt that China can continue to benefit from the broadened experiences both from its large country peers such as the US and the BRIC nations and from its more successful regional neighbors with a shared culture heritage such as Japan, Singapore, Republic of Korea, and Hong Kong (SAR).

References

Agrast, M. D., Botero, J. C., Ponce, A., Martinez, J., & Pratt, C. (2012). *The Rule of Law Index 2012–2013 Report*. Washington: The World Justice Project.

Alford, W. (2003). Exporting the pursue of happiness. In S. Hsu (Ed.), *Understanding China's legal system: Essays in honor of Jerome A. Cohen*. New York: New York University Press.

Austin, J.L. (1962). How to do things with words. Oxford: Oxford University Press.

Beissinger, M. R. (2002). *Nationalist Mobilization and the Collapse of the Soviet State*. New York: Cambridge University Press.

Bell, D. A. (2005). A communitarian critique of liberalism. *Analyse & Kritik,27*, 215–238.

Bentley, Arthur. (1949). *The Process of Government*. Evanston: Principia Press.

Bergsten, C., Fred, F., Charles, L., Nicholas, R., & Mitchell, D. J. (2008). *China's Rise: Challenges and Opportunities*. Washington: Peter G. Peterson Institute for International Economics and the Center for Strategic and International Studies.

Cao, D. (2004). *Chinese law: A language perspective*. Burlington, VT: Ashgate Puublishing Co.

Carothers, T. (1999). *Aiding Democracy Abroad: The Learning Curve*. Washington: Carnegie Endowment for International Peace.

Chen, C. (2009). Growing Social Unrest in China: Rising Social Discontents and Popular Protests. In G. Wu & H. Lansdowne (Eds.), *Socialist China, Capitalist China: Social Tension and Political Adaptation under Economic Globalization* (pp. 10–28). London and New York: Routledge.

CPDD (2013). *China: Comparative moot court pilot project for China*. Boston: Center for Peace, Democracy and Development (CPDD), the university of Massachusetts-Boston. Retrieved April 13, 2013 from http://www.umb.edu/cpdd/expertise/law_reform/china_comparative_moot_court_pilot_project_for_china

Gold, T., Guthrie, D., & Wank, D. (2002). *Social Connections in China: Institutions, Culture and the Changing Nature of Guanxi*. Cambridge: Cambridge University Press.

Greer, M. A. (2007). *Road Maps for Reform: The Effective Use of Assessment*. Washington: Rule of Law Initiative, American Bar Association.

Habermas, J. (1987). *The philosophical discourse of modernity: Twelve lectures (translated by F. Lawrence)*. Cambridge: Polity Press.

He, N., Pi, Y. (2011). *Strain, Individual Adaption and Collective Incidents: A National Survey in China*. Grant proposal submitted to the National Science Foundation.

Jones, W. C. (2003). Trying to understand the current chinese legal system: Essay in honour of jerome A. Cohen. New York: NYU Press.

Inglehart, R. (1997). *Modernization and Postmodernization: Cultural, Economic, and Political Change in 43 Societies*. Princeton: Princeton University Press.

Kahn, P. W. (1999). *The Cultural Study of Law: Reconstructing Legal Scholarship*. Chicago: University of Chicago Press.

Lee, K., Kim, J.-H., & Woo, W. T. (Eds.). (2009). *Power and Sustainability of the Chinese State*. London and New York: Routledge.

Mao, Z. (1960). *On the Correct Handling of Contradictions Among the People*. Beijing: Foreign Languages Press.

Merton, R. (1938). Social Structure and Anomie. *American Sociological Review,3*, 672–682.

Merton, R. (1957). *Social Theory and Social Structure*. New York: The Free Press.

Parsons, T. (1966). *Societies: Evolutionary and Comparative Perspectives*. Englewood Cliffs: Prentice Hall.

Peerenboom, R. (2002). *China's Long March toward Rule of Law*. Cambridge: Cambridge University Press.

Peerenboom, R. P. (Ed.). (2004a). *Asian Discourses of Rule of Law: Theories and Implementation of Rule of Law in Twelve Asian Countries*. London: RoutledgeCurzon.

Peerenboom, R. (2004b). Competing conceptions of rule of law in China. In R. P. Peerenboom (Ed.), *Asian Discourses of Rule of Law: Theories and Implementation of Rule of Law in Twelve Asian Countries* (pp. 113–145). London: Routledge.

Pusey, J. (1981). Mao Zedong's "Revolutionary Morality" and China's "Moral Development". In R. W. Wilson, S. L. Greenblatt, & A. Auerbacher (Eds.), *Moral Behavior in Chinese Society*. New York: Praeger.

Rokeach, M. (1973). *The Nature of Human Values*. New York: The Free Press.

Searle, J. (1969). *Speech acts: An essay in the philsophy of language*. Cambridge: Cambridge University Press.

Shi, T. (2001). *Cultureal impact on political trust: A comparision of mainland china and taiwan*. Comparative politics, 33: 401–420.

The Economist (2013). China's internet: A giant cage. Special report: China and the internet. Retrieved April 6, 2013 from http://www.economist.com/news/special-report/21574628

Tang, W, & Parish, W. L. (2000). Chinese urban life under market reform: The changing social contract. Cambridge University Press.

Tong, J. W. (1991). *Disorder Under Heaven: Collective Violence in the Ming Dynasty*. Stanford: Stanford University Press.

Wang, J. (2011). *Research on collective incidents in China* (中国群体性事件研究). Doctoral dissertation, Graduate School of the China University of Political Science and Law, Beijing (中国政法大学研究生院).

Wang, X. (2005). *Mainland official hails bloody riots as a sign of democracy*. Beijing: South China Morning Post.

Zheng, Y. (2009). Can the Communist Party Sustain its Rule in China. In K. Lee, J.-H. Kim, & W. T. Woo (Eds.), *Power and Sustainability of the Chinese State* (pp. 186–209). London and New York: Routledge.

Yuan, N. (2003). *Funding the rule of law and civil society*. China Rights Form Vol.3. (pp. 22–33).

Part III
Empirical Inquiry

Chapter 5
Pilot Study

5.1 Introduction

Part I and Part II which have focused on the historical (Chaps. 1–2) and socio-legal (Chaps. 3–4) contexts set the stage for the in-depth empirical inquiry illustrated in Part III (Chaps. 5–8). This chapter 5 offers the necessary background and rationales (see Sect. 5.2), research methodology (see Sect. 5.3), and description and preliminary observations of the data (see Sect. 5.4) from a pilot project funded by the John D. and Catherine T. MacArthur Foundation. This comprehensive study was carried out in J Province located in the southeast region of China from 2009 to 2011. It serves as the major data source for the empirical presentations in Chaps. 6–8.

5.2 Background and Rationales

5.2.1 Studies on Chinese Legal Practices and Judicial Reforms

Cohen (1968, 1970) pioneered the empirical inquiry into Chinese criminal justice practices in the late 1960s, in spite of the insurmountable difficulties in gaining research access to the Chinese judicial apparatus. Very few English language publications on the functioning of Chinese justice system are available in the 1970s and much of the 1980s with the exceptions of Li (1978) and Leng (1985). Major book-length publications on post-Mao Chinese legal reform include works from Lubman (1996, 1999) and Lo (1995) in the 1990s and works from Turner et al. (2000); Clarke (2008); Liang (2008) and McConville (2011) in the following decade.

Although it remains severely limited, empirical research on broad array of topics in the field of Chinese law and legal reform is gaining momentum in the last two decades. Some researchers (e.g., Liang 2008; Lu and Miethe 2002; Lu and Drass 2002; Lu and Gunnison 2003; Zuo 2009) devote attention to assess the

N. He, *Chinese Criminal Trials*, DOI: 10.1007/978-1-4614-8205-5_5,

impact of China's Criminal Law and Criminal Procedure Law reforms in actual court trials. Others focus on studying the symbiotic relationship between the legal institutions and the various legal practitioners during the time of reform (e.g., Halliday and Liu 2007; Liu 2006; Liu and Halliday 2009, 2011; Michelson 2003, 2006, 2007; Michelson and Read 2011).

A unique recent development in empirical legal research in China is worth mentioning. Funding for empirical legal research is strongly tied to experimentations related to Chinese court reform, focusing typically on thorny issues related to criminal due process. From 2002 to 2011, eighteen scholar-led demonstration projects on criminal procedure reform have been funded by the Ford Foundation (Stutsman 2011). These empirical projects cover topics such as police interrogation, pretrial discovery, bail and discretionary non-prosecution, live witnesses, evidence collection, victim-offender mediation, criminal defense, plea bargaining, and sentencing. These projects and research teams were led by eight senior Chinese legal scholars in the field of Chinese criminal procedure law (see Fig. 5.1). There is strong indication that the tradition of empirical legal research is beginning to set roots in China. Application of empirical methods, including experimental design methodology (with varying levels of design sophistication and implementation fidelity), is a common feature of these demonstration projects. Guo's (2011) bilingual book on the Chinese experience based on these empirical studies offers an excellent overview of the design and implementation of experimental methodology in Chinese judicial fields. These projects, however, should not be mistaken for traditional sociological studies due to the obvious absence of any theoretical focus. Also, the statistical analysis used to report the outcomes of these studies remain rudimentary, including mostly simple counts, percentages, and pie/bar graphs. We are not aware of any hypothesis testing being used in any of these studies so far. Research design and statistics are taught in less than a handful of Chinese law schools at the moment. Nevertheless, the awareness and interest have grown substantially in recent years given the promotion of empirical legal research and a series of large-scale empirical methods training workshops co-sponsored by the Ford Foundation, Vera Institute of Justice, and the Institute of Procuratorate Theory, the research arm of the Chinese Supreme People's Procuratorate. In short, it would not be an overstatement that the first decade of the twenty-first century should be remembered as the golden years of empirical criminal procedure reform experiments.

5.2.2 *Why Study Legal Representation and Criminal Processing in Basic People's Court?*

The MacArthur pilot study both benefits from and contributes to the momentum of growing empirical legal research in China in the last decade. It differs from the other studies by focusing primarily on collecting empirical data on legal

Fig. 5.1 Major funded projects in china's golden years of empirical criminal procedure reform experiments

representation and criminal processing in the Basic People's Courts (the lowest level court) in China. According to the recent statistics from the National Statistical Bureau of China (2011a, b), a total of 996,666 criminal defendants are tried in 2009 in all levels of Chinese courts (i.e., Basic People's Courts, Intermediate People's Courts, Provincial Higher People's Courts, and the Supreme People's Court). The largest share of criminal cases is received by Basic People's Court as courts of First Instance in China. Chinese census statistics do not differentiate the exact number of cases tried in these Courts. All levels of Chinese courts can serve as Courts of First Instance, including the Supreme People's Court of China. Except the Basic People's Court, all higher level courts also serve as an appellate court for cases from one level below.

Plagued by the shortage of legal professionals, a socialist twist of the inquisitorial (Continental) legal system and the lack of judicial independence, due process rights protection in Chinese courts has historically been viewed as (grossly) inadequate. Until recently, there is little empirical knowledge on how criminal defendants are represented in Chinese court, especially at the lowest level Basic People's courts. Many may have observed that, in terms of the rule of law in the books, the language used to describe the fundamental and procedural rights granted to Chinese citizens by the Chinese Constitution (1982), Chinese Criminal Law (1997), and Criminal Procedure Law (1996) is increasingly similar to those of the western world.[1]

Chinese Criminal Procedure Law (1996) specifies the importance of legal representation as a procedural right for the criminal defendants in two areas: First of all, the law makes legal representation mandatory for those charged with capital crimes. By comparison, this threshold of providing government-appointed counsel

[1] Debates and discussions on the revisions of both Chinese Criminal Law and Criminal Procedure Law were in the background of the MacArthur pilot study. The 8th revision of the Chinese Criminal Law was adopted by the People's Congress and took effect on 5/1/2011. Similarly, the most recently revised (2012) Chinese Criminal Procedure Law took effect on 1/1/2013.

for indigent defendants involved in capital crime was passed in the U.S. more than half a century earlier. There was the decision made by the U.S. Supreme Court in *Powell versus Alabama* (1932), which applied the right to all criminal defendants charged with state capital crimes. The Court affirmed the right 6 years later in *Johnson versus Zerbst* (1938) and expanded it to be applicable to all indigent defendants charged with a felony in federal courts. In 1963 (i.e., *Gideon vs. Wainwright*), the Court applied the same right to those charged with any state felony crime. The Court extended the right to juveniles in 1967 (i.e., the *In re Gault* ruling). The Court's decision in *Strickland versus Washington* (1984) took a step further by providing a right for effective counsel. The Court's more recent decision in *Alabama versus Shelton* (2002) further extended such right to indigent defendants who are threatened to receive even a suspended prison sentence. The American experience at least demonstrates that the right to counsel evolution is likely to be long and tortuous even in a well-established democracy.

Second, the law gives priority to government-appointed legal counsel to the minors, the elderly, women and those physically challenged who are charged with crimes. We could not find any statistics with regard to the exact number of government-appointed legal representation befitting this particular legal provision. Conversations with J province judges suggest that currently no more than 50 % of juvenile criminal defendants are represented by lawyers, either hired or appointed. We do not have solid evidence to suggest this particular law is being applied substantively.

There are indeed substantial increase in the number of practicing lawyers in China, from 3,000 in 1980 to a total of 173,327 in 2009. This number includes 155,457 full-time and 8,764 part-time lawyers (National Statistical Bureau of China 2011a, b). Altogether, Chinese lawyers provided legal representations in a total of 564,204 criminal cases in 2009. There are 15,888 law firms nationwide. One can certainly argue that the increasing supply of practicing lawyers would make legal representation more available to more people, especially at the lowest level courts where the bulk of all criminal cases are processed. While it is true that Chinese law provides language for legal representation and the actual number of lawyers in China has increased dramatically, there is at this time no solid empirical research to document to what extent legal representation is provided to criminal defendants in Basic People's Courts in China.

5.2.3 What to Study and Why J Province?

The pilot study is intended to investigate the reality of legal representation and criminal processing in Basic People's Courts in J Province. Data are collected on multiple dimensions including case specific information such as the extent and nature of legal representation, the impact of strategies used by defense attorneys on case outcomes, criminal justice practitioners' perceptions of legal representation, judicial practice and criminal justice reforms, and the impact of courtroom culture on case outcomes.

The American PI's research partner-X University's School of Law has established strong ties with the legal communities in J Province. High level of cooperation is expected from the judicial agencies in the province. Many courts throughout the Province are already in partnership with the law school, regularly hosting student internships and faculty research. Many alumni of the law school are now in leadership positions in these agencies, and some are known as reform-minded magistrates. The co-PI also directs a Research Center in the law school and serves as a consultant to several Basic People's Courts on difficult criminal cases.

This project can be seen as a demonstration model of collaborative cross-national legal research. The Chinese researchers are able to identify the most urgent and problematic issues confronting Chinese judiciary in carrying out legal reforms. The American faculty provides empirical research experience to help apply suitable methodology for answering the project's research questions. Project outcomes that are scientifically based and policy relevant are expected to be achieved. Continued close collaborations are also expected between the research partners beyond the current research project. It is fair to say that the MacArthur funding not only helps to achieve substantive results from the current project, it also helps to build an infrastructure that will afford and benefit future criminal justice policy research in China.

5.2.4 *Why Now?*

A unique opportunity presents itself to conduct an empirical assessment of the impact of legal representation on criminal case process and outcome when the Chinese Lawyers' Law was revised on June 1, 2008. The most significant provision of the law provides Chinese criminal suspects the right to legal representation at first police hearing (interrogation). In the past, lawyers have been barred from police investigation stage. Previously, lawyers could be requested by their clients only after all police investigations are completed (often confessions are extracted by this point) and when the prosecutorial agency began their proceeding. The new provision is a significant departure from the previous practices and is being strongly resisted by the Chinese criminal justice agencies (police, prosecution, and the court). Although the new Chinese Lawyers' Law falls short of calling for protection of suspect/defendant rights similar to giving Miranda warning upon arrest, the possibility of legal representation at the earlier stage of police investigation may provide extra protection against torture and coerced confessions. The current study aims to provide empirical data from a Southeast Province.

There are four major areas of empirical study conducted in China in recent years: (1) pretrial detention reform; (2) police interrogation process reform; (3) plea bargaining reform; and (4) reform on alternative sentencing with mediation. It is clear that all these topics reflect a critical need for empirical research for the purpose of promoting judicial reform. However, no large-scale empirical research has been conducted on the topic of legal representation in China.[2] This pilot project fills this void and contributes to an area that needed much empirical evidence and significant improvement.

Legal reform with regard to increasing level of legal representation is not an easy task. The researchers are confronted with both questions of *whether* and *how* criminal defendants are represented in Chinese courts. The lawyer density ratio in China is roughly about 1 per 8,867 citizens (150,000 lawyers in a population of 1,330,044,600), compared to the U.S. ratio of 1 per 281 citizens. No amount of short-term reform can fundamentally change that ratio quickly. In fact, 206 counties in China have no local law firm, making access to legal representation exceedingly difficult. Therefore, the availability of qualified Chinese lawyers remains a long-term goal. Many believe that there is a greater immediacy and perhaps greater likelihood to improve how lawyers perform in Chinese courtrooms. By studying how criminal defendants are actually represented by their attorneys, we may come closer to making realistic recommendations on how to improve their performance within a shorter time frame.

5.3 Research Methodology

5.3.1 Sample, Research Questions, and Hypotheses

The study was conducted in J province which has nine prefectures and 85 counties, with a total population of 35 million at the time of the study. There are three major regions in this southeast coastal province: the south, the north, and the west regions, reflecting different levels of economic development and population size (e.g., the southeast region being the most populous and urbanized, the west being rural and the least developed). Significant differences in court caseload, case types, court infrastructure, allocation of judicial resources, and availability and quality of practicing lawyers may be a reality. It is imperative therefore to include adequate representations from all regions. In the original sampling design proposed to the MacArthur Foundation, one randomly selected Basic People's Court from each of the five major cities (with largest population) is included in the sample, and a master list of all other Basic People's Courts in the province (excluding those from the five major cities) was compiled and the courts are grouped into three regions as explained above. A random sample of three Basic People's courts in each region is drawn. Demographic characteristics of the prefecture-level cities and final court access information are included in Table 5.1.

[2] Terrence Halliday and Sida Liu's National Science Foundation funded project which focuses on criminal procedure law in China coincided with the MacArthur pilot study.

Table 5.1 J Province basic people's courts (N = 82) and registered lawyers (N = 4,208; 2008 data)[a]

Prefecture-level cities	Population	GDP/capita (Yuan)	Basic courts (Total)	Basic courts (Observed)	Registered lawyers (2008)	Lawyer density Ratio	Legal aid lawyers
City A	7,790,000	34,840	10	9	518	15,039	17
City B	6,830,000	33,615	12	11	1,326	5,151	28
City C	3,760,000	18,261	10	8	211	17,820	14
City D	3,030,000	17,851	9	3	148	22,782	21
City E	2,890,000	19,348	10	3	180	16,056	20
City F	2,840,000	21,515	5	5	131	21,679	9
City G	2,770,000	24,334	7	5	173	16,012	10
City H	2,630,000	25,407	12	5	152	17,303	23
City I	2,490,000	62,651	7	6	831	2,996	9
Total	35,030,000	28,647	82	55 (67%)	3,670 (4,208)	7,642	151

[a] Chinese national lawyer density ratio: China National ratio: 1 per 8,867 (US ratio: 1 per 281). Calculations are made based on census population data and the 2008 registered lawyers' figures reported by Provincial Lawyer's Association. Another report puts the total number of lawyers in J Province at 4,584. In 2008, a total of 26,937 criminal cases were represented by lawyers.

Given the paucity and credibility concern of the existing data, the MacArthur pilot project team is forced to start from a blank slate in order to investigate the following questions: (1) *what* is the extent of legal representation for criminal defendants in the lowest level criminal courts? (2) *how* are criminal defendants represented in these courts? (3) *what* are the dynamics of the courtroom working group (judges, procurators, and defense attorneys)? and (4) *how* are the outcomes of criminal cases really decided in these courts? The research starts with the following key hypotheses:

- Level of legal representation in criminal cases is low in Chinese Basic People's Court
- There is a difference in the use of legal representation by case types (e.g., violent crime defendants are more likely to seek legal representation)
- There are variations in both the availability and quality of legal representation across regions of different economic development
- Chinese criminal lawyers have little substantive impact on sentencing outcome based on the defense they provide in court
- Chinese criminal lawyers focus not on acquittal but on presenting mitigating circumstances to impact the sentencing decision
- Extra-legal factors (such as sensitivity of the case, a defendant's residency/employment statuses, an attorney's professional reputation in the courtroom, and political connections) play significant role in determining case process and outcome
- Criminal defense attorneys are marginalized in Chinese court by their professional peers such as judges and prosecutors

- There are political influences on case outcomes

These are some of the baseline questions that should be answered first. One important goal for the pilot study is to also identify and prioritize the research questions. As stated earlier, reform of the Chinese judicial system has started at least two decades ago but scientifically based empirical assessment has lagged far behind. Of course, one of the reasons is due to political sensitivity; among other reasons may very well be the lack of empirical research tradition and expertise. Government publications of Chinese crime statistics and criminal justice process are highly aggregated, reported irregularly and of questionable validity (He 2014). They are of very limited use for policy makers and researchers. Therefore, original empirical studies conducted independently by non-governmental researchers are not only complimentary but also indispensable.

5.3.2 Data Collection

Case Files: In the Basic People's Court, a criminal case is usually tried by two judges with a people's assessor or by a panel of three judges with one presiding judge (i.e., Collegial Panel). Four sections of information are documented in a typical court case dossier (more detailed descriptions in Chap. 6): (1) the defendant's demographics (age, gender, education, employment, residential status) and information on his/her legal counsel (when applicable); (2) pretrial information (dates of detention by the police, single or multiple offenders status, prior record, confession, transfer of the case from prosecution to the Basic People's court, and criminal indictment); (3) documented oral and/or written defense arguments presented by the defense attorneys, stated attitudes of the defendant, and the court's findings on major facts; (4) the court's reasoning and sentencing decisions. Individual case dossier is consisted of various paperwork carrying original seals, signatures, and thumb prints. Parts of the dossier are printouts of files kept in electronic format, for example, demographics and final summary judgment. The availability of summary judgment files (usually no more than three pages for each case) via official publications or court website is increasing but highly uneven across the regions. Collecting complete court case dossiers is exceedingly difficult. A great deal of trust between the courts and the researchers is required. Variable accessibility across regional courts is expected.

Questionnaire Survey: The questionnaire is designed to be applicable to respondents of different criminal justice related careers. The targets are judges, procurators, defense attorneys, and police officers (and those in other professions). These targets are reached either through classroom based surveys of those enrolled in professional *Juris Masters* (*JM*) degree programs offered by law schools in the Province or through questionnaires distributed with the assistance of local lawyers associations.[3] Majority of the *JM* students are legal professionals from different regions of the Province. They are either full-time government employees in justice agencies or attorneys from private law firms who spend 3 months a year to attend graduate professional study at area university law schools. For example, X University Law School enrolls about 150 of *JM* candidates per cohort. Two cohorts of this group of respondents were surveyed during the 24 month study period. The content of the survey is designed specifically for the pilot study. Questions cover (1) demographic information; (2) pretrial issues relevant to legal representation and due process right protection; (3) issues related to court process at the adjudication stage; (4) perceptions of respective organizational environment, job significance, job satisfaction, and resource distribution; (5) courtroom interactions between defense attorneys, procurators, and judges; (6) attitudes toward ongoing legal reforms in China; and (7) open-ended questions at the end for additional comments.

Court Observations: The main goal of court observation is to collect information on how defense attorneys actually function in criminal trials. Trained research associates used structured file to document full-length court trials involving defense attorneys. We collect data on (1) whether and how the attorneys are able to obtain favorable outcome for their clients prior to the trial (e.g., avoiding pretrial detention); (2) whether, what and how arguments (e.g., on the defense of capacity, character and attitude, defense of criminal circumstances, and defense of the fact) are made by the defense attorneys in the court; (3) how well is the defense attorney received by the trial judges and procurators (including pretrial evidence sharing); (4) how often a defense attorney's speech is interrupted by the presiding judge; (5) the proportion of time that is allocated by the court to the defense attorney and the prosecution; and (6) whether and which argument(s) made by the defense attorney is adopted by the judge in the final summary judgment.

Data Analysis: All completed questionnaires and court observation forms are sent to and processed by the U.S. partner of this study. Physical copies of court case dossiers are kept in secured location in the Chinese Co-PI's local office. Digital photograph of the dossier files is sent to the PI in the U.S. Trained doctoral research associates from the U.S. are tasked to perform data entry, data inspection, and data cleaning duties. Both data analysis and report writing are carried out jointly by all research partners.

Summary: The project was planned and successfully completed within a 24 month period, from 2009 to 2011. *Phase I- Project Preparation* took 4 months which includes site selection and meetings with participating court officials, design

[3] Surveying *JM* students in a university setting away from their normal workplaces proves successful. In fact, it may be the better option for the researchers to have relatively unconstrained access to this sensitive population. On the other hand, it is also possible that Chinese criminal justice practitioners who are studying in a *JM* program may have more exposure to western legal literature, have higher career inspiration, and may be more progressive. It may be helpful to keep this possible "positive" bias in mind when interpreting the findings based on their responses.

and pilot testing of all data collection instruments, recruiting and training of faculty and student research associates. *Phase II- Data Collection* which took 10 months includes collection of case-level data, survey of criminal justice practitioners, and observations of selected criminal trials. *Phase III-Data Analysis and Dissemination of Results* took additional 6 months which includes data entry, data cleaning, data analysis, conference presentations, and submission of final grant report.

5.4 General Descriptions of Data Collected

5.4.1 Characteristics of Survey Questionnaire Respondents

A total of 642 completed survey questionnaires have been collected. Among our survey respondents (see Table 5.2), there are 348 (or 54.7 %) practicing attorneys, 177 (27.8 %) criminal justice practitioners (85 from courts, 47 from procurator's office, and 45 from public security agencies), and 111 (or 17.5 %) employees of other government or non-government units. Overall, the demographics of our survey respondents suggest that (1) they are mostly male (64.5 %); (2) they are between 25 and 44 years old (83.5 %); (3) about half of them are Communist Party members (49.1 %); (4) most of them have Bachelor of Law or higher degrees (82.9 %); (5) more than half of them are practicing attorneys (54.7 %); and (6) more than half of all respondents (56.8 %) work in the three largest cities-(a.k.a. Big-3) in the Province and all of the nine prefectural level cities are represented in the sample.

With regard to the key questions about legal representation in criminal trials, we find the followings[4]:

- 39.5 % of the criminal defendants charged for a violent crime, and 32.1 % of the criminal defendants charged for a property crime have used their own attorneys
- In 30.8 % of the cases, criminal attorneys were allowed to represent their clients from the earliest stage of the criminal investigation
- 27.2 % of the criminal defendants are migrant workers
- In criminal trials with legal representation,
  - 3.5 % of the defendants are acquitted.
  - 5.5 % of the cases result in prosecutors changing/correcting the initial charges (supposedly in favor of the defendant).
  - 24.1 % of the criminal defendants receive a reduced sentence at the end of the trial.

[4] These are general responses from all respondents included in the survey. More in-depth comparisons of occupational group specific responses are presented in Chap. 8.

Table 5.2 Major Demographics of Survey Respondents (N = **642)**

	Frequency	Valid percent[a]
Gender		
–Male	413	64.5
–Female	227	35.5
Age		
–Under 25	57	8.9
–25 to 34	355	55.4
–35 to 44	180	28.1
–45 & above	49	7.6
Political Status		
–No affiliation	219	34.7
–Democratic Party Members	50	7.9
–Communist party member	310	49.1
–Other	53	8.4
Highest Legal Education		
–Bachelor's degree	390	61.2
–Master's degree	136	21.4
Current Job		
–Lawyer	348	54.7
–Court	85	13.4
–Procurator	47	7.4
–Bureau of Public Security (police)	45	7.1
–Other	111	17.5
Monthly Income (yuan)[b]		
–Under 2000	98	16.0
–2000 to 4000	224	36.6
–4000 to 6000	132	20.1
–Above 6000	167	27.2
Region (J Province)		
–Three largest cities	360	56.1
–All other cities	153	23.8
–Unidentified	129	20.1

[a] *Valid Percent*: percentage calculated without missing data
[b] Exchange rate at about US$1 = 6.7yuan

- Areas of improvement: 30.6 % of them argue for improvements on *both* effectiveness and prevalence of legal representation; 49.3 % of the respondents think it is more important to improve the *effectiveness* of legal representation

5.4.2 Court Observation Data

A total of 325 criminal trial observations have been conducted between 2009 (286 cases observed, or 88 %) and 2010 (39 cases observed, or 12 %). Figure 5.2 illustrates the distribution of the type of court cases observed in the pilot study.

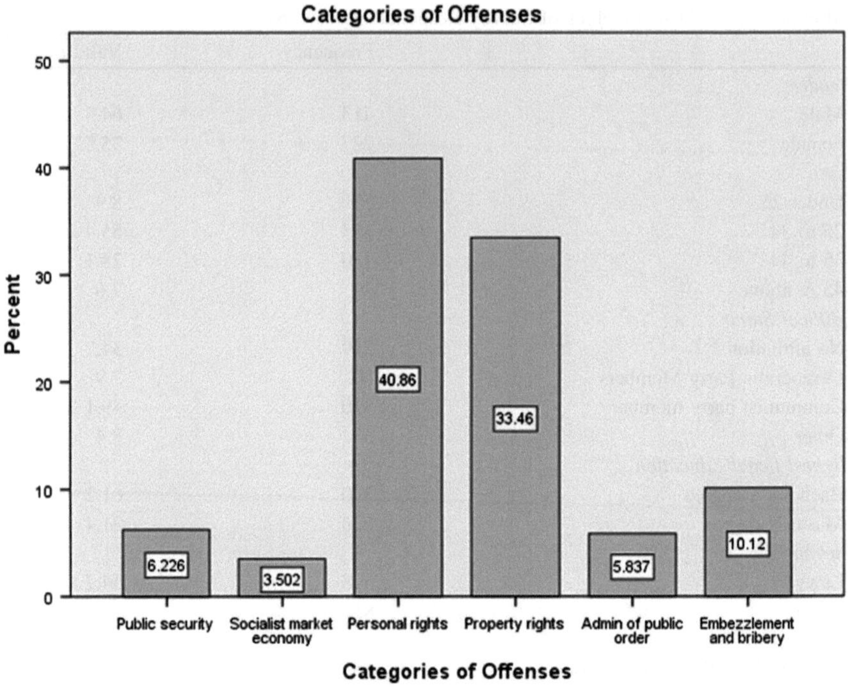

Fig. 5.2 Categories of offenses observed in criminal trials

About 75 % of the observed cases are of two types: Crimes against personal and property rights as specified in the Chinese Criminal Law. Majority of these court observations were conducted in the summer (August-47 % and July-10 %) and winter (December-16 %, November-10 %, and January-10 %) months, when student research assistants are available (see Fig. 5.3). The distribution of days (in any month) for court observation seems to spread out relatively evenly (see Fig. 5.4).[5] For example, the least chosen day is the 9th (1.2 % of the time) and the most chosen day is the 5th (6.2 %). The breakdown in any month when court hearings were conducted and observed is: 26.2 % (1st to 7th), 19.0 % (8th to 14th), 24.6 % (15th to 21st) and 28.3 % (22nd to 31st). The observations conducted by the research team covered 55 (or 67 %) of the total number of Basic People's Courts in J Province ($N = 82$). Every Prefecture-level city (a total of nine) in each major region of the province is included. This outcome has far exceeded our original goal of gaining access to 15 (or about 18 %) courts province-wide (See Table 5.1 for more details).

A preliminary examination of our court observation data suggests that, among the 325 criminal trials observed:

[5] The relatively even distribution reduces possible biases such as the month-end case processing rush to meet reporting deadlines.

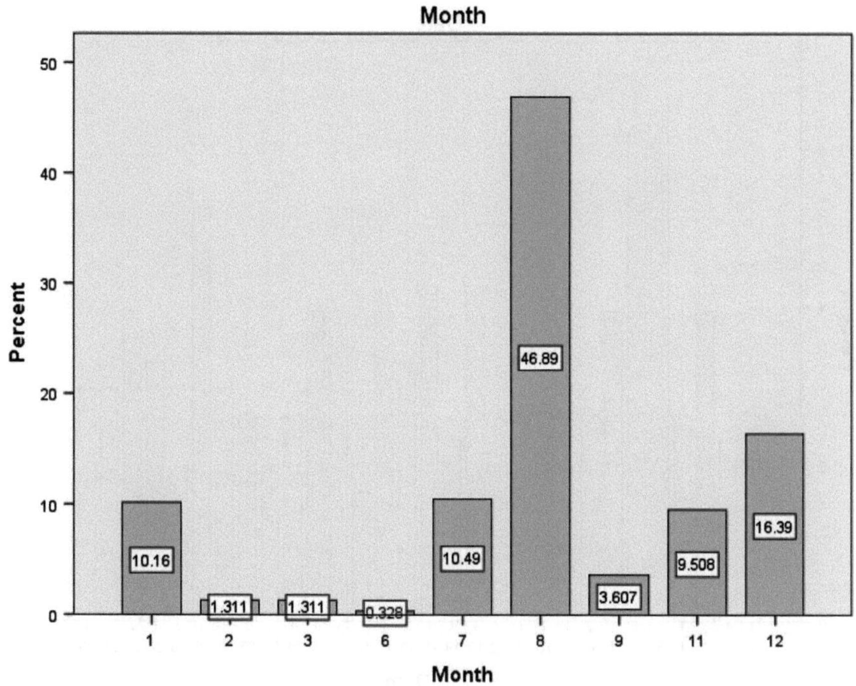

Fig. 5.3 Month of the year court observations conducted

- 294 (95.1%) cases were brought by the state (i.e., public prosecution); 15 (4.9 %) cases were brought by private parties (i.e., private prosecution due to refusal of the state to bring criminal charges)
- The duration for the observed trials averaged 114 min (standard deviation = 86.36 min) (see Figs. 5.5 and 5.6 for breakdowns of trial time per case or per defendant across different offense types)[6]
- On average, the defense side was allowed 18 min to speak while the prosecution was allowed 27 min
- 172 (53.9 %) of the trials observed involved a single defendant; 147 (46.1 %) involved multiple defendants
- Majority of all the observed cases were tried by a (three) judge panel (266 or 88.1 %); 36 cases (11.9 %) were tried by a single judge
- 54.5 % of the observed trials involved two or more prosecutors; the other 45.5 % involved a single prosecutor

---

[6] Lengthier trial times appear to be associated with cases involving public security, socialist market economy, personal rights and administration of public order. We will not elaborate given the small sample size.

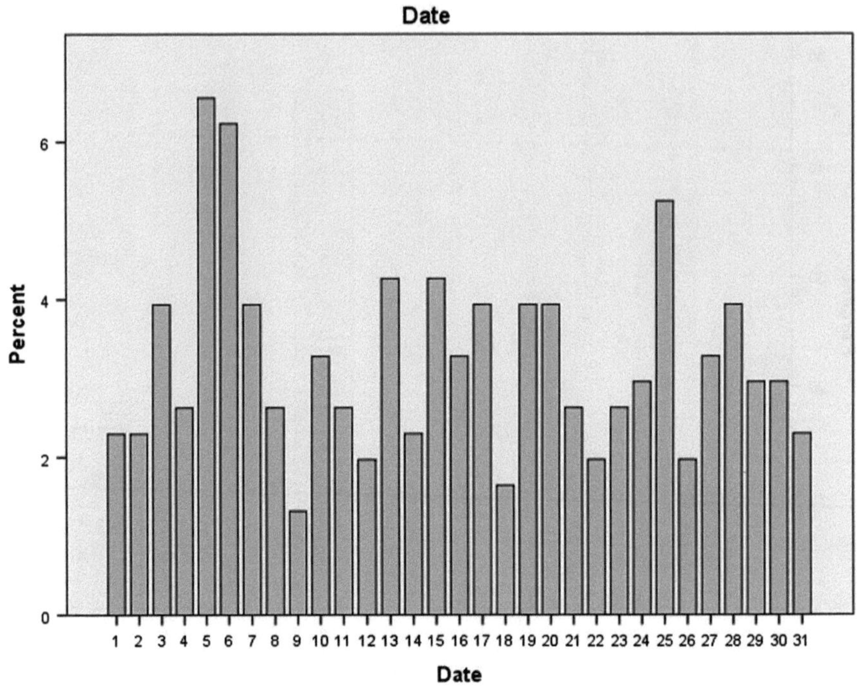

Fig. 5.4 Date of the month court observations conducted

- 43.5 % of the defense counsels spent less than 5 min questioning the accused; 39.7 % of them spent between 5 and 10 min and, 16.7 % of them less than 10 min
- 55.2 % of the defense counsels spent less than 5 min questioning the victim; 34.3 % of them less than 5 min and, 10.4 % of them more than 10 min
- The number of times the defense questions the witness averaged about 2.75 per trial
- The number of times when the defense calls upon an expert witness averaged 0.22 or less than 1 per trial (minimum = 0 to maximum = 6 times)

5.4.3 Criminal Case File Reviews

The research team collected a total of 149 complete criminal case files from ten Basic People's courts in five of the nine prefectural level cities. Data collection from criminal case files proved to be the most challenging aspect of the pilot study. The original plan was to send the research assistants to the courts file rooms to read and code those files onto an existing data recording sheet. This became unrealistic when we found out that various extents of the case files provincial wide remain

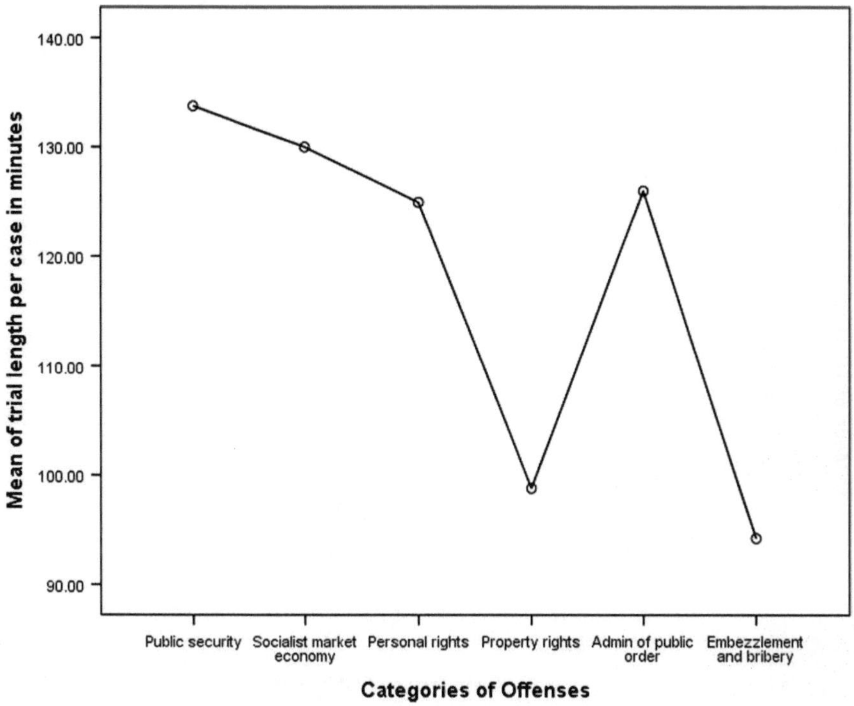

Fig. 5.5 Average trial time for categories of offenses (per case)

hand written. An average complete case file for one defendant contains more than 50 pages. It became cost prohibitive to follow the original plan to process the files onsite. A reasonable compromise was reached to collect photocopies of the complete court case files first and then process them offsite on a more flexible schedule. The PIs now have in their possession all these cases in digitized format.

Although most of the collected cases are limited to trials conducted in the past 5 years, the researchers are fortunate to have collected valuable historical data from two national model Basic People's courts. There are a total of 35 criminal cases in various categories from one Basic People's court from 1994 to 2010. We also have 25 cases from one Basic People's court, ten of which were tried (in 2007 and 2008) before the court was designated a national sentencing guideline trial site and 15 cases were tried (in 2009–2010) using the sentencing guideline worksheets.

5.5 Summary and Conclusion

With regard to how criminal defendants are represented and tried in J Province Basic People's courts, the first lesson learned is that the majority of criminal defendants did *not* receive any legal representation. Responses from the survey of

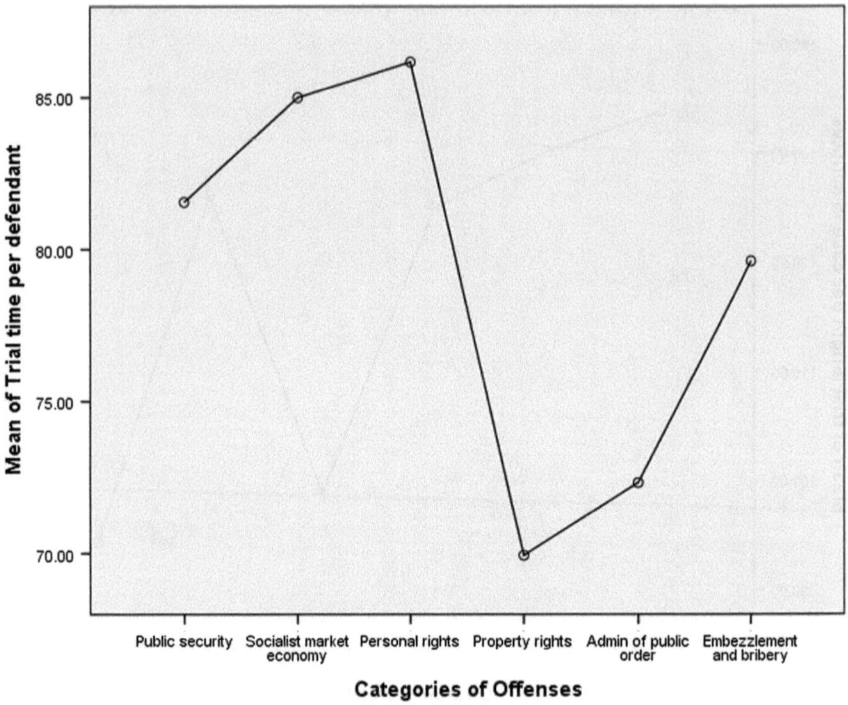

Fig. 5.6 Average trial time for categories of offenses (per defendant)

criminal justice practitioners (including defense attorneys) suggest that criminal defendants do not hire a lawyer for two major reasons: either they cannot afford one (78.8 %) or they are ambivalent about the usefulness or effectiveness of an attorney (61.5 %). The overall rate of criminal legal representation in J Province is about 40 %, higher than that of 30 % estimated for China as a whole. However, in less developed regions of the Province (six out of the nine prefectures), the average rate of legal representation is substantially lower; especially in property crime cases (9 %). In cases where a defendant does hire an attorney (or is eligible to receive a court appointed attorney), findings from the study provide insights on why attorneys have *not* been more effective in criminal trials:

- Defense attorneys were *not* involved in the early stage of (police) criminal investigation
- Coerced confessions are *not* addressed openly and adequately by the court, the prosecution, and the defense
- Major system impediments for effective counsel in criminal trials include:
  - Difficulty in scheduling meetings with clients in custody
  - No privacy when meeting with clients in custody
  - Difficulty in getting bail for clients
  - Difficulty in getting witnesses to testify in court (lack of witness protection)

  - Difficulty in collecting evidences
  - Prosecution withholding evidences from the defense
  - Difficulty in viewing and photocopying court case files
  - Power imbalance inside the courtroom (defense attorney has the least power)
  - No remedy for violations of lawyers' rights

- Criminal justice practitioners often disagree on reform initiatives:
  - Plea bargaining
  - Pretrial conferencing (among judge, procurator, and the defense)
  - Defendant's right to remain silent
  - Victim-offender mediation
  - Bifurcated criminal court process (trial and sentencing hearings)
  - Media presence in the courtroom.

With regard to these (westernized) reform initiatives, we found a similar pattern that: slightly over one-third of the respondents are supportive of them, slightly less than one-third are undecided, and another one-third are opposed. This observation is not at all surprising to us given the current climate of the Chinese criminal justice reform. China has enacted (or revised) more laws in the past two decades than the system could possibly digest and incorporate in a relatively short period of time. Professionalism among Chinese criminal justice practitioners has improved steadily but still leaves much to be desired. The westernization (or Americanization) of criminal justice reform has evoked mixed reactions (from admiration to suspicion) in the Chinese legal community.

The pilot study and the survey of the myriad criminal justice reform projects conducted in recent years led to the following observations: (1) local governments in China can be open to all kinds of criminal justice reform ideas; (2) some progressive local practices can be quickly recognized by the provincial and even the national government; (3) many justice reform experiments have been conducted without necessary scientific evaluation of their impact (i.e., outcomes unknown); (4) there are a lot of sponsored research projects but very little partnership and communication among researchers (i.e., accumulation of scientific knowledge is not made possible; investment in research not optimized); and (5) there are more ad hoc, piecemeal studies than well-coordinated systematic research projects with clear implementation plans (i.e., unrepresentative and non-translational research). It is thus recommended that future research could address some of these issues by (1) absorbing the positive energy and system knowledge from the reform advocates; (2) capitalizing the established partnership between legal scholars and criminal justice community; and (3) taking a systematic approach that allows scientific assessment, accumulation of knowledge and policy implementation.

The MacArthur Pilot Study is not only unique in design but also unprecedented in its scope of inquiry. Focusing on the lowest level trial court practices, this study helps answer the question on how the lower courts are actually functioning and how legal representation is actually implemented in China. It also demonstrates both the necessity and feasibility of conducting comprehensive empirical legal research in China. Empirically and scientifically based legal research is indeed gaining momentum in China (Zuo 2007, 2010; Guo 2011). We see a positive sign that evidence-based policy making is beginning to be accepted by criminal justice practitioners and policy makers. The international teams of faculty from China and the U.S. have brought both local access and knowledge of local cultural norms as well as experience with conducting similar studies in the United States. This study offers some of the most in-depth empirical evidences on the subject of legal representation at grass-roots level. It also reveals criminal process in lower courts through observational data reflecting the actual interactions between judges, prosecutors and defense attorneys in everyday criminal trials. This pilot project has thus succeeded in achieving one of its most important intended goals, that is, to provide a reliable and empirical benchmark on the subject matter of legal representation in criminal trials. As a result, chapters that follow (Chaps. 6–8) draw heavily from this rich data in order to make better sense of Chinese criminal trials (Chap. 9).

References

Clarke, D. C. (2008). *China's Legal System: New developments, new challenges*. Cambridge: Cambridge University Press.

Cohen, J. A. (Ed.). (1970). *Contemporary chinese law: Research problems and perspectives*. Cambridge: Harvard University Press.

Cohen, J. A. (1968). *The criminal process in the People's Republic of China, 1949–1964: An introduction*. Cambridge: Harvard University Press.

Guo, Z. (2011) *The Chinese Experience: A Survey of Pilot Projects on Criminal Justice Reform* (中国经验:以刑事司法改革试点项目为蓝本的考察). Beijing, PR China: Beijing University Press (北京大学出版社).

Halliday, T. C. & Liu, S. (2007). Birth of a liberal moment? Looking through a one-way mirror at lawyers' defense of criminal defendants in China. In T. C. Halliday, L. Karpik, & M. M. Feeley (Eds.), *Fighting for political freedom: Comparative studies of the legal complex and political liberalism*. Oxford: Hart Publishing.

He, N. (2014). The politics of numbers: Crime statistics in china, chapter 12. In L. Cao, L. Sun, I. & W. Hebenton (Eds.). *The Routledge Handbook of chinese criminology* (pp. 147–159). New York: Routledge Publishers.

Leng, S. (1985). *Criminal justice in post-mao china: Analysis and documents*. Albany: State University of New York Press.

Li, V. (1978). *Law without lawyers: Comparative view of law in china and the united states*. Boulder: Westview Press.

Liang, B. (2008). *The changing chinese legal system, 1978-present: Centralization of power and rationalization of the legal system*. New York: Routledge.

Liu, S. (2006). Beyond global convergence: Conflicts of legitimacy in a chinese lower court. *Law and Social Inquiry,36*, 75–106.

Liu, S., & Halliday, T. C. (2009). Recursivity in legal change: Lawyers and reforms of china's criminal procedure law. *Law and Social Inquiry,34*, 911–950.

Liu, S., & Halliday, T. C. (2011). Political liberalism and political embeddedness: understanding politics in the work of chinese criminal defense lawyers. *Law and Society Review,45*, 831–864.

Lo, C. W. (1995). *China's legal awakening: Legal theory and criminal justice in deng's era*. Hong Kong: Hong Kong University Press.
Lu, H., & Drass, K. A. (2002). Transience and the disposition of theft cases in china. *Justice Quarterly,19*, 69–96.
Lu, H., & Gunnison, E. (2003). Power, corruption, and the legal process in china. *International Criminal Justice Review,13*, 28–49.
Lu, H., & Miethe, T. D. (2002). Legal representation and criminal processing in china. *British Journal of Criminology,42*, 267–280.
Lubman, S. B. (1996). *China's legal reforms*. New York: Oxford University Press.
Lubman, S. B. (1999). *Bird in a cage: Legal reform in china after mao*. Stanford: Stanford University Press.
McConville, M., Choongh, S., Wan, P., Hong, E., Dobinson, I., & Jones, C. (2011). *Criminal justice in china: An empirical inquiry*. Cheltenham: Edward Elgar.
Michelson, E., & Read, B. (2011). Public attitudes toward official justice in beijing and rural china. In M. Y. Woo, & M. E. Gallagher(Eds.), *Chinese justice: Civil dispute resolution in contemporary china*. (pp. 169–203). New York: Cambridge University Press.
Michelson, E. (2007). Lawyers, political embeddedness, and institutional continuity in china's transition from socialism. *American Journal of Sociology,113*, 352–414.
Michelson, E. (2006). The practice of law as an obstacle to justice: Chinese lawyers at work. *Law and Society Review,40*, 1–38.
Michelson, E. (2003). *Unhooking from the state: Chinese lawyers in transition*. Ph.D. dissertation, Department of Sociology, University of Chicago.
National Statistical Bureau of China. (2011a). *Criminal defendants in chinese courts or first instance*. Beijing: National Statistics Press.
National Statistical Bureau of China. (2011b). *Statistics on lawyers, notary service and mediation*. Beijing: National Statistics Press.
Stutsman, T. (2011). The use of demonstration projects to advance criminal procedure reform in china. *Columbia Journal of Asian Law,24*, 335–366.
Turner, K. G., Feinerman, J. V., & Guy, R. K. (Eds.). (2000). *The limits of the rule of law in china*. Seattle: University of Washington Press.
U.S. Supreme Court (1932). *Powell vs. Alabama*, 287 U.S. 45.
U.S Supreme Court (1938). *Johnson vs. Zerbst*, 304 U.S. 458.
U.S Supreme Court (1963). *Gideon vs. Wainwright*, 372 U.S. 335.
U.S Supreme Court (1967). *In re Gault*, 387 U.S. 1.
U.S Supreme Court (1984). *Strickland vs. Washington*, 466 U.S. 668.
U.S Supreme Court (2002). *Alabama vs. Shelton*, 535 U.S. 654.
Zuo, W. (2010). The landscape of chinese criminal procedure law and practice (刑事诉讼的中国图景). Beijing: SDX Joint Publishing Company (三联书店).
Zuo, W. (2009). A domestic model building of china's criminal litigation (in chinese). *Chinese Journal of Law,2*, 107–120.
Zuo, W. (2007). Empirical study on the operation mechanism of criminal procedure in china (中国刑事诉讼运行机制实证研究). Beijing: Law Press (法律出版社).

Chapter 6
Court Case Dossier: Anatomy of Chinese Criminal Trials

6.1 Introduction

A Chinese court case dossier reveals much about the routine criminal justice practice with the associated organizational structure and power dimensions. It not only contains the *selective* evidential files from earlier stages of police and prosecutorial investigations,[1] it also includes major documentations resulting directly from the actual trial itself. In addition, checklists and copies of signed documents that change hands between the criminal justice agencies (e.g., police, detention center, prosecution and court) are included. Therefore, court case dossier can be used to reveal the anatomy of Chinese criminal trials and at the same time, as an analytical tool for multiple sociological purposes.

Contemporary Chinese criminal court case dossier is a product of both imperial legal tradition and modern legal development with heavy influence from Civil-law legal family. We are hesitant to draw the influence on Chinese case dossier from the former Soviet Union. Although the impact on the Chinese socialist legality from the Soviets is recognizable in Chinese law, case dossier system used in China is perhaps more likely the blend of Chinese imperial tradition and the inquisitorial legal tradition with heavy focuses on codified laws and dossier based trials. This chapter brings to bear both Chinese imperial and socialist legal traditions and demonstrates their impact on contemporary Chinese criminal trials.

[1] Terminologies such as "police" and "public security" are used interchangeably in reference to common police functions at local level. Contents included in this book do not touch upon the "national security" aspect of the Chinese policing.

N. He, *Chinese Criminal Trials*, DOI: 10.1007/978-1-4614-8205-5_6,

6.2 Case Dossier: Confluence of Culture and Nomenclature

6.2.1 Historical Lineage

Hegel (2009) who compiled and translated twenty case histories from the eighteenth-century China offers an authentic look at the format and content of Imperial criminal case dossier. He gained access to these case materials from historical archives in Beijing and Taipei. He describes the so-called "routine memorials" as following an identical form, i.e., clear scripts written on white paper that is folded in accordion style, with six lines written on each folded page. These judicial reports, according to Hegel, "reveal both the formulaic structure and the standardized rhetoric". The offender is always introduced in the first paragraph with characterization of the person and criminal act carefully shaped by the ruling magistrate. Following a brief summary of the case, the procedures used for the investigation are described. Testimonies with varying lengths are then introduced in the document followed by the final judgment (recommendation of punishment) rendered by the magistrate. Included in a memorial prepared by the Three Judicial Offices for the Qing Emperor in 1803, Hegel (2009:73) shares with us the translation of a local magistrate's summary and recommendation of sentence that encapsulates the dramatic ending of a shocking murder case:

> According to the culprit, he conceived the idea of rape, but when she did not comply, he took her life to silence the victim. He acknowledged the accuracy of each detail of the case without objection and confessed that he had not succeeded in the rape attempt, nor had he any accomplices. I conclude that Cao Ligong, failing in his attempt to rape Mrs. Cao Wang, decided on the spot to strangle her, having been overcome by immoral desires. Because Mrs. Cao Wang is an aunt by marriage to a distant relative, her murder should be considered the same as an ordinary murder. Disregarding the relatively minor offense of moving a corpse, for which he should be forgiven, I recommend that he be punished according to law concerning the immediate murder of a woman after failing in an attempt to rape her, the penalty for which is beheading without delay. In accordance with the substatute, the culprit should first have the characters "vicious criminal" tattooed on the left side of his face. Because she had resisted rape even unto her wrongful death, Mrs. Cao Wang was most certainly an exemplar of chastity. Therefore, I recommend that the request be appended that imperial recognition be awarded her in order to further public morality.[2]

Hegel's (2009) carefully selected work succeeded exceptionally well in bringing the Chinese Imperial history to the present. In fact, if the reference of time were to be omitted, Hagel's cases can be easily mistaken to have taken place

[2] Each of Hegel's (2009) carefully selected and translated Imperial criminal cases offers a window of opportunity to peek into and piece together the contour of a fast changing Chinese society three centuries earlier that appears remarkably similar to the one we live in today. The human tragedies illustrated in the twenty murder cases are valuable raw materials for criminologists. The Imperial Magistrate's judgment cited here can be seen as a "quintessential official speech in the name of and to everyone." (Bourdieu 1987: 838) Likewise, contents included in the court case dossier illustrated in this chapter could be viewed in the same light.

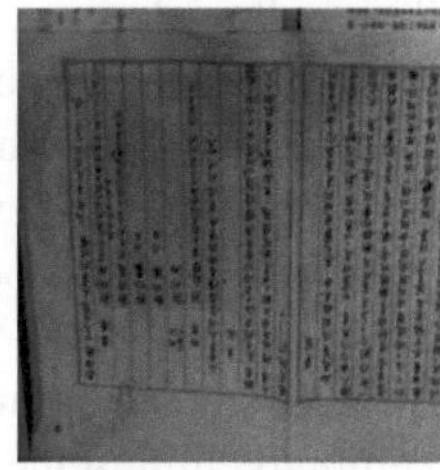

Photo 6.1 Court judgment brushwork

somewhere we know and to someone we could identify.[3] Through written records such as the official court document, the past is not only preserved but also revisited. Fast-forward to the year 1950, 1 year after the establishment of the PRC, a hand-written court final judgment (in fact the outcome of the very first civil trial from a Basic People's Court in 1950) with brush from G Province in Southern China unfolds a page of the tradition and offers a glimpse of the imperial past (see Photo 6.1).[4]

6.2.2 Case Dossier System

The structure of the current court case dossier is the product of professionalization movement in the Chinese legal system. The content format is jointly designed by the Supreme People's Court and the National Bureau of Archives in 1984 (i.e., Regulations on People's Court Case Dossier Archiving Methods and File Management). The application of this joint regulation is made mandatory throughout China. All cases related documentations are to be written with brush or ink pen, says Article 3 of the Regulation. The order of the contents to be included in the case dossier is clearly defined in Article 9. A total of 30 categories of case related materials are to be kept in the dossier, including documents that are considered confidential, for example, private notes taken by the judges while reading the case

[3] Crimes committed by migrants and among migrants, official corruptions, domestic violence and other family tragedies (often outcomes of greed, love and lust) are familiar storylines that seem to transcend time and space. These 18th century cases can indeed be found in the 21st century.

[4] Brush writing has long been abandoned in the production of formal court documentation. Calligraphy written in brush, however, remains omnipresent inside Chinese courthouses as a form of artistic expression. Photography and calligraphy produced by the court officials are major ingredients of a Chinese courtroom culture that showcases the soft side of the judicial environment. Our visits to many Chinese courthouses in recent years form the base for this impression. This may be seen as an extension of the authentic Chinese scholar-official tradition from the Imperial time. The same observation is much less applicable to the other branches of the justice apparatus, i.e., the People's Procuratorate or the Public Security Bureaus.

files, collegial panel discussion record, court adjudication committee meeting minutes and major decisions. Eleven more categories are to be included in cases involving capital crimes (Article 10) and, another 24 categories could be added by the court of appeal, when applicable. The Regulation also goes into details by specifying that all documents are to be punched through with three to five holes and properly secured with strong thread at the length of about 18 cm (Article 22). Case dossier also should not exceed 200 pages in general (Article 21). These seemingly minuscule provisions are not at all surprising in a Chinese culture obsessed with preserving written history.

Unlike the practice derived from the Common Law, adversarial trial system such as the U.S., Chinese criminal trials rely heavily on the use of comprehensive, written case dossier constructed with highly specific requirements. In reality, certain parts of Chinese criminal case dossier are not shared openly with the defense attorneys. Chinese criminal law also discourages defense attorneys from collecting and presenting additional evidences in support of their clients. "Sharing" or "withholding" critical trial related information is thus an ever-present contentious struggle between the opposing parties. A closer examination of Chinese criminal case dossier would certainly contribute to an improved understanding of the trial process as "paradigmatic staging of symbolic struggle" within the relational power structure of the juridical field (Bourdieu 1987).

Figure 6.1 places the major contents of court case dossier in the context of the whole criminal proceeding, beginning with the police investigation dossier (A1 to A4), to prosecution dossier (B1 to B3), and finally, to the court dossier (C1 to C9). Materials from the police dossier are far more voluminous and complicated. The

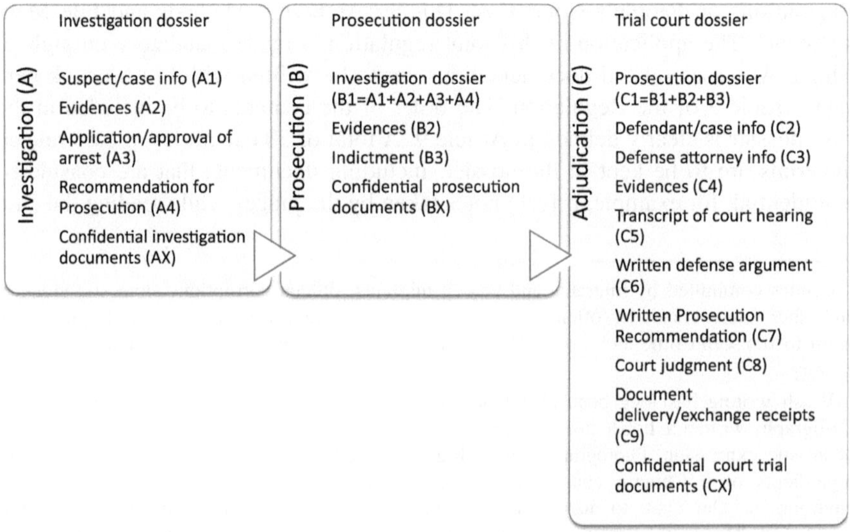

Fig. 6.1 Chinese criminal case dossiers

Chinese Ministry of Public Security specifies and distributes a total of 92 basic legal forms applicable to the police. The forms are tailored to suit four stages of police work: case filing, criminal investigation, criminal detention, and execution. The forms include fill-in-the-blank (such as Decision to Initiate a Criminal Investigation), descriptive (such as Application to Make a Formal Arrest), and a combination of the two (such as Crime Scene Investigation Report). The most striking observation of the police forms is the level of detail required for documenting the approval process, including the hierarchy of approval with explicit instructions on the forms for a specific next level of approval (e.g., from line officer to line supervisor to division Head and to the Bureau Head, as appropriate) and, the placement of the seals of the Public Security Bureau, the personal seal and signature of the Head of the Public Security Bureau.

It is worth noting that, similar to the Regulation on Court Case Dossier construction and management, there are equally specific Regulations on police dossier and prosecution dossier. A court case dossier necessarily includes the major contents from the two earlier dossiers; however, confidential documents (AX, BX, and CX) in each of the dossiers are not necessarily shared across these criminal justice agencies and certainly never shared with the defense attorneys. Chinese defense lawyers' access to any or all of the three dossiers is intentionally, structurally limited by the provisions that are more explicitly stated in these archive Regulations than included in the Criminal Procedure Law.[5]

Article 14 of the court case dossier Regulations provides that higher level courts and the Public Security and Procuratorate agencies at the same level may check out court case files with formal letter of request signed and approved by proper officials in charge. Borrowed items are to be promptly returned within a specified time limit and they are strictly prohibited from being shared with outside parties. In principle, no other agencies/units/individuals are allowed to check out any materials from an archived court case dossier. Defense attorneys and all other non-justice agencies parties may only review selected files on site and under certain conditions. Approvals are required at various stages of the case review application process. For example, a defense attorney can only access a file with the approval of the presiding judge of the case. Lawyers may hand copy judgment and other terminal documents. Approval is required from the court file room official if the attorney is to access other case materials. Review and signature from court official are required before the hand copied materials are taken out of the file room by defense attorney (Article 15). Like in many areas of Chinese criminal justice system, the actual practices may be quite different from the legal provisions. Variations across different jurisdictions are also likely. In addition, a defense attorney's personal connection with court officials and his or her prior work

5 We will save more detailed discussions on the different perceptions of access to police evidentiary files, contrasting the views from the criminal justice officials (i.e., judges, prosecutors, and the police) and the defense attorneys, for a later chapter (Chap. 8) focusing on Bourdieusian power and control.

experience inside the criminal justice system, especially prior employment experience as a court official afford him/her the much-needed trust and advantages.[6]

6.3 Network of Power and Criminal Trial Process

Zuo (2010) provides a nuanced analysis of the construction and use of case dossier in Chinese criminal trials. He focuses particularly on when and how evidences are built in the dossier through each stage of the formal legal process (i.e., moving from police investigation to prosecution and finally to court trial). Using 50 randomly selected case dossiers from one local court across three decades (1984, 1994 and 2004), Zuo finds that about half of the case dossier contain evidences such as the suspect/defendant statements, victim(s) statement(s), witness written testimonies, forensic evidences and etc., the other half are mainly procedure related, administrative documents characterizing clearly-defined and tightly controlled inter-agency transactions in a powerful and complex administrative-judicial bureaucracy.

Two interesting contrasts in the compilation of evidential materials for case dossier are most revealing, according to Zuo (2010). First of all, evidences collected by the police (and to a far less extent, by the prosecution and the court) constitute about 99 % of the total pool of evidential materials used in a trial. It is suggested that Chinese defense attorneys rarely conduct additional independent investigation nor produce any evidences of their own. One major source of deterrence has been the perceived threat of prosecution from Article 306 of the Chinese Criminal Law (see Li, Sun and He 2012), which states that:

> If, in criminal proceedings, a defender or agent ad litem destroys or forges evidence, helps any of the parties destroy or forge evidence, or coerces the witness or entices him into changing his testimony in defiance of the facts or give false testimony, he shall be sentenced to fixed-term imprisonment of not more than 3 years or criminal detention; if the circumstances are serious, he shall be sentenced to fixed-term imprisonment of not less than 3 years but not more than 7 years. Where a witness's testimony or other evidence provided, shown or quoted by a defender or agent ad litem is inconsistent with the facts but is not forged intentionally, it shall not be regarded as forgery of evidence.[7]

---

[6] Political Embeddedness and the work of Chinese criminal defense lawyers are well articulated in Liu and Halliday's (2011) recent work.

[7] English translation of the Article 306 of the Chinese Criminal Law was accessed on 5/17/2012 from the web site of the U.S. Congressional Executive Commission on China. To avoid unnecessary confusions on the use of different legal terminologies, we will apply the same English translation source when citing Articles from the Chinese Constitution, Chinese Criminal Law and Chinese Criminal Procedure Law. Grateful acknowledgement is made to the excellent translations posted on CECC web site. http://www.cecc.gov/pages/newLaws/criminalLawENG.php. See also New York Times editorial titled "Big Stick 306 and China's Contempt for the Law (5/6/2011) http://nytimes.com/2011/05/06/opinion/06fri3.html?_r=0.

Secondly, it is discovered that from 92 % (for 1984) to 95 % (for both 1994 and 2004) of the police evidences are actually generated *before* the formal arrest was made (emphasis added). Zuo's (2010) succinct empirical observations demonstrate amply the total dominance of administrative power in Chinese criminal processing. Criminal evidences collected predominantly by the police, accepted uncritically by the prosecution and the court and unchallenged (or unchallengeable) by the defense attorneys virtually make the prosecution and court trial a mere façade. A Chinese criminal trial, to a great extent, is reduced to formality with the fate of a criminal defendant largely shaped at the point of formal arrest and literally sealed at the end of the police investigation.

Figure 6.2 places Chinese court system inside an intricate and interactive network of power systems. To the far right is the People's Congress at all levels of the government, which by the Constitution represents the highest government power. To the far left is the Political-Legal Committee which exerts tight controls on day-to-day justice administration and maintenance of social order at all levels. Within the Political-Legal Committee structure and at each corresponding level, the head of the police organization usually chairs the committee while Presidents (and Vice-Presidents) of the People's Court and People's Procuratorate serve as members. The operation of the court thus is surrounded by powerful forces that permeate from both sides and from top to bottom. By design, the Chinese courts are the weakest among all justice organizations. The courts by law are under supervision by the People's Procuratorate for their lawful operation, a vertical relationship. Yet, at the same time, the People's Courts are also expected to interact with the People's Procuratorate at horizontal level. Major or sensitive

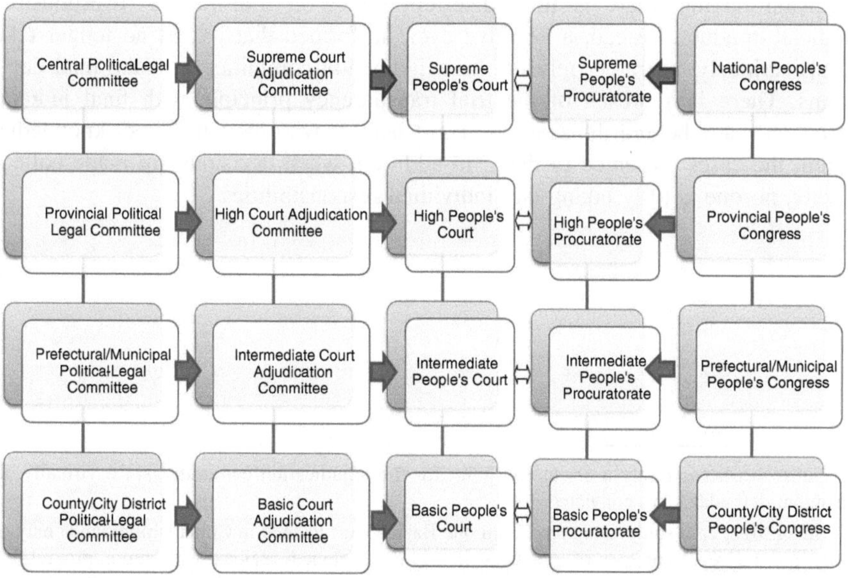

Fig. 6.2 Contemporary Chinese court system and Its *de jure* and *de facto* relational structure

cases are first discussed by the highest decision-making group within the court-the Adjudication Committee which is consisted of Presidents and Vice-Presidents of the court and the chief judges of the civil, criminal, and administrative trial courts. It is without exception that all important, difficult, sensitive cases at all levels of the Chinese courts arc decided by the corresponding adjudication committees well before the trials begin.

A highly valuable empirical study was conducted by He (2012) using 1 year worth of meeting minutes (n = 47) from an adjudication committee of a basic court in Shaanxi Province. A total of 430 (among which 363 are criminal) cases were brought to discussion at these meetings, averaging 20 min per case. The researcher finds no record of any votes taken at these meetings. The adjudication committee approved about 54 % but made revisions on 41 % of the sentences made by the judge panels.[8] These revisions are mainly concentrated in the amount of fine and the years of probation granted by the court. The recommendations made by the adjudication committee are consistently one-directional, that is, with increased fine amount and years of probation. The President of the court who chairs the committee has the overwhelming authority in guiding the discussions and making final decisions. Those holding dissenting views either failed to speak up or made to agree with the majority led by the President of the court. The researcher concludes that adjudication committee is not being used to deal with (and learn lessons from) difficult cases as intended by law but rather used as a routine mechanism to process case decisions collectively to avoid individual responsibilities. It did not serve as a mechanism to curb corruption as suggested by some scholars (e.g., Su li from Beijing University Law School). On the contrary, because of the superficial nature of the adjudication committee discussions and decision-making, there is little deterrent effect on trial judges' irresponsible judicial conduct. Instead, a negative cycle is formed that judges no longer take trials seriously but rather rely on the adjudication committee to make final decisions. There is a breach of the trial transparency principle with final judicial decision made behind the scene by court leaders who have no direct knowledge about the cases presented to them. In addition, when decisions are made collectively, no one is truly taking any individual responsibilities.[9]

[8] Guilty verdict is rarely a discussion point for the adjudication committee since virtually all criminal defendants are convicted.

[9] He's (2012) case study using data from one Basic Court located in China's hinterlands may or may not be representative of practices in more developed regions with more progressive judiciary. In fact, exploring the regional variations in Chinese court practices is a challenging but meaningful research topic.

6.4 The Contour of Court Case Dossier

A case involving obstruction of justice from a Basic People's Court in J Province is used for this exercise. The dossier begins with a front page that includes the following key information:

XX Province XXX Basic People's Court
Criminal Trial of First Instance (Official Dossier)
[20XX] XXX (Letter Code),[10] XXX (Numeric Serial #)
Criminal Charge: Obstruction of Justice
Public Prosecution: XXX Basic People's Procuratorate
Criminal Defendant(s): XXX (A), XXX (B), XXX (C)[11]
Judge Panel: XXX (Presiding Judge), XXX (Judge), XXX (Judge), XXX (Court Clerk)
Date Case Received: February XX, 20XX
Date Case Closed: March XX, 20XX
Original Trial Court (Case ID): N/A
Trial of First Instance Sentencing Outcome: 1 year and 3 months (Defendant A); 1 year and 3 months (Defendant B); 1 year (Defendant C)
Court of Appeal Outcome: N/A
Retrial Outcome: N/A
Date Case Dossier Archived: September XX, 20XX
Archive Category: Short-term[12]

The second page of the court case dossier is a Table of Contents with two columns labeled "document title" and "page number." A total of 72 pages (counting the front page and table of contents page) are included in this case dossier, among which 37 pages are procedural, administrative paperwork (i.e., checklists, summons, receipts, copies of defense lawyers' licenses[13] and trial date public announcement). The remaining 35 pages are distributed in the following categories:

Copy of Arrest Warrant (1 page)
Criminal Indictment (2 pages)
Evidences (including witnesses and victims written statements) (4 pages)
Trial Proceeding Transcript (14 pages)

[10] The three letters indicate the location of the trial court (using the first letter of the city name), criminal trial (indicting where it is a criminal or civil or administrative case) and a trial of first instance (to separate trial of first instance from appeal or retrial), respectively. The method of designation is standardized nationwide.

[11] It is common that multiple criminal defendants share the same case dossier and are tried together on the same date. Co-defendants are separated during the court questioning and cross-examination phase.

[12] A square stamp indicating that this dossier is to be kept as a "short term" (30 years) item. Two other categories are "long term" which is for 60 years and "permanent.".

[13] Lawyer's license is issued for one-year duration only. Annual registration is required. The Lawyer's Association is subject to the control of Bureau/Department of Justice at corresponding levels. The three defense lawyers involved in this case all have the same registration due date stamped on their licenses. They are from three different law firms.

Written Defense Scripts (7 pages total), submitted by three defense attorneys representing the three defendants
Sentencing Recommendation from the Prosecution (1 page)
Court Final Judgment File (including both verdict and sentence) (5 pages)

There is no doubt that pretrial stage is critical to the outcome of a Chinese criminal trial. A great deal of knowledge can be gained by following the footprints of the case from one stage to another. It is certainly interesting to recall Feeley's (1979) U.S. based conclusion which suggests that in the local (misdemeanor) courts "the process is the punishment." Can the same conclusion be drawn in the Chinese context? So far, we have detected that the distributions of contents in the sampled criminal case dossier to be largely consistent with Zuo's (2010) empirical observations. To elaborate on Zuo's insightful summary based discussion on Chinese criminal case dossier, we examine the details of this case with regard to arrest warrant (from the police), recommendation for prosecution (from the police), Criminal Indictment (from prosecution), written materials provided by the criminal defense, and the court final judgment with sentencing decisions.

6.4.1 *Arrest Warrant*

XXX Bureau of Public Security

Arrest Warrant[14]

Serial Number (Year)XXXX[15]

According to Article 59 of the Criminal Procedure Law of the People's Republic of China and with the approval of XXX Basic People's Procuratorate,[16] police detectives XXX and XXX are dispatched to execute this warrant and make an arrest of XXX, residing at XX City, XX Township, XX Village.

XXX
Chief of Public Security Bureau[17]
September XX, 19XX

I hereby acknowledge that this arrest warrant has been read to me on September XX, 19XX

Arrestee Signature XXX[18]

(Arrest warrants for the other two suspects are omitted)

---

[14] A round XXX Bureau of Public Security stamp is placed in the middle of the titles for both documents.

[15] Six digits number with the first two indicate the year of arrest.

[16] Article 59 of the Chinese Criminal Procedure Law states that: "An arrest of a crime suspect or a defendant must be approved by the People's Procuratorate or decided by the People's Court, and it shall be executed by the Public Security organ".

[17] A square stamp of the name of the chief of Public Security Bureau is place to the right of the signature.

[18] The arrestee's thumb print in red ink is placed on top of her signature.

6.4.2 Recommendation for Criminal Prosecution

Following the arrest and detention of all three criminal suspects involved in this case on September XX, a recommendation for criminal prosecution is filed by the XXX Bureau of Public Security with the corresponding level Basic People's Procuratorate 12/XX/19XX. It reads:

XXX Bureau of Public Security Recommendation for Criminal Prosecution

[19XX] Serial Number XXX

Criminal suspect A,[19] female, Han nationality, born in 19XX, September XX, elementary school education, unemployed prior to arrest, resides in XX Province, XX City, XX Township, and XX Village.

Relevant Background: detained on Feb., XX, 19XX for obstruction of justice; arrest warrant issued by the XXX City Basic People's Procuratorate on Sept., XX, 19XX and executed on Sept., XX, 19XX; currently in custody at XXX City Detention Center.

Criminal suspect B, male, Han nationality, born in 19XX, July XX, elementary school education, peasant prior to arrest, resides in XX Province, XX City, XX Township, and XX Village.

Relevant Background: identical with the description provided for criminal suspect A.

Criminal suspect C, male, Han nationality, born in 19XX, November,[20] high school education, unemployed prior to arrest, resides in XX Province, XX City, XY Township, and XZ Village.

Relevant Background: identical to the description provided for criminal suspects A & B.

Case Facts: On February X, 19XX about 11 pm, police officers from XXX Bureau of Public Security were dispatched to serve a warrant of detention to an aggravated assault criminal suspect XYZ[21] residing at XX Township, XX Village. Criminal suspects A, B, and C punched, kicked and bit the police officers on duty, causing the criminal suspect XYZ to escape with handcuff on. According to the facts illustrated above, criminal suspects A, B, and C have violated Article 277-Obstruction of Justice as specified in the Criminal Law of the People's Republic of China.[22] According to Article 129 of the Criminal Procedure Law of the People's

---

[19] She is the sister-in-law of the escaped criminal suspect XYZ.

[20] No precise date was given.

[21] XYZ is the younger brother of the second criminal suspect/defendant (B) in this case.

[22] Article 277 in the Chinese Criminal Law (1997) is under Chapter VI Crimes of Obstructing the Administration of Public Order, Section I Crimes of Disturbing Public Order. It contains four paragraphs. The first paragraph states that "Whoever by means of violence or threat, obstructs a functionary of a State organ from carrying out his functions according to law shall be sentenced to fixed-term imprisonment of not more than three years, criminal detention, or public surveillance or be fined." The second paragraph applies to obstructing a deputy to the National People's Congress from carrying out his functions (omitted). The third paragraph deals with obstructing the workers of

Republic of China,[23] we hereby recommend that criminal prosecution and investigation be launched against the three suspects by the People's Procuratorate.

Respectfully submitted to

XXX Basic People's Procuratorate

Chief of XXX Bureau of Public Security[24]
December XX, 19XX

Enclosed:

1. Two copies of police case dossier
2. Two copies of Recommendation for Prosecution

6.4.3 Criminal Indictment

XXX City Basic People's Procuratorate

Criminal Indictment
XXX (Letter Code) [20XX] Serial Number XXX

Criminal Defendant A, female, 35 years old (born on June, XX, 19XX).[25] Birth place: XX City, XX Township, Han nationality, elementary school education, unemployed, resides at XX City, XX Township, and XX Village before arrest.

Criminal Defendant B, male, 36 years old (born on July, XX, 19XX). Birth place: XX City, XX Township, Han nationality, elementary school education, peasant, resides at XX City, XX Township, and XX Village before arrest.

Criminal Defendant C, male, 35 years old (born in November, 19XX) Birth place: XX City, XX Township, Han nationality, high school education, unemployed, resides at XX City, XY Township, and XZ Village before arrest.

(Footnote 22 continued)
the Red Cross Society from performing their functions during natural calamities/emergencies (omitted). The fourth paragraph states that "whoever intentionally obstructs officers of a State security organ or a public security organ from maintaining State security in accordance with law and causes serious consequences, though without resort to violence or threat, shall be punished in accordance with the provisions of the first paragraph".

[23] Article 129 of the Chinese Criminal Procedure Law (1996) states that "when a public security organ concludes the investigation, it shall make sure that the basic facts of the case is clear and the evidence is reliable and sufficient, shall write a recommendation for prosecution, and transfer the case, together with case files and evidences, to the people's Procuratorate at the same level for examination and decisions".

[24] A square stamp of the name of the chief of the Public Security Bureau is placed atop the signature.

[25] There is an inconsistency in the birth month for suspect A: in the Recommendation for Prosecution submitted by the police, her birth month was listed as September, in the Criminal Indictment produced by the prosecution it becomes June. The year and exact date of birth are consistent. None of the parties involved in the case seems to have noticed this discrepancy.

The above three criminal defendants were charged with obstruction of justice and detained on February XXth, 19XX by XXX Bureau of Public Security. On September XX of the same year, their formal arrests were authorized by this Basic People's Procuratorate. All three criminal defendants are currently detained at XXX City Detention Center.

XXX Bureau of Public Security has completed their investigation of the case involving criminal defendants A, B, and C, and submitted a recommendation for prosecution to the People's Procuratorate. The following facts are gathered according to proper legal procedures:

On February XX, 19XX about 11 pm, police officers from XXX Bureau of Public Security were dispatched to serve a warrant of detention to an aggravated assault criminal suspect XYZ, who resides at XX Township, XX Village. The criminal facts are applicable to all three criminal defendants A, B, and C that they have intentionally committed obstruction of justice with physical force against police officers on duty and who had made known of their official identifications. These criminal defendants made up and shouted lies such as these police officers "rape", "rob" villagers. They instigated a riot with large crowd, resulting not only in physical injuries of the police officers but also the escape of the criminal suspect XYZ.

The facts illustrated above are clear and evidences included are reliable and sufficient to bring this prosecution forward.

It is our determination that criminal suspects A, B, and C have violated the Criminal Law of the People's Republic of China and should be subject to criminal liability under Article 277-Obstruction of Justice. According to Article 141 of the Criminal Procedure Law of the People's Republic of China,[26] we hereby file this criminal indictment of obstruction of justice against each of the three criminal suspects. Please render proper judgment according to the law.

Respectfully submitted to
XXX City Basic People's Court

Procurator: XXX
January XX, 20XX

Enclosed:

1. List of Evidences (1 copy)
2. List of Witnesses (1 copy)
3. Photocopied major evidence files (1 folder)[27]

[26] Article 141 of the Chinese Criminal Procedure Law states "when the People's Procuratorate believes that the facts of a crime committed by the crime suspect have been ascertained, that the evidence is reliable and sufficient and that criminal responsibility shall be investigated according to law, the People's Procuratorate shall make a decision to initiate a prosecution, and shall, in accordance with the provisions on trial jurisdiction, initiate a public prosecution in the People's Court".

[27] The table of contents provided by the prosecution indicates that this folder contains a total of 138 pages (for all three defendants). Apparently, the prosecution evidences (originated from the police investigation) are only selectively included in the formal court case dossier.

6.4.4 Criminal Defense

Each of the three criminal defendants has hired his or her own defense attorney. The three attorneys (two males and one female) are from three different law firms in the same city. Written criminal defense scripts submitted by the three attorneys are included in the court case dossier. The attorneys (male, aged 60 and 35) representing Defendants A and B provided hand-written scripts (both clean and legible) while the youngest attorney (female, aged 30) representing Defendant C offered a typed-up script. We translate the major arguments made by each attorney below.

6.4.4.1 Criminal Defense from Attorney A

Dear Presiding Judge and Judges,

I am the criminal defense attorney representing Defendant A in this case. I hereby submit the following defense opinions according to the facts and the law for your consideration:

The defense does not dispute the criminal indictment filed against my client. However, this defense does find partial inconsistency, inadequacy, and inaccuracy in the facts of this case presented by the prosecution. Detailed below are the defense opinions with specific regard to these disputable facts and our suggestions for the sentencing consideration by the court.

1. Defendant A did not directly involve in obstructing justice with physical force. Her role in this case is trivial. At the night of the event, two plain-clothed police officers suddenly appeared at a home where a wedding event is taking place. Although she was at the scene, my client-Defendant A did not interfere with the function of the police using physical force; at least there is no credible evidence to support the accusation. According to the Chinese Criminal Procedure Law, the prosecution has to present clear and sufficient evidence beyond the reasonable doubt in support of the criminal charge. In this case, all eye witness testimonies (from five witnesses) were extracted when the witnesses themselves were under coercive measures (detention) carried out by the Public Security Bureau. None of the five witnesses has appeared in court to testify in person. There is at least a theoretical possibility that the written statements provided by the victims-police officers from the Public Security Bureau are exaggerated. Once again, none of the officers appears to testify in court. My client-Defendant A did shout the words "rape" and "rob" at the scene. She could be faulted for her poor judgment to certain degree but should not be held responsible for the full extent of the criminal charge.
2. Defendant A's action is not directly related to the escape of XYZ. According to the Criminal Indictment, this case of obstruction of justice resulted in two

serious consequences: (1) the escape of criminal suspect XYZ, and (2) the injuries of police officers. With regard to the latter, there is absolutely no credible evidence to support the claim of injuries suffered by the police officers. With the former, it is the result of the involvement of a large crowd that night. According to the information provided in the case dossier, 10–20 people were already at the scene (most of them are XYZ's relatives and friends who are attending his wedding that night) when Defendant A shouted the words. Therefore, my client's verbal action is neither the reason for the gathering of the crowd nor the reason for XYZ's escape.

3. There is clear procedure violation by the officers of the Public Security Bureau. The officers who were on duty that night did not wear uniforms, did not show their IDs, and did not show the warrant for detention to XYZ or anyone at the scene. Objectively speaking, my client-Defendant A had no reason to believe the strangers at the door were police officers.
4. My client-Defendant A had no prior criminal record. Therefore, a lighter sentence may be warranted.
5. The defense urges the court to ascertain the applicability of the provisions in the Article 277 of the Criminal Law to my client in this case.

Combining all the aforementioned arguments, the defense respectfully requests that the court apply leniency to Defendant A in this case.

Respectfully submitted to
XXX Basic People's Court

XXX Law Firm
Attorney XXX (March XX, 20XX)

6.4.4.2 Criminal Defense from Attorney B

Attorney B representing Defendant B made two almost identical arguments with Attorney A that (1) there is no evidence to support that his client had used force against the police officers; and (2) there is procedure violation by the officers on duty at the night of executing a warrant of detention to XYZ. Attorney B does reveal one additional piece of information to the court which was not found in the defense arguments made in Attorney A's script. The new revelation concerns specifically the treatment of Defendant B since his own criminal detention.

Attorney B writes: "My client-Defendant B was detained by the Public Security Bureau on February XX, 19XX but was not formally arrested until September XX, 19XX. How come such a simple case with clear facts gets dragged on forever and made into such a complicated one? During meetings with my client, I was told that the police forced him to confess to the charge or would let him rot in jail. The police actually did exactly that. They dragged on the case for 8 months before a formal arrest was made. It has been a full year since the time of the incident".

The court case dossier has no documentation of any bail request made or denied. There is also no mention about the current status of the escapee XYZ-Defendant B's younger brother and Defendant A's brother-in-law. In spite of the sharp words used against the police actions in the defense script, Attorney B (like Attorney A), did not dispute the Criminal Indictment against his client. He concludes his written defense argument with the same plea for leniency anchored on two reasons: the minor role played by his client in the incident and the first-time nature of the accused crime.

6.4.4.3 Criminal Defense from Attorney C

The female and the youngest attorney among the three made a not-guilty plea for her client-Defendant C. Her written defense script is typed rather than handwritten, longer (3 pages) than that of the Attorneys A and B (each with 2 pages only), and included more citations and discussions of various legal provisions.

Attorney C's first defense argument is that the prosecution has the burden of proof to justify the legality of the official action that took place on the night of February XX, 19XX serving the warrant of detention. She writes: "after reviewing all the evidences included in the dossier, the only basis for the officers' action serving the warrant of detention was the order, directive or notice from the leader of the Public Security Bureau. Only 5 or 6 out of a total of more than 10 officers on duty that night wore uniforms. The only documentation that the police have made known their official identifications is through their shouting of the words "we are from the Public Security Bureau. Don't Run!" when XYZ was running away. There is absolutely no other evidence showing the police have a legitimate Warrant of Detention that night, nor are there any witnesses who have seen any display of identifications by the police. Therefore, the defense argues that due to the unclear facts and insufficient evidence, whether the police were executing a lawful order on the night of Feb., XX, 19XX is questionable".

Attorney C made her second defense argument focusing on the exact behavior of her client-Defendant C. She suggests that no clear evidence has linked her client to the use of force against the police officers that night and that her client-Defendant C only grabbed one of the officers but did not punch, kick or bite anyone as suggested in the criminal indictment. Attorney C concludes her defense script by stating that "according to Article 163, paragraph 3 of the Criminal Procedure Law, when facts are not clear and evidence insufficient, the court shall render a judgment of not guilty".[28]

[28] Defense Attorney C apparently made a mistake here by citing the wrong Article in the Criminal Procedure Law. It should be Article 162, paragraph 3 which states that a judgment of not guilty should be rendered for lack of sufficient evidences.

6.4.5 Criminal Judgment

The court final judgment on the case including verdicts and sentences applicable to each defendant is rendered on March XX, 20XX. The five-page judgment document uses a large sum of materials from earlier police and prosecution documents (i.e., arrest warrant, recommendation for prosecution and criminal indictment). This document also summarizes the major defense arguments made by the three attorneys, followed by addressing whether these arguments have been accepted by the court (none was accepted). Sentences are provided at the very end of the judgment, followed by the brief instruction on the defendant's right to appeal. Translation of the major contents of the final judgment is provided below.

XX Province XXX Basic People's Court
Criminal Judgment
[20XX] XXX (Letter Code), XXX (Numeric Serial #)[29]

Public Prosecution Organ: XXX People's Procuratorate

Criminal Defendant A, female, born in 19XX, September XX,[30] Han nationality, elementary school education, peasant, resides in XX City, XX Township, and XX Village.

Defense Attorney A XXX, XXX Law Firm

Criminal Defendant B, male, born in 19XX, July, XX, Han nationality, elementary school education, peasant, resides in XX City, XX Township, and XX Village.

Defense Attorney B XXX, XXX Law Firm

Criminal Defendant C, male, born in 19XX, November XX,[31] Han nationality, high school education, small business owner,[32] resides in XX City, XY Township, and XZ Village.

Defense Attorney C XXX, XXX Law Firm

The above three defendants were detained on Feb., XX, 19XX by XXX Bureau of Public Security for obstruction of justice. They were formally arrested on Sept., XX, 19XX and are currently in detention at XXX City Detention Center.

XXX People's Procuratorate rendered indictments against the three defendants for the crime of obstructing justice. Upon receiving the request for trial from the People's Procuratorate on February XX, 20XX, this court formed a collegial panel

[29] The letter code and numeric serial number match those on the front page of the court case dossier.

[30] The court has made the correction of Defendant's birth month from June as stated in the prosecution's Criminal Indictment to September as stated in the police Recommendation for Prosecution. The court also enters Defendant A's occupation as "peasant," not "unemployed" as stated in all prior documents.

[31] The exact date of birth for Defendant C is now added. In all previous documents, only the birth year and month for Defendant C were listed.

[32] The court seems to have independently verified Defendant C's occupation which was listed as "unemployed" in all earlier documents.

to administer the open trial. Procurator XXX from the People's Procuratorate, the three defendants and their attorneys have participated in the trial. This trial is now completed.

The prosecution stated that: On February X, 19XX about 11 pm, police officers from XXX Bureau of Public Security were dispatched to serve a warrant of detention to an aggravated assault criminal suspect XYZ, residing at XX Township, XX Village. The criminal facts are applicable to all three criminal defendants A, B, and C that they have intentionally committed obstruction of justice with physical force against police officers on duty and who had made known of their official identifications. These criminal defendants made up and shouted lies such as these police officers "rape", "rob" villagers. They instigated a riot with large crowd, resulting not only in physical injuries of the police officers but also the escape of the criminal suspect XYZ.[33]

Evidences provided by the prosecution include: eyewitness testimonies from XXX, XXX, XXX, XXX, and XXX; victim's statements from XXX, XXX, XXX, and XXX; statements from all three criminal defendants, and administrative decisions made by the Bureau of Public Security. It is determined by the prosecution that criminal suspects A, B, and C have violated the Criminal Law of the People's Republic of China and should be subject to criminal liability under Article 277-Obstruction of Justice.

Against the criminal indictment, Defendant A argues that "I did shout the word 'robbery' and did not know they were police officers." Her attorney provides the following defense arguments: (1) Defendant A was not directly involved in obstructing justice with physical force. Her role in this case is trivial; (2) Defendant A's action is not directly related to the escape of XYZ; (3) there is clear procedure violation by the officers of the Public Security Bureau; (4) Defendant A should be considered as a first-time offender. A lighter sentence may be warranted; and (5) the defense urges the court to ascertain the applicability of Article 277 of the Criminal Law to this case.

Against the criminal indictment, Defendant B argues that "I did not see the police arresting my younger brother. I did not do anything. But, I didn't stop anyone else from doing anything". His defense attorney did not dispute the crime as charged. He made the following suggestions: (1) part of the facts against Defendant B is neither clear nor sufficient; (2) police officers did not follow proper procedures, and Defendant B only played a very minor role in the incident; and (3) Defendant B has good attitude, has no prior criminal record and should be granted leniency in court judgment.

Against the criminal indictment, Defendant C argues that "I participated in the incident without knowing what's going on. I grabbed someone but did not hit anyone". His defense attorney suggests that no clear evidence has linked Defendant C to the use of force against the police officers that night and that according to

[33] This paragraph is virtually word-to-word repeat of the same statement by the prosecution in the Criminal Indictment.

Article 163,[34] paragraph 3 of the Criminal Procedure Law the court should render a judgment of not guilty.

According to the court trial, the following facts have been substantiated: On February XX, 19XX about 11 pm, police officers from XXX Bureau of Public Security were dispatched to serve a warrant of detention to an aggravated assault criminal suspect XYZ, residing at XX Township, XX Village. The criminal facts are applicable to all three criminal defendants A, B, and C that they have intentionally committed obstruction of justice with physical force against police officers on duty and who had made known of their official identifications. These criminal defendants made up and shouted lies such as these police officers "rape", "rob" villagers. They instigated a riot with large crowd, resulting not only in physical injuries of the police officers but also the escape of the criminal suspect XYZ.[35]

Evidences in support of the aforementioned facts are: (1) victim's statements from XXX, XXX, XXX, and XXX, identifying all three defendants' involvement; (2) eyewitness testimonies from XXX, XXX, XXX, XXX, and XXX, placing the three defendants at the scene; (3) relevant documents from the Bureau of Public Security; and (4) the three criminal defendants' own statements admitting their involvements in the crime of obstructing justice.

All the above listed evidences have been substantiated in court and are sufficient to support the criminal charges as filed. The defendants' recantations of earlier confessions are not consistent with the established facts and are therefore rejected by the court. Majority of the arguments made by the defense attorneys are inconsistent with the facts and are therefore not adopted.

The court finds sufficient evidences to determine that criminal defendants A, B, and C have committed the crime of obstruction of justice which caused social harm and should be punished according to law. The public prosecution filed by the People's Procuratorate against all three defendants is therefore fully supported. During the court trial, Defendants A and B attempted to circumvent the correct charges against them by pleading to a lesser charge thus deserves aggravated sentencing consideration according to the law. In order to maintain normal social order, we render the following judgment according to Article 277 and Article 25[36] of the Criminal Law:

1. Criminal Defendant A is convicted of the crime of obstruction of justice and sentenced to imprisonment of 1 year and 3 months (Defendant A's jail time while on criminal detention is counted towards the total length of this sentence,

[34] The court did not make any mention of the mistake made by the Defense Attorney C who cited Article 163, instead of Article 162 of the Criminal Procedure Law (1996).

[35] This is a second repeat of the identical statement made by the prosecution in the Criminal Indictment (which in turn is almost a "copy and paste" from the statement made by the Public Security Bureau in its Recommendation for Prosecution).

[36] Article 25 of the Chinese Criminal Law specifies that "a joint crime refers to an intentional crime committed by two or more persons jointly".

i.e., the duration of her prison term is to be counted as from Feb., XX, 19XX to May XX, 20XX).

2. Criminal Defendant B is convicted of the crime of obstruction of justice and sentenced to imprisonment of 1 year and 3 months (Defendant B's jail time while on criminal detention is counted towards the total length of this sentence, i.e., the duration of his prison term is to be counted from Feb., XX, 19XX to May XX, 20XX).
3. Criminal Defendant C is convicted of the crime of obstruction of justice and sentenced to imprisonment of 1 year (Defendant C's jail time while on criminal detention is counted towards the total length of this sentence, i.e., the duration of his prison term is to be counted from Feb., XX, 19XX to Feb., XX, 20XX).

In case of appeal, please notify through this court or through XXX Intermediate People's Court within 10 days after receiving this judgment. In case of filing a written appeal, please submit one original and three copies of your appeal document.

Presiding Judge XXX[37]
Judge XXX
Judge XXX
March XX, 20XX
Court Clerk XXX

6.5 Conclusion

The anatomy of Chinese criminal trial is revealed in this chapter. Using the confluence of culture and nomenclature as a backdrop, we dissect a real court case involving three criminal defendants who are charged with obstruction of justice. The case dossier itself reveals much about the internal logic of a normal Chinese criminal justice process. As much and as detailed as we are able to present this sample case dossier, we are still left in dark with a multitude of decisions that went into making the case and this case dossier. The most noticeable observation of this dossier is the penetrating impact of the police evidences on the whole trial process. The evidences required to bring up a string of police actions are quite different in the Chinese criminal justice system compared to that of other countries. A substantial amount of evidences (far beyond the need for a simple probable cause) is required before a Warrant of Detention can be issued. A substantial amount of time is also needed to gather additional evidences while the suspect is in police custody. Limited empirical data suggest that about 40 to 70 % of those criminal detentions resulted in formal arrests. A formal arrest decision is highly correlated to the decision for formal prosecution, from 85 to 99 %, according to Zuo (2007). As we

[37] A round court stamp is placed on top of the judges' names.

have seen in the case illustrated in this chapter, criminal conviction is virtually a certain result from the Chinese court.

Generalizability based on a single case and limited empirical data will always be problematic. However, what we have hoped to achieve in this chapter is to take a quick glimpse of the roles played by the parties involved in a criminal trial. Using this case, we have seen a Chinese criminal trial process dominated by written materials included in the dossier that are largely shaped by evidences provided by the police and that are unchallenged and/or unchallengeable in court. Languages used in the original police documents are used verbatim at the prosecution and court trial stages. Neither eyewitnesses nor victims have appeared in court to testify. In spite of the legitimate arguments made by the defense attorneys, no cross-examination was conducted. The court also fails to acknowledge the fact that Defendant C who received his sentence on March XX, 20XX should have been released from jail on February XX, 20XX (i.e., 20 days prior to the final sentence) based on the court judgment.

This particular case of obstruction of justice remains mysterious in other aspects. The coincidence in the timing of the original police action (i.e., serving a Warrant of Detention to suspect XYZ who eventually escaped) that led to the ensuing incident is intriguing. With all the considerations, time and efforts needed by the police to make a decision of serving the Warrant, the head of the Bureau of Public Security chose to dispatch officers at 11 pm on the night of XYZ's wedding and more than 10 officers were sent to serve a single Warrant to a single suspect. Although police administrative decisions were made to detain five other villagers together with the three defendants for their involvements in the alleged incident of obstructing justice, these villagers were quickly released from a short-term detention after signing written testimonies against the three defendants. The three defendants, two of whom are the escapee XYZ's closest relatives were kept in jail awaiting their formal arrests (8 months later) and trial (one full year later). Findings from this particular case give credence to Feeley's (1979) conclusion made three decades ago in the U.S. that the process *is* the punishment (emphasis added). The seemingly converging conclusions drawn from two different countries, two different legal systems and two different time periods beg for explanation. From a Bourdieusian perspective, it may be argued that, in a liberal democratic society where the rule of law is the norm, a criminal trial can be seen as a battleground where relatively equal and independent actors (e.g., judges, prosecutors, and defense attorneys) confront each other to interpret a corpus of texts (the criminal law) in order to sanctify a legitimized vision of the social world (Bourdieu 1987). Can the Bourdieusian assumption and expectation hold true in criminal trials conducted in a legal system featuring socialist rule of law with Chinese characteristics? People's justice and law's embattled empire are the main thrusts of the next chapter.

References

Bourdieu, P. (1987). The force of law: Toward a sociology of the juridical field. *Hastings Law Journal*, 38, 805–53 (Translated by Richard Terdiman).

Feeley, M. (1979). *The process is the punishment: Handling cases in a lower criminal court*. New York: Russell Sage Foundation.

He, X. (2012). Black hole of responsibility: The adjudication committee's role in the chinese court. *Law & Society Review*, 2011. Available at SSRN: http://ssrn.com/abstract=2038216.

Hegel, R. (2009). *True crimes in eighteenth-century China: Twenty case histories*. Seattle: University of Washington Press.

Li, L., Sun, J. & He, N. (2012). An empirical assessment of the impact of chinese penal code 306: Voices from the field (刑法306条存与废: 倾听法律人的心声) *He Bei Law Science* (河北法学), 29, 17–26.

Liu, S., & Halliday, T. (2011). Political liberalism and political embeddedness: Understanding politics in the work of Chinese criminal defense lawyers. *Law & Society Review, 45*, 831–864.

Zuo, W. (2010). *The landscape of Chinese criminal procedure law and practice (*刑事诉讼的中国图景). Beijing: SDX Joint Publishing Company (三联书店).

Zuo, W. (2007). *Empirical study on the operation mechanism of criminal procedure in China* (中国刑事诉讼运行机制实证研究). Beijing: Law Press (法律出版社).

Chapter 7
People's Justice and Law's Embattled Empire

7.1 Introduction

Having used case dossier as a vehicle of physiological introspection in the last chapter, we now shift focus to studying the psychological aspects of Chinese criminal trials. Since its original enactment in 1979, Chinese Criminal Law has undergone the first major revision in 1997 and a series of minor revisions (last being in 2011). However, it has not been scrutinized as closely or as publically as the Chinese Criminal Procedure Law (CPL96) in the legislative arena and public opinion. The result of the domestic and international critical attentions on criminal due process and human rights is the most recent major revision of the Criminal Procedure Law in 2012 (CPL12). There are clear signs that certain articles in CL97 are increasingly contested in courts as well as in public opinions nationwide. This can be viewed as a manifestation of the inherent contradiction in the socialist legal orthodoxy and liberal market economy inspirations. Socialist law with Chinese characteristics is now more than ever an embattled empire.[1] Both the legal provisions and the practical interpretation of these legal texts (in this case, Chinese Criminal Law) through trial represent a "paradigmatic staging of the symbolic struggle" between antagonistic world views (Bourdieu 1987). This chapter provides nuanced observations of selected provisions of the law and their practical interpretations. In addition, we use a two-prong approach to demonstrate how the government is coping with the dilemma of maintaining legitimacy of the legal system (delivering people's justice through fair, transparent, and efficient trials) on the one hand adhering to the increasingly confused and challenged orthodox socialist legality on the other. First, we illustrate the application of the newly installed Chinese sentencing guidelines (2010) with actual cases and sentencing worksheets from the Basic People's Court. Second, we dissect a typical court organizational structure in a Basic People's Court based on observations made during our site visits to China.

[1] Dworkin's (1986) book is an inspiration for the title and theme of this chapter.

N. He, *Chinese Criminal Trials*, DOI: 10.1007/978-1-4614-8205-5_7,

7.2 Segmented Criminal Law

During our multiple site visits while working on the MacArthur pilot project in China, we noticed that those Basic People's Courts with large criminal caseload often designate judges to specialize in two case groups with corresponding courtrooms assigned.[2] For example, Criminal Courtroom #1 might be designated to handle all cases involving crimes of infringing upon citizens' personal and democratic rights, crimes of endangering national public security, crimes of obstructing the administration of public order, crimes of robbery and snatching, and crimes of endangering national security committed by non-military persons. Criminal Courtroom #2 would then be designated to process all property related crimes, crimes of disrupting the order of socialist market economy, crimes of embezzlement and bribery, and crimes of dereliction of duty. The division of labor is likely due to several major considerations. Cases tried in Courtroom #1 do not normally involve monetary values while those tried in Courtroom #2 certainly do. The overall caseload maybe somewhat evenly distributed with the use of case groups, although the rationales and mechanisms to group cases (and the number of rooms assigned) may vary from court to court. The designation of specialized courtrooms may be helpful to utilize and increase judges' professional knowledge and, to improve efficiency in case processing.

The Chinese Criminal Law (CL97) follows a similar format used in the Continental legal tradition that, there are both "General Provisions" and "Specific Provisions" sections. The General Provisions of the Chinese Criminal Law are covered in five chapters and 101 articles (or 22 % of the total articles in CL97). These provisions provide the basic principles and the scope of the application of the law, general definitions of crimes, types of punishments, and concrete instructions on the application of punishments. The General Provisions set the tone for the Specific Provisions in the Criminal Law that socialist legality is to be actualized through the legal texts used in individual Articles. The Specific Provisions include 11 chapters and 351 articles (or 78 % of the total articles in CL97), articulating detailed descriptions of various punishable criminal acts with associated punishments.

It is apparent that two chapters dominate the Specific Provisions of the CL97: "crimes of disrupting the order of the socialist market economy" (Chap. 3 with 92 articles, or 20 % of the total articles in CL97) and, "crimes of obstructing the administration of public order" (Chap. 6, 91 articles, or 20 % of the total articles in CL97). Titles of all the major chapters and sections and the relative distribution of the number of articles included in the CL97 are listed in Table 7.1.

The hefty concentration of the CL97 in two large categories of criminal activities, i.e., those against the socialist market economy and the administration of public order, can be seen as an unmistakable display of "symbolic power"

[2] Due to its overwhelming caseload, civil cases have long been tried in multiple courtrooms simultaneously.

Table 7.1 Chinese criminal law (1997)

	Title	No. of articles	Percentage (%)
Part I	General provisions	101	(22.4)
Chapter I	Aims, basic principles, and scope of application	11	2.4
Chapter II	Crimes	20	4.4
Chapter III	Punishments	29	6.4
Chapter IV	Application of punishments	29	6.4
Chapter V	Other provisions	12	2.7
Part II	Specific provisions	351	(77.7)
Chapter I	Crimes of Endangering National Security	12	2.7
Chapter II	Crimes of Endangering Public Security	26	5.8
Chapter III	Crimes of Disrupting the Order of Socialist Market Economy	92	20.4
Chapter IV	Crimes of Infringing Upon Citizens' Rights of Person and Democratic Rights	31	6.9
Chapter V	Crimes of Property Violation	14	3.1
Chapter VI	Crimes of Obstructing the Administration of Public Order	91	20.1
Chapter VII	Crimes of Impairing the Interests of National Defense	14	3.1
Chapter VIII	Crimes of Embezzlement and Bribery	15	3.3
Chapter IX	Crimes of Dereliction of Duty	23	5.1
Chapter X	Crimes of Servicemen's Transgression of Duties	32	7.1
Chapter XI	Supplementary Provisions	1	0.2
Total		452	100 (100)

(Bourdieu 1987) and dominance of "orthodoxy" (Bourdieu 1977) in the universe of legal discourse. Criminal Law as the "quintessential form of the symbolic power" is now being challenged more openly on a daily basis in the field of juridical practice in China. Criminal defense arguments illustrated in the case of "obstruction of justice" included in the previous Chap. 6 offer a glimpse of growing public contention against the arrogance of government power. In the current chapter, we use examples to accentuate the ongoing struggles in the practice of defending (by the government) or disputing (e.g., by the free spirited entrepreneurs) one specific definition of crime—the "crimes of disrupting socialist market economy."

We are certainly aware that the sheer number of Articles does not necessarily correspond to the frequency of their daily applications. The relative distribution of the legal provisions in the Chinese Criminal Law is perhaps more so a reflection of the intent of the lawmakers (in order to construct a preferred social reality) than a reflection of the authentic social reality. Chinese national court statistics (Supreme People's Court 2010a, b; seen in Figs. 7.1 and 7.2) reveal two interesting realities. First of all, criminal cases only occupy 3 % of the total case volume, in contrast to

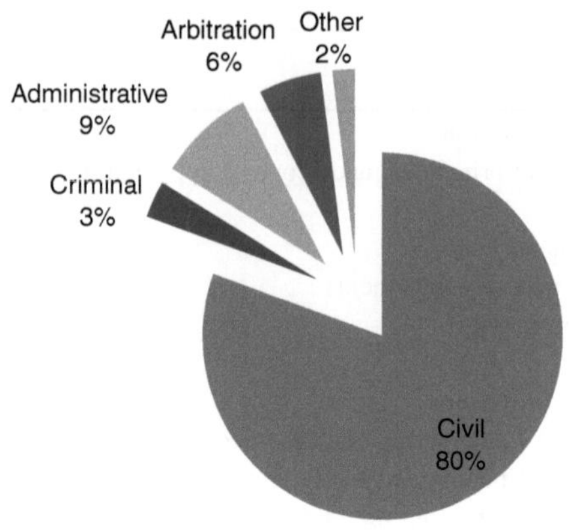

Fig. 7.1 Case distribution (all courts; 2009)

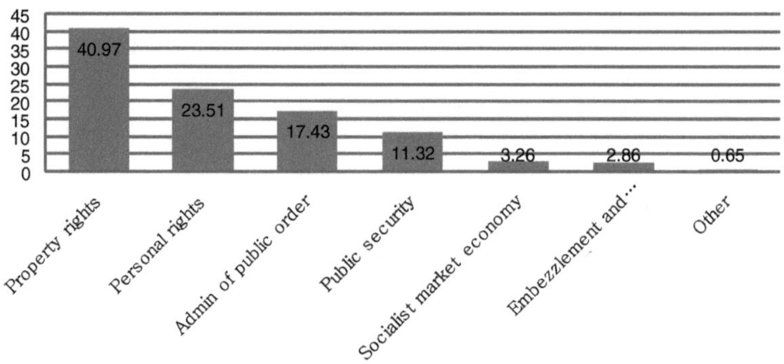

Fig. 7.2 Distributions of criminal trials of 1st instance (PRC, 2009)

the dominance of civil cases (80 %). The volume of criminal cases is even less than administrative cases (9 %) and arbitration cases (6 %). Second, within the profile of criminal cases tried in the courts of first instance, property offense category has the largest share (41 %). Third, crimes against administration of public order together with crimes against public security would account for about 29 % of the total case volume nationwide (the second highest category if so combined). This figure is in correspondence with public contentions arising out of the multitude of social problems discussed in Chap. 3. The inevitable clash between socialist ideal portrayed in the legal texts and the actual social reality provides the context for the cases we highlight below.

7.3 Crimes of Disrupting Socialist Financial Order

Three articles provided in the CL97 provide legal language that stretches the limits of criminal sanctions applicable for disrupting socialist financial order from up to 3 years imprisonment to life imprisonment or death penalty.

Article 176 states that:

> Whoever *illegally takes in deposits from the general public or does so in disguised form*, thus disrupting the financial order, shall be sentenced to *fixed-term imprisonment of not more than three years* or criminal detention and shall also, or shall only, be fined not less than 20,000 yuan but not more than 200,000 yuan; if the amount involved is *huge*, or if there are other serious circumstances, he shall be sentenced to *fixed-term imprisonment of not less than three years but not more than 10 years* and shall also be fined not less than 50,000 yuan but not more than 500,000 yuan (italics added)

Article 192 provides that:

> Whoever, for the purpose of illegal possession, *unlawfully raises funds by means of fraud* shall, if the amount involved is *relative large*, be sentenced to *fixed-term imprisonment of not more than 5 years* or criminal detention and shall also be fined not less than 20,000 yuan but not more than 200,000; if the amount involved is *huge*, or if there are other serious circumstances, he shall be sentenced to *fixed-term imprisonment of not less than five years but not more than 10 years* and shall also be fined not less than 50,000 yuan but not more than 500,000 yuan; if the amount involved is *especially huge*, or if there are other especially serious circumstances, he shall be sentenced to *fixed-term imprisonment of not less than 10 years or life imprisonment* and shall also be fined not less than 50,000 yuan but not more than 500,000 yuan or be sentenced to confiscation of property (italics added).

Article 199 adds that:

> Whoever commits the crime mentioned in Articles 192, 194, or 195 of this Section shall, if the amount involved is *especially huge*, and especially heavy losses are caused to *interests of the State and the pe*ople, be sentenced to *life imprisonment or death* and also to confiscation of property (italics added).[3]

7.3.1 A Case with National Publicity

Legal battle on the applicability of either Article 176 or Article 192 is the focus of one of the most influential criminal cases in China in recent years. The "Wu Ying case" (2012) involves a young business woman, a 27-year-old billionaire at the time of her arrest in 2007. Although she was arrested under Article 176, Wu was

[3] Articles 194 and 195 in the CL97 specify in similar format with similar sentences frauds by the means of "financial bills" (Article 194) and "letter of credit" (Article 195). In the latest revised version of Chinese Criminal Law (which took effect in May, 2011), Article 199 is revised to read as "Whoever commit the crime mentioned in Article 19 of this section shall, if..." without any mentioning Articles 194 and 195.

charged and tried under Articles 192 and 199 for illegally raising funds in excess of 770 million RMB yuan from eleven private investors and for causing "heavy (financial) losses of the State and the people." She was accused of intentionally defrauding the public with the lure of high interest rate in spite of having already accumulated substantial debt (14 million RMB yuan) at the time of her new borrowing. The government argued that Wu knew or should have known that she would not be able to repay her loans. Wu's defense team rebutted that Wu is the owner of multiple legitimate businesses (investing in cosmetics, store space in shopping malls, recreation centers, and hotels) and the loans she borrowed were not targeting at the general public. The eleven investors are all relatives and acquaintances. The high interest rate she promised the investors is the outcome of youthful inexperience and over-ambition.[4] It was further argued that Wu had made no attempt to illegally possess the investment for personal consumption and that she had already made great effort in returning the principle and interest of the loans to the investors. At time of the trial, Wu has paid off nearly half of her debts from the eleven investors. The defense team ended its argument by stating that "This is a completely normal private business matter."[5]

After 2 years of highly publicized trial, Wu received a death sentence with immediate execution in December 2009 from the Intermediate People's Court of Jinhua City (Zhejiang Province), the trial court of first instance. The defendant appealed the decision to the next level court and, in January 2012, Zhejiang Province High People's Court upheld the death sentence and submitted the case to the Supreme People's Court for final approval. In April 2012, the Supreme People's Court sent the case back to the Zhejiang Province People's High Court for retrial which resulted in a final judgment of death sentence with two-year suspension. In February 2013, Wu's defense team filed a petition to the Supreme People's Court against the now legally effective final judgment from the High People's Court of Zhejiang Province, invoking the procedure for trial supervision allowable in the Chinese Criminal Procedure Law (1996).[6] It seems that Wu and her defense team are courting the ambivalent Supreme People's Court who did not grant approval to the original death sentence with immediate execution rendered by the lower court. Given the substantial media exposure, live discussions in the blog sphere and good deal of sympathy from the public toward the defendant in the case, the Chinese Supreme People's Court has a very difficult decision to make. Whether or not the highest court in China would take on this criminal case again,

[4] It is interesting that the defense made a point that Fortune 500 companies operate in a similar way, i.e., borrowing from investors while already in debt and without certainty for the margin of return for the new investors.

[5] Complete defense scripts filed at all stages of Wu Ying' trial are posted on the website of King and Capital Law Firm http://www.king-capital.com/templates/second/index.aspx?nodeid=182.

[6] Article 203 of the CPL96 provides that "A party or his legal representative or near relative may file a petition to a People's Court or People's Procuratorate against a legally effective judgment or ruling, notwithstanding, the execution of the judgment or ruling may not be suspended.".

the intensified struggle is completely exposed between a banking and investment sector largely monopolized by the government and the insatiable needs for capital investment from an increasingly uncontrollable market economy.[7] While Wu and her defense team rekindle their hope for a reversal of fate in the hands of the Supreme People's Court Justices in the coming months, the world continues to search for the true meaning of the legal provisions made in the name of preventing crimes of disrupting the order of socialist market economy.

7.3.2 A Local Case Without Publicity

At the local level and completely outside the national limelight, crimes prosecuted according to CL97 Article 176 have become frequent affairs in the more developed southeast region since the late 1990s. Many trials of such cases are now conducted by the Basic People's courts applying a simplified trial procedure (i.e., conditioned on a guilty plea). We offer an intriguing case below that illustrates the nature of such offense, a reflection of the evolution of the relevant legal provisions, the logic of the defense argument, and the court's rationale in rendering the final judgment. Close attention is paid to the timing of the case process which began with this defendant's arrest in 1995 (2 years before the CL97 was enacted) and her eventual trial and conviction in 20XX.

XXX Bureau of Public Security

Recommendation for Prosecution

[19XX]Serial Number XXX

Criminal suspect XXX, female, Han nationality, born in 19XX, July XX, elementary school education, running underground loan shop prior to arrest, resides in XX Province, XX City, XX Township, and XX Village.

Relevant Background: arrest warrant issued by the XXX City Basic People's Procuratorate on Nov., XX, 19XX and executed on Jan., XX, 19XX; currently in custody at XXX City Detention Center.

Case Facts: Since 199X, criminal suspect XXX has operated from her home an underground loan shop, defrauding a total of 214 customers with the lure of interest rate of 3 to 3.5 % and taking in total deposits in the amount of 72 million RMB yuan and 1.2 million Hong Kong dollars. Criminal suspect XXX used partial

---

[7] Majority of the non-government owned businesses in China have great difficulty in borrowing loans from the government owned banks. For these types of businesses, only ten percent of the needed loans are acquired from the government owned banks (Chinese Industry-Commerce Times 2012-3-13). Private fund-raising and loan relationship thus run a constant risk between the lines of legality and illegality. Criminalizing failed business (private loan) relationship and selective enforcement are brewing frustration and contention among small business owners. Many of the provisions in CL97 are regarded as outdated. Likewise, socialist market economy is increasingly a contested concept and a diluted orthodoxy.

fund to pay off high interests owed to XXX, XXX, and others in addition to financing her own lavish lifestyle. According to the facts illustrated above, criminal suspect XXX has violated Article 7—"illegally takes in deposits from the general public" (italics added)[8] as specified in the Decision on Punishing Crimes Against Disruption of Financial Order made by the Standing Committee of the National People's Congress.[9] According to Article 129 of the Criminal Procedure Law of the People's Republic of China, we hereby recommend that criminal prosecution and investigation be launched against this suspect by the People's Procuratorate.

Respectfully submitted to
XXX Basic People's Procuratorate
Chief of XXX Bureau of Public Security
July XX, 19XX
Enclosed:

1. Four copies of police case dossier
2. One copy of Recommendation for Prosecution

The prosecution finally moved the case forward on Nov., XX, 20XX, charging the defendant under CL97 Article 176 for illegally taking in deposits from the general public. The defendant secured two attorneys to represent her case on Feb., XX, 20XX. The trial was finally completed on Dec., XX of 20XX, almost 5 years after her arrest. In spite of the defense arguments that the defendant committed much of her "crime" before July 1, 1995 when the "Decision on Punishing Crimes Against Disruption of Financial Order" made by the Standing Committee of the National People's Congress was issued and long before the CL97 took effect, the court sentenced the defendant to 9 years and 9 months imprisonment, plus a fine of 500,000 RMB yuan. The sentence, which is almost to the fullest extent provided by law (i.e., 3–10 years imprisonment and 500,000 in fines), was also rendered despite the defense arguments that the defendant had surrendered herself to the Public Security Bureau voluntarily and had returned a substantial amount of the deposits she took in. The length of her detention in jail waiting for trial was close to 4 years, an inexcusable breach of due process, unwise use of state resources, and unnecessary decision against an old woman with no prior criminal history.[10]

[8] The original recommendation for prosecution is a typed document. The XXX Bureau of Public Security visibly crossed off in ink the original legal provisions cited (in italics). The substituted provision of law was added in handwritten form with the Bureau's official stamps placed atop of each revised spot. Articles 7 and 8 included in the Decision of the Standing Committee of the Chinese National People's Congress would later become Articles 176 and 192 in the CL97 which went into effect on October 1, 1997.

[9] Time (July 1, 1995) of the issuance of the National People's Congress decision was not indicated in this document.

[10] The court calculated her sentence length as from Jan., XX, 19XX to Oct., XX, 20XX. The defendant would be 67 years old when released from prison.

The two cases illustrated above offer a sobering reminder of the gravity of state power in the making and enforcement of laws in defense of the socialist legal order. Chinese market economy, especially the interest rates (e.g., bank deposit and loan) used in the banking system, is subject to total control by the central government. Interest rate is used as a mechanism to manipulate the market for the maximal benefit of the socialist state: the government reduces it to encourage consumption by the public and increases it to encourage deposit and increase capital supply for socialist force of production.[11] Although its proportion has been gradually reduced since the beginning of the reform era (1978), state-owned enterprises (and disguised "private" enterprises) continue to dominant key areas of the Chinese economy. Government crack-downs on private, non-governmental lending practices are facing increasing resistance and public contention. The selective enforcement of the law has been detrimental to the legitimacy of the criminal justice system. The two cases exemplified above reveal only the tip of the iceberg. Ultimately, it seems that differentiating intentional fraud (as described in CL97 Article 192) from unwanted and unpredictable challenges of the official banking mechanism by the private sector in market place (as described in CL97 Article 176) may rest more with lawmaking than with law enforcement.

7.4 Trial of Corruptive Official: The Curious Case of CL97 Article 395

Article 395 of the CL97 states that:

> Any State functionary whose possession of assets obviously exceeds his lawful income (if the difference is enormous) may be ordered to explain the sources of his property. If he cannot prove that the sources are legitimate, the portion that exceeds his lawful income shall be regarded as illegal gains, and he shall be sentenced to fixed-term imprisonment of not more than 5 years or criminal detention, and the portion of assets that exceeds his lawful income shall be recovered.

This Article falls under Chapter VIII "Crime of Embezzlement and Bribery" in the CL97. Article 395 is often filed when charges of embezzlement and bribery are difficult to prove in court due to lack of witnesses and material evidences. This Article shifts the burden of proof from the State to the criminal defendants who are public officials and member of CCP. Who actually gets charged for this crime? How does the State investigate such cases? And, what types of sentences are

---

[11] Similarly, in the international business arena, the U.S. and other nations have repeatedly raised serious issues about the government manipulation of the value of RMB, China's currency. Foreign business entities sometimes take for granted the nature of Chinese socialist market economy, seeing more of the "market" but missing the critical word "socialist.".

rendered? These are all interesting questions. We present a transcript below based on the (open) court hearing of a case tried under Article 395.[12]

At 8:30 am, 20XX, December XX, the court clerk on duty made the following announcement to the audience before the judges, the procurator, defense attorney, and the defendant entered the courtroom.

"In order to maintain court order and assure the normal trial proceeding, I hereby make the following announcement on the rules of the courtroom:

All citizens are allowed to attend an open trial except the following individuals:

(1) Those who are under 18 years old;
(2) Those who are mentally ill or drunk;
(3) Those who are deprived of political rights; those who are currently serving a sentence outside prison; and those who are under public surveillance;
(4) Those carrying a weapon or other dangerous object;
(5) Other individuals who may disrupt court order.

All must obey the following court rules:

(1) Do not enter the specific space designated to relevant parties involved in the trial;
(2) Do not tape-record, video-tape, photograph, or take notes;
(3) Do not talk loudly, applaud, walk about, shout slogan, or interrupt speech given by any party involved in trial;
(4) Do not use cell phone, beeper, and walkie-talkie in the courtroom;
(5) Do not smoke or spit on the floor.

The judicial police will enforce the rules of the courtroom. Those who violate any of these rules may be asked to leave or be taken out of the courtroom under the order of the collegial panel." (End of announcement by the court clerk)

Clerk: the procurator and the defense attorney(s) please enter the courtroom.

Clerk: All rise! The presiding judge and judges on the collegial panel please enter the courtroom.

Presiding Judge: Please sit down.

Clerk: Presiding Judge, all preparations related to the trial of criminal defendant XXX (charged with crime under CL97 Article 395) are in order.

Presiding Judge: The court is now in session. Please bring defendant XXX into the courtroom.

Presiding Judge: Defendant XXX, state your personal background to the court.

Defendant: My name is XXX, male, born in XXX City on 19XX, (month) and (date), formerly a manager of XXX department, XXX Corporation, home address: XXX City, (Number) XXX Road, Apartment # XX.

Presiding Judge: Do you have any previous criminal record?

---

[12] Article 395 is intended to target crimes committed by the so-called "state functionary." The line becomes blurred since the downsizing and the conversion of the former State Enterprises into flexibly structured private–public joint ventures.

Defendant: No.

President Judge: When and why were you detained?

Defendant: I was detained on August XX, 19XX by the XX City Custom Office Smuggling Crime Investigation Bureau.[13] I was formally arrested on September XX, 19XX as a crime suspect under Article 395.

Presiding Judge: Did you, and when did you receive a copy of the Criminal Indictment?

Defendant: Yes, I did. I received it on 20XX, December XX.

Presiding Judge: According to Article 152 of the Chinese Criminal Procedure Law, this court is holding an open trial of criminal defendant XXX charged under CL (1997) Article 395. The Collegial Panel is consisted of three judges: XXX serves as the Presiding Judge; the other two judges are XXX and XXX.[14] The court clerk is XXX. Representing the XXX Basic People's Procuratorate is Procurator XXX. Representing the defendant is criminal defense attorney XXX.

Presiding Judge: According to the relevant provisions of the CPL (96), as a defendant you have the following rights during the trial:

(1) You may request any member of the Collegial Panel, court clerk, Procurator to recuse himself/herself from the trial;
(2) You may provide additional evidences, apply to the court to call any new witnesses to testify, to gather new evidences, or to re-examine and re-evaluate existing evidences;
(3) You may provide self-defense or seek representation by defense attorney;
(4) You may make final statement at the end of the court trial investigation.

Presiding Judge: Defendant, did you hear clearly the aforementioned rights? Do you seek the court to apply the rule of recusal?

Defendant: Yes, I have heard all my rights clearly. No, I have no cause to apply for recusal.

Presiding Judge: The court investigation now begins. Would the prosecution please present the Criminal Indictment to the court?

Procurator: (read the Criminal Indictment 20XX Serial Number XXXXX; omitted)

---

[13] The defendant was first detained for suspected bribery charge by a specialized investigative unit within the Chinese Custom local branch. The court case dossier includes the Approval Form for Criminal Detention, the Search Warrant, the written record of the home search, signed, and thumb-printed by the defendant's wife, a list of all personal items seized at the defendant's home (bank deposit books, saving account numbers, deposit slips/receipts, gold jewelries, cash in the amount of RMB 180,000). Also included in the dossier are the case filing decision letter prepared by the Anti-corruption division of the XXX Intermediate People's Procuratorate, the Arrest Warrant, and the copies of Asset-Freezing Orders issued by the State (this applies to each bank account held by the defendant and his wife).

[14] Although the senior judge is named as the Presiding Judge for the case, one of his junior colleagues is documented to have actually conducted all the questionings in this court hearing. The senior judge did sign off on the court transcript at the end. We are not certain how common this practice is.

Presiding Judge: Defendant, do you disagree with the facts stated in the Criminal Indictment against you?

Defendant: No.

Presiding Judge: The procurator may question the defendant now.

Procurator: Defendant, what was your occupational status with XXX Corporation?

Defendant: I was a division manager for XXX Department with XXX Corporation.

Procurator: What were the sources for your legitimate income?

Defendant: My salary.

Procurator: Do you receive gifts from your relatives?

Defendant: Very rarely.

Procurator: What was the source for the RMB 580,000 of your assets seized by the criminal justice agency?

Defendant: I could not recall clearly now.

Procurator: Under whose name do you make bank deposits?

Defendant: In my name and my wife's name.

Procurator: How much of your assets were seized after your criminal detention?

Defendant: I don't remember clearly now.

Procurator: Presiding Judge, I am finished with my questions.

Presiding Judge: Now the defense attorney may question the defendant.

Defense Attorney: Defendant, in your prior employment with XXX Corporation, what major types of business did you engage?

Defendant: My employer acts as an agent in providing shipping services related to foreign trade.

Defense Attorney: Presiding Judge, I have no other questions.

Presiding Judge: Does the Procurator have additional investigatory questions?

Procurator: No.

Presiding Judge: The prosecution and the defense may present evidences. Now, the prosecution may begin to provide the court evidences.

Procurator: With the court permission, the prosecution would like to present the following three written documentations: (1) the Business License of XXX Corporation; (2) the defendant's Certificate of Employment from the XXX Corporation; and (3) the personal file of defendant XXX.[15]

Presiding Judge: Permitted.

Procurators: (read all three documents; Omitted)

Presiding Judge: Defendant, do you disagree with the written documentations presented by the prosecution above?

Defendant: No.

[15] The defendant joined the Communist Youth League in the early 1970s and became a Chinese Communist Party (CCP) Member in late 1980s. The file is kept by the branch office of the CCP embedded in the company and the 13 page personal file carries the stamp of the CCP branch.

Presiding Judge: Defense attorney, do you disagree with the written documentations presented by the prosecution above?

Defense Attorney: No.

Presiding Judge: The prosecution may continue presentation of additional evidences.

Procurator: With the court permission, the prosecution would like to present the following two additional written documentations: (1) written record of the search conducted at the defendant's home; and (2) a list of all items seized.

Presiding Judge: Permitted.

Procurator: (read and display both documentations to the court).

Presiding Judge: Defendant, do you disagree with the written documentations presented by the prosecution above?

Defendant: No.

Presiding Judge: Defense attorney, do you disagree with the written documentations presented by the prosecution above?

Defense Attorney: No.

Presiding Judge: The prosecution may continue presentation of additional evidences.

Procurator: With the court permission, the prosecution would like to present the following copies of bank deposits.

Presiding Judge: Permitted. (The presiding judge asked the judicial police officer on duty), please bring these items to be recognized by the defendant and the defense attorney.

Procurator: Defendant, were these bank deposits kept and found in your home?

Defendant: Yes.

Presiding Judge: Defense attorney, do you disagree?

Defense Attorney: No.

Presiding Judge: The prosecution may continue presentation of additional evidences.

Procurator: With the court permission, the prosecution would like to present the following asset freezing order.

Presiding Judge: Permitted. (The presiding judge asked the judicial police officer on duty), please bring the item to be recognized by the defendant and the defense attorney.

Presiding Judge: Defendant, do you disagree with the documentation presented by the prosecution above?

Defendant: No.

Presiding Judge: Defense attorney, do you disagree with the written documentation presented by the prosecution above?

Defense Attorney: No.

(Similar segments of evidence presentation followed that included the evidences: home purchase agreement, various invoices, photographs of gold jewelries, market value assessment of these jewelries, pay stubs from both the defendant

(16 years in total)[16] and his wife (28 years in total),[17] estimated yearly average family (of 3) consumption in the defendant's city of residence,[18] record of written testimony provided by the wife of the defendant, and written statement provided by the defendant himself).

Procurator: The prosecution has now completed all presentations of evidences.

Presiding Judge: Now the defendant may present any or all evidences.

Defendant: I have none.

Presiding Judge: Does the defense attorney have additional evidences to be presented to the court?

Defense Attorney: None.

Presiding Judge: Do the defendant and defense attorney request for new witnesses to testify in court or for gathering additional evidences?

Defendant: No.

Defense Attorney: No.

Presiding Judge: The court investigation phase is now completed. The court debate now begins. The prosecution may proceed by making a statement first.

Procurator: (read the statement. Omitted)[19]

Presiding Judge: Defendant, you may provide self-defense.

Defendant: I have none.

Presiding Judge: the defense attorney may provide defense on behalf of the defendant.

Defense Attorney: The defense does not dispute the criminal facts as stated in the Criminal Indictment. However, the defense would like to make the following requests for consideration by the court: (1) the defendant's employment status does not, strictly speaking, qualify as a "state functionary" as specified in the applicable

---

[16] The defendant made less than RMB 4000 a year in the late 1980s and early 1990s. Beginning from the mid-1990s, his official annual income increased to five digits and ended at about RMB 120,000 a year prior to his arrest. Altogether, his employer certified that the defendant made a total of RMB 430,000 during his employment with the company from 19XX to 19XX.

[17] The defendant's wife retired at the age of 49 as a low-level municipal government employee. Her income record corresponds with the national economic growth in the last three decades of the twentieth century and its impact on ordinary government employees. She made a little over RMB 200 a year in 19XX and a little over RMB 26,000 in 19XX when she retired.

[18] A certificate from the XXX City Statistics Bureau is included in the dossier, stating the average yearly rate of consumption based on a family of 3 (such as the defendant's-both parents and a single child) living in the city (survey based estimate). It is estimated that the defendant and his family would have spent a total of RMB 140,000 during the years from 19XX to 19XX.

[19] A small detail is noticed in the hand-written statement read by the Procurator (which is included in the case dossier) that the word "bribery" was scratched off and replaced with words indicating the charge based on CL97 Article 395. A bribery charge under CL97, if substantiated, carries a far more serious sentencing outcome, from 10-year imprisonment (for taking in bribery in a minimum amount of RMB 100,000) to life imprisonment or death sentence, plus confiscation of property. It all depends on various statutory and discretionary circumstances. Certainly, in a case charged under the bribery clauses (CL97 Articles 385 and 386), the State has much of the burden of proof, unlike using the Article 395 where the burden of proof rests solely with the defendant.

law underlying the criminal indictment. The defendant does not exercise state power nor derive state-backed authority over others from his employment. His actions as charged do not pose threat to the society. Application of probation for his sentence may be warranted; (2) the defendant has plead guilty with good attitude. In addition, he has always been a model employee at work. Combing all above, the defense requests that the court grant lenient sentence to the defendant.

Presiding Judge: It's now the procurator's turn to make statement.

Procurator: There is no doubt that the defendant qualifies as a "state functionary" according to the law. Therefore, Article 395 is applicable to the defendant in this case. About the request for probation raised by the defense, the prosecution defers to the court's discretion according to all the facts and circumstances involved in this case.

Presiding Judge: The defense may make another statement.

Defense Attorney: The defense requests that the court grant lenient sentence to the defendant according to the circumstances argued above.

Presiding Judge: Does the prosecution have further statement to make?

Procurator: No.

Presiding Judge: The court debate is now completed. The defendant may make the final statement.

Defendant: I am very regretful now. Because of my age, I sincerely request that the court consider probation as my sentence.

Presiding Judge: The court hearing is now completed. (Turn to the judicial police on duty) Take the defendant back to XXX City Detention Center. The court is in recess.

The court transcript provided above is all true.

XXX (Defendant signature with red thumbprint)

20XX, December XX

XXX (Presiding Judge signature)

20XX, December XX

XXX (Court Clerk signature)

20XX, December XX

One week later, the court returned the final judgment sentencing the defendant to 1 year and 6 months of imprisonment. The calculation of the sentence length credits the time the defendant spent on criminal detention. The defendant would be released from prison 3 months after receiving his final sentence. The defendant's unexplained asset in the total amount of RMB 580,000 is recovered by the State. The drastically varying prison sentences associated with the three sample cases give rise to the necessity of a discussion on Chinese sentencing practices. We highlight the rationales and practices of Chinese sentencing guideline reform in the section below.

7.5 Sentencing Guidelines in Criminal Processing

The sentencing guideline that went into effect on October 1, 2010 nationwide provides an opportunity to decipher the Chinese government's attempt to control judicial discretions. Although sentencing guidelines implemented in the U.S. Federal and State courts served as an inspiration, the Chinese legal system adapted rather than adopted the U.S. practices. The goals articulated by the Chinese Supreme People's Court for the new sentencing guideline include: to regulate judicial discretion, to implement criminal justice policy that combines 'severity' and 'magnanimity', to increase transparency in judicial decision-making, to enhance the legitimacy of the criminal justice system, to promote uniform and consistent sentencing, and to safeguard judicial fairness (SPC 2010). We will not elaborate on the systematic comparisons of the Chinese and the U.S. sentencing guidelines. Such exercise would be difficult because there will not be a typical U.S. practice that is representative of the complicated American judicial system. For example, research suggest that by 1999, the 18 U.S. States that have adopted sentencing guidelines did so with varying goals including but not limiting to the followings: reduce judicial disparity in sentencing, promote more uniform and consistent sentencing, project the amount of correctional resources needed, prioritize and allocate correctional resources, increase or decrease punishments for certain categories of offenders and offenses, establish truth in sentencing, make the sentencing process more open and understandable, reduce prison crowding, provide a rational basis for sentencing, increasing judicial accountability (Lubitz and Ross 2001).

Consistent with its Continental Legal influence, the Chinese sentencing guideline includes two major chapters: (1) General Provisions (10 sections; 47 articles); (2) Specific Provisions (30 sections; each section covers one type of criminal offense; each section includes multiple articles detailing highly specific and quantifiable sentencing related elements (both mitigating and aggravating circumstances). Although we have a valuable collection of a broad variety (15+ types of crimes) of case dossiers ($N = 149$) that contain all materials including final sentencing outcomes, the number of cases we currently obtained remains undersized for us to conduct reliable statistical comparisons of crime-specific sentencing outcomes pre- and post-guidelines. Only with a substantial larger pool of cases across multiple years (and perhaps multi-jurisdictions) shall we be able to gauge the possible impact of the application of the sentencing guidelines. Using two categories of criminal cases with high frequencies in trials of 1st instances at Basic People's Courts, we provide a rudimentary introduction of the construction and use of Chinese sentencing guideline worksheets. It is worth noting that the worksheets that help judges derive the final sentencing outcome are not shared with the defense attorneys. In fact, withholding critical information by the Chinese criminal justice apparatus from the defense attorneys constitutes one of the patterned modalities of power and control in Chinese juridical field (more discussions to come in Chap. 8).

Tables 7.2 and 7.3 are examples of standard worksheets used to facilitate and document sentencing decision-making for the crimes of larceny and assault (two of the most frequent crimes) from a Basic People's Court located in M city, J Province. Similar worksheets are created by local courts to cover all the major crime types they face on regular basis. These worksheets need to follow a general format; however, they are also made adaptable to local conditions. It is worth pointing out that the national sentencing guideline instruction allows not only adjustments made at provincial-level but also further minor adjustments made at lower level courts. Through the two examples we are to illustrate below, we hope to shed light on the intended and practical purposes for the application of sentencing guideline in China today. The Supreme People's Court not only allows but also encourages local adaptation of the sentencing guidelines. Three courts (at both the Basic and Intermediate levels) included in our study were designated as experimental sites prior to the adoption of the national sentencing guideline. The sentencing guideline worksheet is a reflection of the collective wisdom from the local court personnel and is instrumental to establishing prototype models at the Provincial and National levels. It would certainly be interesting for future studies to gather and compare sentencing worksheets from courts located in different provinces.

7.5.1 Sentencing Worksheet-Larceny

The sentencing worksheet includes two general sections: Section I concerns the statutory sentence which covers all major categories applicable for a particular offense type as stipulated in a particular article in the Criminal Law. For example, for the crime of larceny, four categories of sentences (under column 1) are potentially applicable, three of which concern the adult offenders, i.e., Category A covers a sentence that is under three years of imprisonment; Category B covers a sentence that ranges from 3 to 10 years of imprisonment; and Category C covers a sentence that is longer than 10 years of imprisonment. Each category of the larceny sentences corresponds to a detailed list of statutory provisions (see under column 2). Columns 1 and 2 are pre-made in print form, Column 3 needs to be filled out by the Presiding Judge of a criminal case after the trial. This is the section where numeric values are entered based on the judge's determination of the applicability of the statutory provisions, which begins with the statutory minimum sentence associated with a specific Category of sentence (i.e., in this case 18 months). The combination of the statutory minimum sentencing with applicable statutory adjustment adds up to the final statutory sentencing (i.e., 120 months + 24 months = 144 months). This statutory sentence then becomes the base for the calculation of discretionary sentences shown in Section II of the sentencing worksheet.

The applicable circumstances which might impact the final sentence are included under the first column of Section II in the worksheet. Just like the statutory provisions included in Section I, major categories of such discretionary circumstances are printed on the standard worksheet. However, space is saved for

Table 7.2 Example Chinese sentencing worksheet: Larceny J Province M City Basic Court Sentencing Processing Form (Criminal Defendant XXX; Property value: RMB 472,640; # of Incident: 1) (Year) XXX Serial # XXX

	Statutory provisions	Determination of statutory sentence (Month)		
		Statutory minimum	+Statutory adjustment	Statutory sentence
Section I: Statutory sentence				
Youth offenders	(a) Aged 16–18, committed the crime less than 3 times, confessed, and returned the illegal proceeds, and one or more of the followings: – Deaf, or blind, or mute – Accomplice – Other minor circumstances (b) Aged 16–18, attempted or terminated crime (c) Aged 16–18, stealing from family or relatives and, family and relatives do not press for criminal charge	Not		
regarded as crime				
Adult Offenders				
Category A: under 3 years imprisonment and/or fine	(a) Stolen amount RMB 2,000, statutory minimum = 4 months; 1 additional month per additional RMB 500 (b) Stolen amount RMB 6,000, statutory minimum = 1 year; 1 additional year per additional RMB 10,000; 1 additional month per additional RMB 600			
Category B: 3–10 years imprisonment and fine	(c) Stolen amount RMB 20,000, statutory minimum = 3 years; 1 additional year per additional RMB 10,000; 1 additional month per additional RMB 800 for the remainder amount			
Category C: 10+ years or life imprisonment, plus fine or confiscation of property	(d) Stolen amount RMB 90,000, statutory minimum = 10 years; 1 additional year per additional RMB 200,000	120	24	144
Section II: Discretionary sentences (Month)				

(continued)

Table 7.2 (continued)

Statutory provisions	Determination of statutory sentence (Month)		
	Statutory minimum	+Statutory adjustment	Statutory sentence
Applicable circumstances	Adj. (± %)	Months (±)	Outcome after Adj.
Repeat offender; May add 5–30 %			
Breaking and entering household; May add 10–20 %	+15 %	+21.6	
Destruction of properties causing additional losses; May add 10–20 %			
Targeting disabled and/or widowed elderly household; May add 10–20 %			
Serial offending; May add 10–20 %			
Crime committed in support of drug and/or gambling habits; May add 10–20 %			
Crime committed due to substantiated financial difficulties in paying for family support, school tuition, and medical expenses; May deduct up to 30 %			
Voluntarily returned criminal proceeds to the original place and/or victim(s); May deduct 30–50 %			
Stealing from own home or from close relatives; May deduct 50–80 %			
Other statutory and Total or discretionary circumstances			
Meritorious performance	−20 %	−28.8	
Confession	−10 %	−14.4	
	−15 %	−21.6	122.4

Formula: Statutory Sentence ± Adj. Outcome = 144 + 144(−15 %) = 122.4 (months)
Note Final Announced Sentence is 10 years (using the whole number)

Table 7.3 Example Chinese sentencing worksheet: Assault J Province M City Basic Court Sentencing Processing Form (Criminal Defendant XXX; Injury: minor, 10th degree; Locations of Injury: 3) (Year) XXX Serial # XXX

	Statutory provisions	Determination of statutory sentence (month)		
		Statutory minimum	+ Statutory adjustment	Statutory sentence
Section I: statutory sentence				
Category A: under 3 years imprisonment or detention	(a) Average circumstance, intentional assault causing minor injury of one person, statutory minimum = 6–18 months	18	2	20
	(b) Depending on the extent of injury, 1–2 additional month(s) per additional person of very minor injury or 3–6 months per additional person of minor injury			
	(c) 1–3 month(s) additional sentence per increase in 1 degree of injury category			
Category B: 3–10 years imprisonment	(a) Average circumstance, intentional assault causing major injury of 1 person, statutory minimum = 3–4 years			
	(b) Depending on the extent of injury, 1–2 additional month(s) per additional person of very minor injury, or 3–6 months per additional person of minor injury, or 1–2 years per additional person of major injury			
	(c) 1–3 month(s) additional month(s) per increase in 1 degree of average handicap category, or 6 months to 1 year per increase in a degree of serious handicap category, or 2–3 years per increase in a degree of most serious handicap			
Category C: 10 + years imprisonment	(a) Intentional assault causing cruel injury of 1 person, causing 6th degree of serious handicap, statutory minimum = 10–12 years			
	(b) Depending on the extent of cruelty, 1–2 additional month(s) per additional person of very minor injury, or 3–6 months per additional person of minor injury, or 1–2 years per additional person of major injury			
	(c) 1–3 month(s) additional month(s) per increase in 1° of average handicap category, or 6 months to 1 year per increase in a degree of serious handicap category, or 2–3 years per increase in a degree of most serious handicap			

(continued)

Table 7.3 (continued)

Statutory provisions	Determination of statutory sentence (month)		
	Statutory minimum	+ Statutory adjustment	Statutory sentence
Section II: Discretionary sentences			
Applicable Circumstances	Adj. (± %)	Months (±)	Outcome after Adjustment
Associated with gangs or organized crime; May add up to 20 %			
Against vulnerable group such as the elderly, children, the physically challenged, pregnant women, etc.; May add up to 20 %			
Using guns, knives or other weapons; May add up to 20 %	+10 %		
Assault occurring during commission of other crime; May add up to 20 %			
Able but refuse to provide financial compensation to victim(s); May add up to 20 %			
Criminal assault as a result of marriage, family, neighbor disputes; May deduct 10–30 %			
Criminal assault occurred in the heat of moment without premeditation; May deduct 10–30 %			
Other statutory and/or discretionary circumstances			
Providing financial compensation voluntarily and acquired forgiveness by the victim(s)	−20 %		
Confession	−10 %		
Total	−20 %	−4	16

Formula: Statutory sentence ± Adj. Outcome = 20 + 20 (−20 %) = 16

Note Final Announced sentence is 16 months

possible new entries of "Other statutory and/or discretionary circumstances." In our larceny example, a 15 % increase in the sentence is added due to the nature of the offense, i.e., "breaking and entering household." However, discretions by the judge are also made to reduce 20 % of the sentence for "meritorious performance" and 10 % of the sentence for making a "confession." The net result of the discretionary sentencing consideration (as illustrated in Section II) is a reduction of 15 % (or 21.6 months) of the statutory sentence (illustrated in Section I). This criminal defendant should have received a final sentence of 122.4 months to be exact. The Presiding Judge, however, made a note at the end of the sentencing worksheet that a whole number will be used and the final announced sentence is to be 10 years (or 120 months) of imprisonment.[21]

7.5.2 Sentencing Worksheet-Assault

Sentencing worksheet used for Assault looks similar to that for Larceny, except that in the statutory provisions, levels of personal injury substituted the monetary value of the stolen property. Potential statutory adjustments could be made according to both the extent of injury and the additional number of victims. In the sample case illustrated here, the defendant falls under Category A of the offense type, resulting in the application of 18 months imprisonment as the statutory minimum sentence. Due to multiple locations of injuries suffered by the victim, two additional months of sentences were added to make a total of 20 months as the final statutory sentence. Under discretionary circumstances considered by the court, 10 % increase of the sentence was added due to involvement of weapon in the commission of assault. The defendant, however, also received a total of 30 % reduction in the total sentence, with 20 % reduction credited to having provided financial compensation to the victim voluntarily and acquiring forgiveness by the victim. A net reduction of 20 % of the statutory sentence is applicable, resulting in the final announced sentence of 16 months.

7.6 Basic People's Court: Rhetoric and Reality

The physical and the organizational structures of the Chinese court have no doubt evolved with history. Separating façade and substance, rhetoric and reality would tell a fuller story of the true spirit of the Chinese court. In contrast to the Imperial Magistrate's court (Fig. 2.1, Chap. 2), the contemporary Chinese court is decidedly

---

[21] This is within the allowable additional discretionary sentencing length adjustment (up to 10 %) that a single presiding judge or a Collegial Panel could make according to the Chinese Sentencing Guidelines (SPC 2010).

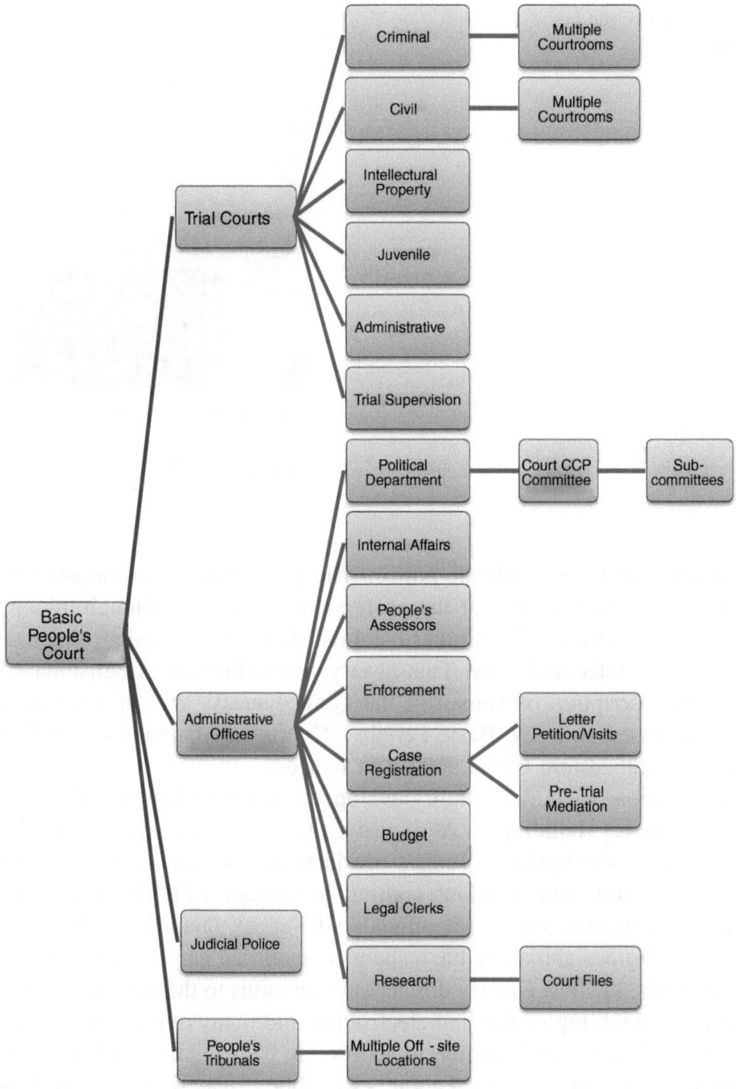

Fig. 7.3 Basic People's Court Structure

more complex. Its charges are more sophisticated, befitting a modern professional organization in a fast-developing nation. Figure 7.3 provides the functional structure representative of a typical Basic People's Court. Trial courts within a Basic People's Court are divided into multiple specializations: civil, criminal, intellectual property, administrative, juvenile, and trial supervision. People's tribunals are auxiliary court facilities located within the jurisdiction but outside the main court building. Court personnel usually include judges, court clerks,

Photo 7.1 Enforce the law with gusto

administrative staff, and judicial police. The proportion of administrative personnel usually outweighs that of the professional judge.[22] Although minor variations do exist, most of the Chinese courts share very similar organizational structure and architectural plan. This observation echoes the Englishman Meadows' (1970) description of yamen in the Qing dynasty. We offer the following observations based on a few Basic People's Courts we visited between 2009 and 2011 in two southeastern China coastal provinces.

A Basic People's Court in more developed coastal regions usually features a stately multi-storey building.[23] A security check-point is now standard at the entrance to the court building. Judges use internal corridors to travel from their offices to the courtrooms without coming in contact with the public. Foreign visitors are accompanied by court officials who speak fluent English (some have received law degrees abroad or have spent time abroad as a visiting scholar). On one of our visits, the host eagerly directs our attentions to the marble floors, multipurpose auditorium, top-of-the-line electronics, and many other modern amenities appointed inside the court building, in addition to boasting the evolving history of his court from earlier time of the People's Republic.[24] The sense of pride from our host is as unmistakable as indelible.

---

[22] For example, in a Basic Court we visited, there are a total of 362 court personnel among which only 141 are judges.

[23] Our site visits in southeast coastal provinces in China reveal the typical construction cost of about RMB 200 million for the building. Office furniture and courtroom equipment are state-of-the-art. Courtroom interior design is increasingly westernized.

[24] Courts with sufficient resources are asked to designate a room as the court history museum that puts on display documents and photos from the past. These materials help to make connections of the Imperial legal tradition and the evolving socialist ideology.

Court house can be seen both as a physical space and as a "field" of juridical practice in Bourdieusian sense. There are reasons to believe that the physical presence itself is made highly symbolic. The architectural design presents us a place where the façade is given as much attention as the substance. We took the following notes after a visit to one Basic People's Court in J Province.

Viewing from the street level, the eyes of the public meet with the gate guarded by the judicial police and find the front entrance of the court house elevated high above the street level, at the end of long and spacious stone steps.[25] Before taking the first step on an ascending journey to the front entrance, however, it is impossible for anyone to miss the stares from two large stone lions (each measuring 10 feet tall) sitting 30 feet apart with the same astute faces. The half exposed foundation of the court house is decorated with stone carvings that feature portraits of both prominent Chinese legal reformers and major western legal philosophers. We were told that this design idea came from the President of this court, a young judge in his early 40s whom we met on the trip.

One should be free to imagine the other aspects of the courthouse design concept. We certainly did. The courthouse and our sense of justice are what we think they are and what we think they should be. The entire front wall of the six-storey court building is covered by large floor-to-ceiling glass panels. The glass wall gleams with light blue color reflecting the sky and the city below. After all, "Blue Sky" (青天) is a name and the highest honor bestowed to a righteous judge in the Imperial time. The glass wall projects a sense of transparency and modernity and, the elevated building and steps leading to its entrance are often found in temples and in Emperor's Palace. Justice is to be sought there inside the courthouse. The magnificent physical presence is right in front of everyone. However, it seems that one could not get there without taking the steps on that uphill journey.

Inside the air-conditioned modern courthouse, one sees the Chairman Mao's writing "To Serve the People" (为人民服务) on the wall in the middle of the great hall.[26] An 8 feet tall and 10 feet wide large digital bulletin board displays trials that are currently taking place (see Photo 7.2).[27] The rolling display clearly provides the basic trial information including the case ID, the cause for civil dispute or criminal charge(s), and parties involved in the civil suit or the name of the criminal defendant, date when case was received by the court, trial date and time (detail to the hour and minute), and location of the trial courtroom. By law, all trials should be open to the public with exceptions of cases involving minors, privacy, and broadly defined security issues.[28] On the main floor of the courthouse, the case

[25] 45 steps from the street level to the court house entrance door were counted at one of our visits to a Basic People's Court in a Southeast province.

[26] Inside the People's Procuratorate building, we noticed that Chairman Mao's other writing "Enforcing the Law with Gusto" (严肃执法) is posted on the wall instead (see Photo 7.1).

[27] We have seen digital bulletin board placed inside or outside of the court building, and sometimes in both locations.

[28] There is a clear historical continuity here. Interrogations and trials have always been conducted in the public since imperial time. Van Gulik's (1956 1997) fascinating rendition of

Photo 7.2 Large digital board

filing hall resembles the ticketing counter of the airport. Instructions on how to file cases for civil, administrative, and private initiated criminal prosecution and, the responsibilities of case filing division of the court can be easily found. Index chart is posted prominently, indicating locations of various courtrooms.

The court we visited has five criminal trial rooms, all located on the first floor, right above the garage. The first floor provides an easier and secure access for the judicial police who need to transport handcuffed criminal defendants to and from the courtrooms. Located from the second to the fourth floors there are 20 civil trial rooms, 2 administrative trial rooms, 2 intellectual property trial rooms, and 1 juvenile courtroom. Court offices are located away from the trial section of the building and generally insulated from the public access.

A strong smell of incense emits from one end of the corridor where holding cells are located for criminal defendants awaiting trial. The air was stifling in the afternoon as the area was apparently not adequately air-conditioned. Upon coming closer to the area, we found a restroom located adjacent to a room with holding cells aligned with each side of the (three) walls. Each cell is small, cage like, measuring no more than 4 ft wide, 8 ft high, and 8 ft deep. A severely cramped space and depressing mood gave the general impression, not a pleasant sight at all. Visitors were led away from the area very quickly. One fleeting eye contact was made with one prisoner in the cell, a young man with slim build and dull facial expression. We realized that incense might be burned to neutralize the odor from the restroom. Nonetheless, one cannot help but link the smell of incense to the echoes of prayers heard inside a Buddhist temple. The incense burner was not found.

The mood lightened when we entered the floor where multiple so-called mediation rooms are located. These rooms are clean with white walls and bright florescent lighting. Chairs and a round table are placed in the room in a way to

---

(Footnote 28 continued)
Chinese detective stories features crime solving by Judge Dee (modeled after a real imperial magistrate who lived from 630 to 700 AD in Tang dynasty), who demonstrates ample wisdom in applying shrewd psychological insights in open court trials. The customs and costumes of van Gulik's crime novel are borrowed from Ming Dynasty (1368–1644 AD), however.

Photo 7.3 Calligraphy work1

Photo 7.4 Calligraphy work2

produce a feeling of causal, household-like environment. No court insignia is displayed but there are tea pot and tea cups.[29] One calligraphy work encased in glass frame is hung in the room. These works (and other artistic works including water color paintings and photographs are hung on the walls along the corridors in the court office section) are produced by court officials. One of those (see Photo 7.3) we found in the mediation room says "All humans are susceptible to mistakes; there is no greater good than to mend one's erred ways." (人孰无过, 过而能改, 善莫大焉) On another (see Photo 7.4), we found "Wind and wave always die down after the storm; Take a step back so you could embrace the open sky." (忍一时风平浪静, 退一步海阔天空)

In sum, anyone who has ever entered a Chinese courtroom recently can attest to the astonishing physical transformations that have occurred. People's justice underlying socialist legality has always been a fluid concept and a moving image, however. Photo 7.5 depicts "trials" conducted in the 1970s in front of village

[29] In describing late Qing mediation practice in China, Katz (2009) cites a tea ceremony called chi*jiangcha* in which teahouse is used as a sort of public court where disputes are resolved.

Photo 7.5 Court photo exhibit

squares by "judges" often with little formal education, let alone legal background.[30] Justice is often delivered to the villages and villagers. A "courtroom" can be anywhere and everywhere. Needless to say the ambience of a solemn courtroom and the formality of a proper trial we witness today were not in existence three decades earlier. The process and presentation were deemed necessary only when they were part of the public propaganda as evident in the extensive use of public hearings and sentencing rallies. People's justice thus has little to do with individuals involved in the trial but with the general public to whom political messages are to be sent. There are contradictions "within the people" and "between the people and their enemies." The former is to be handled with persuasion, patience, and education. The latter is met with a clenched iron fist.

Some might argue that the politicized justice of the past is disappearing from civil trials and being diluted in criminal trials that take place today. The political structure, however, remains largely intact within the court organization. For example, in courts we have visited, more than 80 % of the court personnel are communist party (or communist youth league) members. CCP members' first royalty is to the Party not to the letter of law. Each court has a political department that is tasked to keep an eye on everyone, not just the party members. Important

[30] All but one of the five photos was taken in the 1970s. The more recent photo has a stage and a curtain in an auditorium setting. It showcases a sentencing rally with symbolic public announcement of sentences that have already been given in court. The rally is one of the major components of any anti-crime campaign that puts the faces of the criminals and their crimes in front of the public (see also Trevaskes 2007, 2003).

and sensitive cases are often determined and decided in principle first by the adjudication committee consisted of key members of the court leadership before being handed over to the designated judges for the actual trial.[31]

7.7 Conclusion

We conclude this chapter by suggesting that a unique perspective can be had if we link Bourdieu's (1987) "paradigmatic staging of the symbolic struggle" with the Maoist mass-line people's justice within a changing Chinese socio-legal context. It remains true that the criminal justice apparatus including the court continue to serve as an instrument of the Party. The Marxist contempt for all bourgeois laws and the pragmatic Chinese pursuit for a socialist legality with Chinese characteristics continue to introduce jarring noises in the production of a live rule of law symphony. Behind the façade of magnificent courthouse and modern hardware, preciously little has happened that can fundamentally challenge how Chinese criminal trials are conducted. The contrasting perceptions of power and control held by key actors in the Chinese juridical field are presented in the next chapter within a Bourdieusian framework.

References

Bourdieu, P. (1977). *Outline of a theory of practice*. Cambridge: Cambridge University Press.

Bourdieu, P. (1987). The force of law: Toward a sociology of the juridical field. *Hastings Law Journal, 38*, 805–853.

Dworkin, R. (1986). *Law's empire*. London: Fontana Press.

Katz, P. R. (2009). *Divine justice: Religion and the development of chinese legal culture*. London and New York: Routledge.

Lubitz, R., & Ross, T. W. (2001). Sentencing guidelines: Reflections on the future. In *Sentencing & Corrections: Issues for the 21st century* (Research in Brief, No. 10).

Michigan Judicial Institute (2012). *Sentencing guidelines manual*. State of Michigan.

Supreme People's Court, the People's Republic of China (2010a). *People's court sentencing guidelines*. Beijing.

[31] Variations of practices do exist across jurisdictions. For example, local courts may implement internal policy that sorts out important/sensitive cases that would either require judicial review (by a Vice-President of the court) or judicial intervention (by the criminal/civil/administrative section chief judge) prior to being considered by the full Adjudication Committee as a last resort. The former is a cautious response to the potential impact of the case outcome (e.g., cases that involve foreigners, retrial, judgment against an administrative agency, civil/commercial cases with more than RMB 2 million in dispute, or cases of concern by superior agencies or court leadership. The latter is typically targeted intervention prompted by "problematic cases" or "problematic judges" or serious disagreements with regard to the facts and/or the application of law. These internal decisions would be documented in confidential court case files (CX) included in Fig. 6.1 in the previous chapter.

Supreme People's Court, the People's Republic of China (2010b). *2009 Annual report*. Beijing.

Trevaskes, S. (2003). Public sentencing rallies in China: The symbolizing of punishment and justice in a socialist state. *Crime, Law and Social Change, 39*, 359–382.

Trevaskes, S. (2007). *Courts and criminal justice in contemporary China*. Lanham: Lexington Books.

van Gulik, R. ([1956] 1997). *The Chinese Maze Murders: A Judge Dee Mystery*. Chicago: University of Chicago Press.

Chapter 8
Modalities of Power and Control: Perceptions of Chinese Juridical Practice

8.1 Introduction

Legal scholars have long realized that "foreign observers will continue to be challenged by difficulties in ascertaining practice rather than the texts of norms, and by the distance between them." (Lubman 2003, p. 35) Although there is no shortage in the supply of piecemeal, anecdotal evidences of the Chinese legal practices in public media and in government reports,[1] very little empirical research and even less theory guided empirical inquiries have been carried out. Bourdieu's (1987) sociological theory of *practice* could be applied to the case of China for obvious reasons. Bourdieu's conception of "field" is wide-ranging, including any area of structured, socially patterned "practices" that are professionally and disciplinarily defined. Prior to the application on the juridical field, Bourdieu has already demonstrated the utility of his "theory of practice" in the academic field, intellectual field, religious field, field of market in symbolic goods, and the field of intersection of literature and power (Terdiman 1987).

Bourdieu's theory is particularly relevant to China given its focus on practice—a position endorsed by Karl Marx and a pragmatic philosophy embraced by Mao (and his successors in generations of Chinese leadership). The broadly defined Chinese legal scholarship (particularly those on legal history, legal texts and legal reforms) has received far more attention from law professors and historians than from social scientists. It seems, in our view, that Bourdieu's (1987) theory of practice in juridical field, although briefly mentioned in sociological studies of Chinese lawyers in general (e.g., Michelson 2006, 2008) and Chinese criminal defense lawyers in particular (e.g., Liu and Halliday 2011), has been under-utilized overall.

We make no claim that our pilot study (on legal representation and criminal processing in Chinese lower courts) was designed specifically to test Bourdieu's (1987) theory. However, our data that include questionnaire survey of legal

[1] For example, we often see either the disproportional portray of "criminal justice reform successes" in reports released by the Chinese government or reports of "incidents of human rights abuses" by foreign governments or NGOs.

N. He, *Chinese Criminal Trials*, DOI: 10.1007/978-1-4614-8205-5_8,

practitioners (including judges, procurators, and attorneys), observations of actual criminal trials and access to court criminal case dossier offer a rare opportunity to explore the potential applicability of Bourdieu's theory of juridical practice in the Chinese context. Therefore, Bourdieu's theoretical framework and some of the key concepts will be borrowed for our current examination that extends beyond the case dossier-based analyses and site visits illustrated in Chaps. 6 and 7. We are curious to discern whether Bourdieu's (1987) work which is intended to expound the force of law in modern liberal societies can indeed transcend the specificity of a liberal-democratic, (western) rule of law-based assumption in order to adequately explain the power dynamics among legal professionals in a non-democratic, non-western society with overwhelming socialist State power. We ask how the struggle for control in each stage of criminal trial process challenges the perceptions of the modalities of power and control within the Chinese juridical field. Our inquiry shares the creative spirit of Dezalay and Madsen's (2012) reflective sociological exercise inspired by Bourdieu's (1987) work. Like theirs, we focus more on what *are* the practices under observations rather than what the right practices *should be*.

8.2 Principles of Division

The Chinese juridical field can be seen as a site of struggle for power and control. The hierarchical system of power among Chinese legal professionals defined by the current law and influenced by the ancient legal tradition may be reflected both explicitly and implicitly in the Chinese legal culture. The dictates of the Chinese criminal justice system, the intricacies of the Chinese criminal trial process, the clashes between State power and individual rights, and the evolving norms of conduct among legal professionals make a Bourdieusian analysis not only necessary but possible.

Professionals involved in the Chinese criminal trial process typically include the judges, the procurators, the police, and the defense attorneys.[2] Because they are state employees representing the best interest of the party-state, the judiciary, the procuracy, and the police form what is often called the "iron triangle" in the Chinese criminal justice system.[3] To apply Bourdieu's principles of division, one could look into the structured ways professional groups differentiate and relate to each other. In the Chinese case, for example, political party affiliation, perceptions of power,

[2] The group of professionals involved in a criminal trial could be far more complicated in an adversarial legal system where jury consultants, expert witnesses, private investigators, and other professionals may be included.

[3] Jones (2003) offers a good discussion on the 'political-legal system' (that is consisted of the Security Administration, the Procuracy, and the Courts) which essentially is the same as the 'Iron Triangle' referred here.

Table 8.1 CCP membership by occupations among survey respondents ($N = \mathbf{627}$)

	Lawyers (%)	Ct-Pr–P (%)	Other (%)
CCP member	32.1	79.7	52.7
Non-CCP	67.9	21.3	47.3

Chi square = 106.23, $p < 0.05$

status, and obstacles may be used as distinguishing attributes that set the "iron triangle," the "defense attorneys", and the "other" group apart from each other.

Table 8.1 indicates that, the majority of our survey respondents (about 80 %) who are employed as judges, procurators, and police officers are CCP members, in contrast to a much smaller (but still sizeable) percentage (about 32 %) among respondents who are professional attorneys. In China's current social context, membership in the CCP continues to be an indispensable condition for career advancement if not career entry into the vast empire of government bureaucracy.[4] The CCP has seen a dramatic shift in the composition of its membership in the last three decades and it continues to evolve into a more inclusive party. Gone are the days when the majority of the CCP members are peasants and workers (e.g., in 1956, they were 83 % of the party). The CCP has officially admitted private entrepreneurs into the party membership since 2001 and has become a "catch-all" party ever since (Zheng 2009). Figure 8.1 (the distribution of professions among CCP members) provides a glimpse of such transformation.[5]

It may be argued that the revolutionary fervor is so evident among the CCP membership and leadership in the past has been gradually diluted by younger, better educated party cadres with a toned down socialist rhetoric and a more neutral, pragmatic approach to people and matters.[6] In all aspects, however, the CCP as an organization remains deeply embedded in every vein and pore of the Chinese society. It is not only the "orthodoxy" (Bourdieu 1977), the correct and socially legitimized belief that everyone is obliged to follow, it may have become a "doxa" (Bourdieu 1977) that the realization of the legitimacy of CCP and its prescribed conduct norm is so smooth to be noticeable. Recent empirically based scholarship has suggested that the bulging critical mass of the Chinese middle-

[4] Branch CCP committees are often expected to be established in non-government organizations as well. By 2012, there are more than 4.2 million CCP committees at all levels nationwide.

[5] The total number of CCP members is reported to be 75 million (or about 6 % of total Chinese population) by the U.S. Congressional-Executive Commission on China 2010 Annual Report (CECC 2010). Data represented in Fig. 8.1 are based on a June 30, 2013 report released by the Chinese Ministry of Organization (accessed via Sina.com news).

[6] For example, the singing of "Red Songs" by the mobilized mass which rekindled the memories of the revolutionary past is nostalgic to some but terror to others. Led by the Party boss Bo Xilai in Chongqing, the purported purity of the leftist revolutionary spirit dissipates as quickly as Bo's political downfall in 2012 that included expulsion from the CCP, charges of corruption and abuse of power. BO is sentenced to life imprisonment in september, 2013.

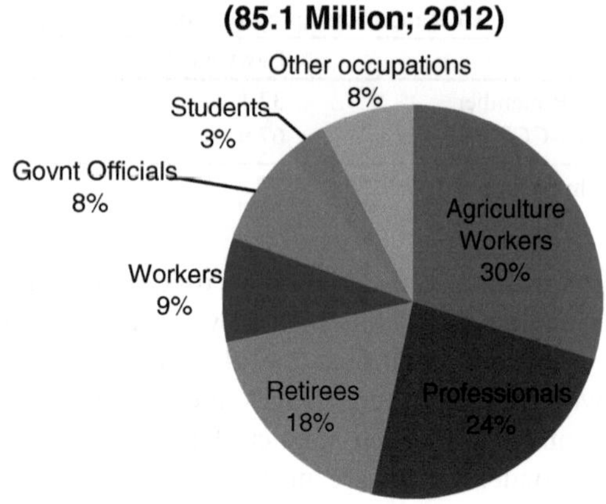

Fig. 8.1 CCP membership compositions

class is the ally of the socialist state led by the CCP (Chen and Dickson 2010).[7] They are more likely the foundation for the *status quo* rather than the movers and shakers for Westernized democracy as predicted by theories of democratic development (see Inglehart and Welzel 2009). There is also a sentiment (or element) of "Chinese Exceptionalism" (in its unique socio-economic and political transformations) that lingers in the air. It challenges the conventional wisdom of modern development trajectory in the spheres of economics and politics. A more in-depth discussion, especially made in the context of a comparison with the so-called "American Exceptionalism," should be an interesting future research topic.

8.3 Legal Representation and Trial Outcomes

Estimates of the rate of legal representation in Chinese criminal cases vary mostly in the range from 20 to 40 % (e.g., Zuo 2007; Lu and Miethe 2002; Belkin 2011; LCHR 1993).[8] Two survey questions in our pilot study were used to gauge the prevalence of legal representation in violent and property crime cases.[9] Breaking down the survey results by the occupational status, CCP membership and city status (i.e., the location and development levels of the cities) yield interesting observations. Table 8.2 suggests that, first of all, no statistically significant differences were found that would differentiate the estimates of legal representation

[7] The authors found that the Chinese entrepreneurs are closely tied to the state politically and financially. These ties shape their views toward democracy. For example, they would favor multi-candidate election under the current one-party system but not advocating for multi-party competition and political liberties.

[8] Lawyers Committee for Human Rights (1993) provides a widest range of estimates, from 20 % to 80 % of all criminal cases, depending on information gathered from individual lawyers.

[9] Estimated rates of criminal legal representation reported in the majority of existing studies do not differentiate between the types of crime charged.

Table 8.2 Analysis of variances: legal representation by occupations, CCP membership, and city status

Variable	Mean	BCa 95 % C.I.#	Std. error	*N*
Pct. legal presentation in violent crime cases	39.58	37.24–42.11	1.20	550
Lawyers	41.69	38.83–44.70	1.52	306
C/P/P	36.03	31.24–40.94	2.46	100
Other	38.33	31.17–45.67	3.55	95
CCP	38.22	34.55–42.14	1.84	266
Other	41.35	38.15–44.68	1.63	281
Big 3	40.60	37.63–43.67	1.58	313
Other	39.30	34.28–44.44	2.57	144
Pct. legal presentation in property crime cases [a,c]	32.35	29.64–35.49	1.44	552
Lawyers	37.67	34.17–41.93	1.90	307
C/P/P	27.64	22.32–32.50	2.73	150
Other	22.58	16.02–30.41	3.67	95
CCP	31.00	27.04–35.35	2.10	268
Other	33.01	32.28–35.40	2.03	281
Big-3	41.92	38.37–45.44	1.89	315
Other	9.04	5.86–12.45	1.73	145

[a] $p < 0.05$, Chi square test (by Occupational groups)
[b] $p < 0.05$, Chi square test (by CCP membership)
[c] $p < 0.05$, Chi square test (by City status)
#BCa (Bias-corrected and accelerated) 95 % confidence interval (results based on 1,000 bootstrap samples)

in violence crime cases across Occupational, CCP or City statuses.[10] The consensus is that about 40 % of criminal defendants charged with violent crimes are represented by legal counsel.

Percentage of legal representation in property crime cases tells a different story that, first of all, lawyers as a group report higher level of legal representation (about 37.7 %) than do the other two groups, respectively (C/P/P-about 27.6 %; Other-about 22.6 %). In addition, substantial difference based on city status is found that in the largest three (coastal and wealthiest) cities included in our pilot study, about 41.9 % of the criminal defendants in property crime cases receive legal representation compared to a mere 9 % in all other cities combined. Judging

[10] Statistical results reported in Tables 8.2 and 8.3 are estimated using Bootstrap resampling methods with 1,000 random samples with replacement form the original dataset. Bootstrapping is based on the idea that inference about a population from sample data can be modeled by resampling the sample data (see Efron 1979, 1982).

by the different results of legal representation for both types of criminal cases, an argument could be made that closer attention should be paid in future discussions (on the prevalence of legal representation) to differentiate the types of crimes and to look for regional, urban–rural impact.

Our assessment of the possible outcomes of criminal trials is measured with three variables: percentage of criminal defendants receiving a lighter sentence, percentage of initial government charges changed, and percentage acquitted (see Table 8.3). Results of one-way analysis of variance reveal a consistent, occupation-specific effect on all three trial outcome variables. Lawyers gave considerably rosier outlook of their trial success. For example, lawyers estimate that about 35 % of criminal defendants receive lighter sentence while the corresponding rates provided by the comparison groups are much lower (about 10 % from the 'iron triangle', and 8.8 % from "other"). Responses from CCP members behave in a similar way like the "iron triangle" that they both report lower percentages of acquittal and lighter sentences (but not in the percentage of initial charge changed).[11] City effects are found in the assessment of percentages of initial charge changed and in acquittal (higher percentages in the more developed cities for both) but not in the percentage receiving lighter sentences.

8.4 Structural Hostility

The structural hostility of a socialist legal system may be studied in both the pretrial and trial stages. According to Bourdieu (1987), the hostility does not preclude complementary exercise of functions held by holders of different juridical capitals. In Chinese criminal justice field in general and criminal trials in particular, various Bourdieusian reflections can be found in the following exercises. Perceptions from three groups of respondents in our sample offer contrasting insights on both the structure and negotiation of power among parties endowed with different juridical capitals.

When asked about the motivations for someone to pursue a career as a criminal defense attorney, the "Iron Triangle" group gave a drastically different view from the lawyers. We see from Table 8.4 that these government employees (i.e., judges, procurators and police officers) view financial gain (i.e., 36 %) as the primary motivation for those who pursue criminal defense, in contrast to the more career-centric response from the lawyers that they do so for the challenging nature of the job (i.e., 43 %). There is also a much higher altruistic inclination among criminal defense lawyers that they choose their profession to promote justice (i.e., 18 % response from the lawyers compared to only 4 % from the "Iron Triangle" group).

[11] There is very little empirical data on Chinese criminal acquittal rate. Brown (1997: p. 122) once commented that "…the court merely rubber stamp the procuracy's criminal cases since the criminal acquittal rate is less than 1 percent." The exact source for this estimate is not clearly stated.

Table 8.3 Analysis of variances: trial outcomes by occupations, CCP membership, and city status

Variable	Mean	Std. error	BCa 95 % C.I.#	*N*
Pct. receiving lighter sentence [a,b]	24.34	1.25	22.02–26.65	403
Lawyers	34.64	1.59	31.56–37.74	238
C/P/P	10.01	2.00	6.48–14.04	93
Other	8.82	2.22	5.01–13.05	72
CCP	20.27	1.81	16.67–24.13	195
Other	27.64	1.85	24.00–31.56	207
Big-3	24.67	1.78	21.32–28.34	212
Other	24.70	2.38	20.64–29.43	125
Pct. initial charge changed [a,c]	5.53	0.50	4.65–6.52	388
Lawyers	7.50	0.69	6.24–8.96	221
C/P/P	3.59	1.07	1.83–5.57	96
Other	2.00	0.62	0.97–3.16	71
CCP	4.86	0.76	3.41–6.45	190
Other	6.10	0.61	4.94–7.44	197
Big-3	6.30	0.79	4.89–7.93	196
Other	3.88	0.60	2.92–4.93	128
Pct. acquitted [a,b,c]	3.54	0.42	2.78–4.34	396
Lawyers	4.27	0.57	3.21–5.39	228
C/P/P	1.69	0.58	0.83–2.82	95
Other	3.67	1.23	1.63–6.17	73
CCP	2.44	0.53	1.57–3.45	191
Other	4.51	0.63	3.31–5.77	203
Big-3	3.85	0.63	2.73–5.16	205
Other	1.77	0.36	1.11–2.49	125

[a] $p < 0.05$, Chi square test (by Occupational groups)
[b] $p < 0.05$, Chi square test (by CCP membership)
[c] $p < 0.05$, Chi square test (by City status)
#BCa (Bias-corrected and accelerated) 95 % confidence interval (results based on 1000 bootstrap samples)

Relatedly, when asked why a criminal defense attorney turns down a case (Fig. 8.2) and why a criminal defendant does not acquire a defense attorney (Fig. 8.3), the divergent and convergent responses from the three occupational groups are worth noting. All three groups seem to be in agreement that lawyers would turn down a case simply because they do not foresee that they can make any difference in the case outcome. Both lawyers themselves and other respondents

Table 8.4 Motivations to become criminal defense attorney ($N = \mathbf{541}$)

	Lawyers (%)	Ct-Pr–P (%)	Other (%)
High income	9.9	35.5	26.4
Promote justice	17.6	4.3	22.0
Reputation	10.9	24.6	15.4
Challenging	42.9	23.9	28.6
Other	18.6	11.6	7.7

Chi square = 80.50 (statistically significant), $p < 0.05$

also report that high personal risk might be a contributing factor (more than 70 % of them agree) to turn down a case, in contrast to a much lower percentage reported by the "Iron Triangle" group (only 34 % of them agree). More than 50 % of the respondents in the non-lawyers (i.e., both the "Iron Triangle" and the other respondents) groups also suggest that lawyers would turn down a case because it is not cost-effective (only 38 % of the lawyers agree with this assessment). From a different angle, when asked why a criminal defendant does not acquire an attorney, the most consistent answer (also with the highest percentages in agreement, i.e., 76, 84, and 80 %, respectively) suggests that it is mainly due to a defendant not able to afford one. The response category receiving (consistently) the second highest percentages from all three groups supports the notion that lawyers are not particularly useful in a criminal trial anyway. This response echoes the key finding from the earlier question and provides converging evidence in support of the view that criminal defense in China is yet to be perceived as effective from both the legal community and from the clientele perspectives.

In spite of the general gloomy view of the effectiveness of legal representation in Chinese criminal trials, respondents do seem to agree that there is "some effect" that can come out of legal representation (see in Fig. 8.4) and that when facing criminal charge themselves (Fig. 8.5), the majority would still consider seeking professional lawyers' assistance first (this is the response category receiving the

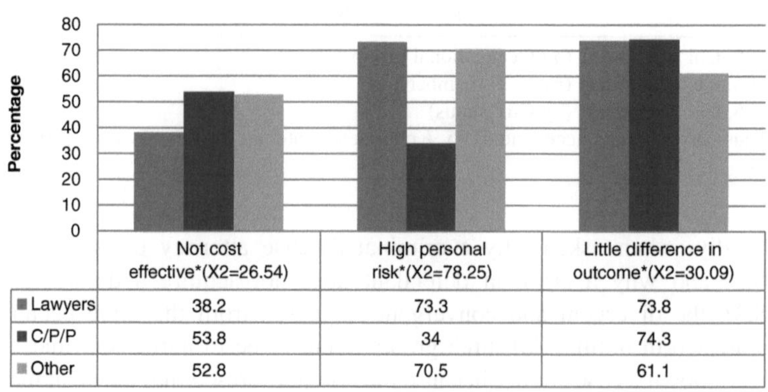

Fig. 8.2 Why does a criminal defense attorney turn down a case?

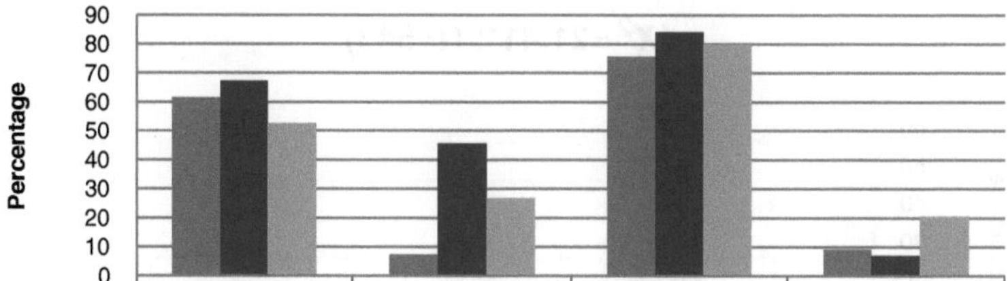

	Lawyer useless* (X2=25.73)	Lawyer irresponsible* (X2=114.78)	Cannot afford one (X2=9.50)	Lawyer not available*(X2=36.25)
Lawyers	61.5	7.3	75.7	9.2
C/P/P	67.3	45.6	84.1	7.1
Other	52.6	26.8	80	20.6

Fig. 8.3 Why criminal defendant does not acquire attorney?

(X^2=26.64*; N=615)

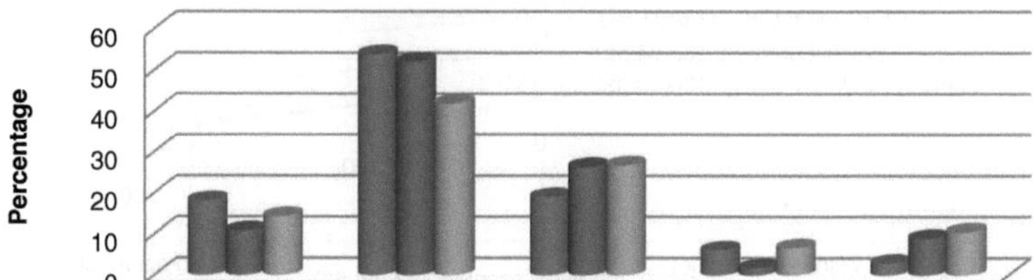

	Great effect	Some effect	No effect	Unsure	Other
Lawyers	18.1	53.9	19	6.1	2.9
C/P/P	10.8	52.1	26.3	1.8	9
Other	14.3	41.9	26.7	6.7	10.5

Fig. 8.4 General impact of legal representation in criminal trials of 1st instance

highest percentage of agreement in each group, i.e., 59 % from the "Lawyers" group; 48.9 % from the "Iron Triangle" group; and 58 % from the "Other" group).

When assessing the major difficulties for practicing criminal defense attorneys (Fig. 8.6), responses follow a consistent ranking order that it is the most difficult to get witnesses to testify in court, it is very difficult to get bail approved for the client, and it is somewhat difficult to even meet one's client. The extent of perceived difficulties in the first two problem areas is more noteworthy across occupation groups and CCP membership status. Making witnesses testify in court remains a criminal justice system-wide issue and may rest largely at the legislature level for improvement. Bail applications, however, are ignored or denied for reasons beyond the defendant's case conditions. The primary reasons appear to be more related to the distrust of the criminal justice agents towards the criminal defendants and the uneasiness for the risk that might be involved in granting a bail decision (see Fig. 8.7).

(X^2=21.41*; N=543)

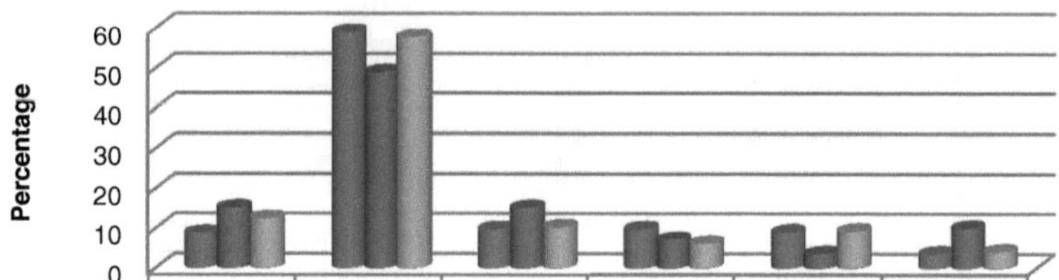

	Relative/friend	Professional lawyer	Court guanxi	Procuratorate guanxi	Govnt official guanxi	Other
Lawyers	8.8	59	9.8	9.8	9.1	3.6
C/P/P	15.1	48.9	15.1	7.2	3.6	10.1
Other	12.4	57.7	10.3	6.2	9.3	4.1

Fig. 8.5 Who would you call for help first?

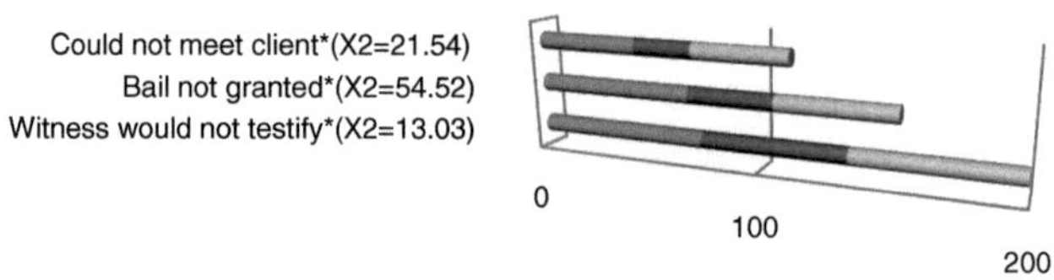

	Witness would not testify*(X2=13.03)	Bail not granted*(X2=54.52)	Could not meet client*(X2=21.54)
Lawyers	74.7	69	45.4
C/P/P	59.9	36.2	24.9
Other	64.9	48.6	41.4

Fig. 8.6 Major difficulties for criminal defense attorneys?

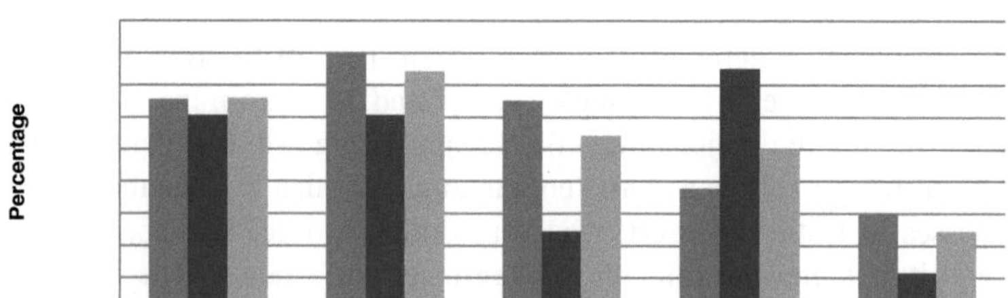

	Distrust of defendant*(X2=17.31)	Risk avoidance*(X2=29.75)	Disapproval of bail*(X2=101.63)	Bail conditions unmet*(X2=77.96)	Misunderstanding of law*(X2=34.47)
Lawyers	65.5	80	65.1	37.8	29.8
C/P/P	60.7	60.6	24.5	75	11.6
Other	65.9	74.2	54.3	50	24.5

Fig. 8.7 Why difficult to get bail?

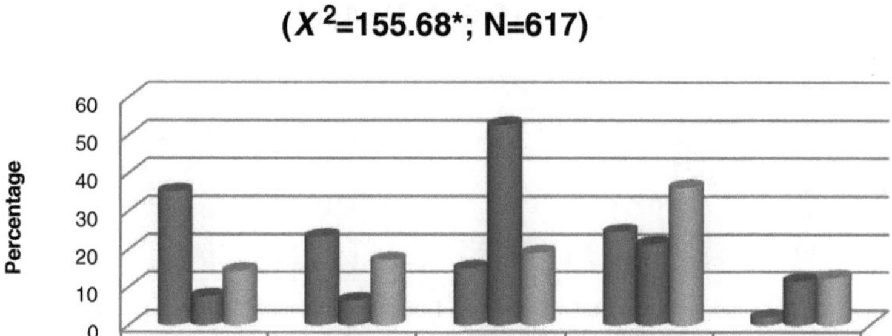

	Getting worse	Unchanged	Getting better	No comment	DK
Lawyers	35.1	23.3	15	24.5	2.1
C/P/P	7.5	6.4	52.6	21.4	11.6
Other	14.3	17.1	19	36.2	12.4

Fig. 8.8 Defense attorney's working environment

To put in context these perceived practical difficulties, we asked our respondents to assess whether Chinese criminal defense lawyers' current working environment has gotten better, or worse, or remained unchanged from the past (Fig. 8.8). The responses are clearly distributed along the occupation lines in that, the "Iron Triangle" group perceives an improvement in the work environment for the lawyers (i.e., 53 % of them say the working environment for the lawyers have improved) while the view from the Lawyer's group is in the opposite direction (i.e., 35 % of the lawyers say it is getting worse).

Attempting to decipher the power dynamic inside the courtroom, we ask three additional questions (1) what is the order of power status in six permutations with three letters each indicating an occupational group, i.e., J-Judges; P-Procurators; and D-Defense attorneys (Fig. 8.9); (2) who and what are the major factors that determine defense attorney's success in a criminal trial (Figure 8.10); and (3) what

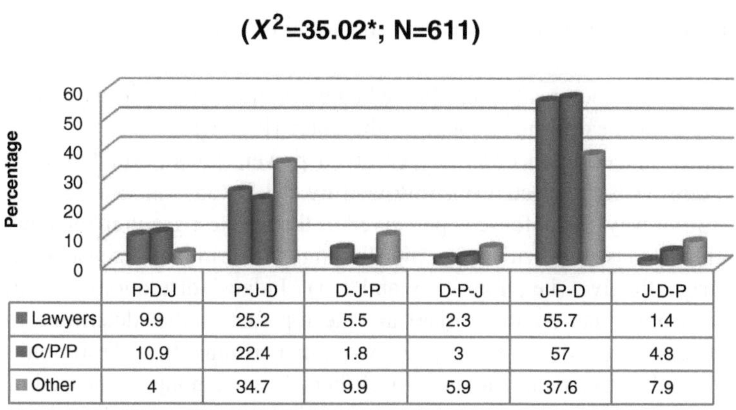

	P-D-J	P-J-D	D-J-P	D-P-J	J-P-D	J-D-P
Lawyers	9.9	25.2	5.5	2.3	55.7	1.4
C/P/P	10.9	22.4	1.8	3	57	4.8
Other	4	34.7	9.9	5.9	37.6	7.9

Fig. 8.9 Power statuses inside the courtroom

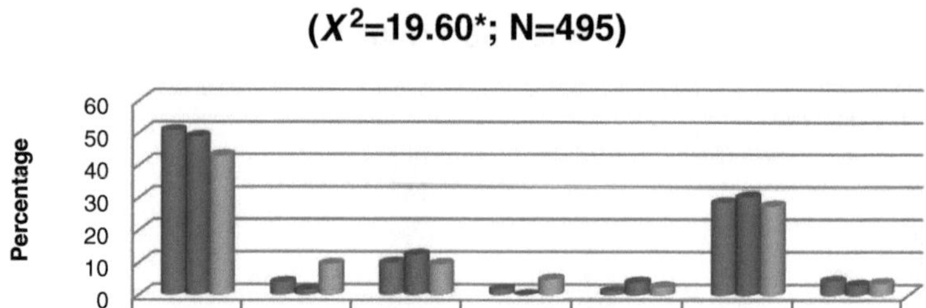

	Judge	Procurator	Defense attorney	Defendant	Witness	Evidence	Other
Lawyers	50.7	3.9	9.9	1.8	1.1	28.4	4.3
C/P/P	48.8	1.6	12.4	0	3.9	30.2	3.1
Other	42.9	9.5	9.5	4.8	2.4	27.4	3.6

Fig. 8.10 Factors impacting defense attorney's success in criminal trial

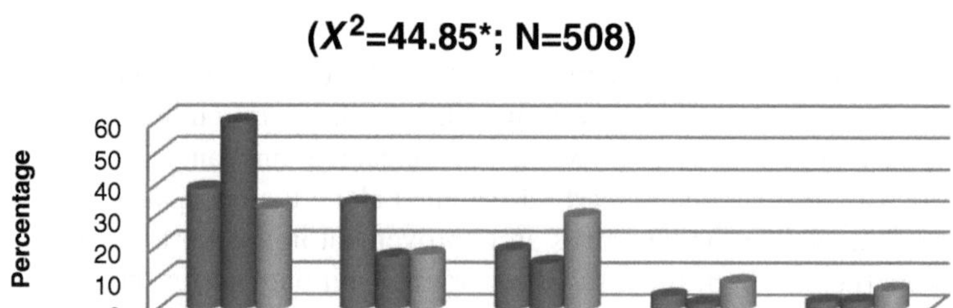

	Merit of defense argument	Trial judge discretion	Adjudication committee decision	Objection from prosecution	Defense attorney reputation
Lawyers	38.4	33.7	18.8	4.3	2.5
C/P/P	59.6	16.6	14.6	2	2.6
Other	32.1	17.3	29.6	8.6	6.2

Fig. 8.11 Deciding factors on the success of criminal defense arguments

are the deciding factors that predict whether or not a defense argument made during the court hearing is adopted by the court (Fig. 8.11).

The most agreed-upon order of perceived power status permutation is J-P-D (56, 57, and 38 %, respectively), followed by P-J-D (25, 22, and 35 %, respectively). Either way, the defense is perceived as the weakest group in the courtroom. Again, this is consistent with the earlier findings that criminal defense work is not particularly effective (i.e., Figs. 8.3 and 8.4). Judges' discretions and material evidences (more than anything else) are the top factors that determine the perceived success of the defense attorney's work in a criminal trial. Testimonies from witnesses and criminal defendant himself/herself are among the least important factors. An interesting contrast is revealed again when we asked whether Article

306 (a.k.a. Big-stick 306) of the Chinese Criminal Law should be repealed, amended, or remain unchanged (Fig. 8.12). We found that almost 70 % of the "Iron Triangle" group would like to keep the *status quo* on this legal provision which subjects defense attorneys to a potential criminal liability. The "Lawyers" group responded in the opposite direction that they would like to see the law appealed (44 %) or amended (32 %). It can be strongly argued that Article 306 remains perhaps the most unique (compared to Western legal systems) and most antagonizing provision in the Chinese Penal Code which grants a decided, unabashed favor on the side of the government.

8.5 Institutional Monopoly and Struggle for Control

In a juridical space such as a courtroom, power relationships between actors rely heavily upon the established rules and practices. Bourdieu's (1987) original discussion on the juridical institution of monopoly has focused on differentiating legal professionals (i.e., judges, prosecutors, and lawyers) from lay persons on the grounds of legal knowledge and acceptance of the specific rules of conduct in the courtroom. It would make sense to argue that within the juridical space shared by the legal professionals, the division of labor among actors also creates subfields with boundaries that are set by law and enforced by practice. In other words, there is a need to look closely at *how* one group of legal professionals manipulates access to information and knowledge to gain unfair advantage against its competition. Response based on a few survey questions from the pilot study can shed lights on this question.

As Fig. 8.13 indicates, lawyers, "iron triangle," and other survey respondents all agree that "materials omitted from case dossier" constitutes the greatest difficulty for criminal defense lawyers (56.6, 51.4, and 61.3 %, respectively). Lawyers report

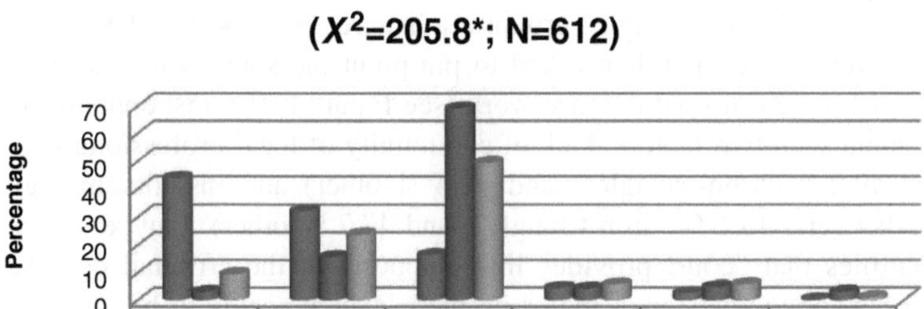

	Repeal	Amend	Unchange	Doesn't matter	Unsure	Other
Lawyers	44	32.3	16.4	4.4	2.6	0.3
C/P/P	3	15.7	69.3	4.2	4.8	3
Other	9.5	23.8	49.5	5.7	5.7	1

Fig. 8.12 Views of proposed change in Article 306 of the Chinese criminal law

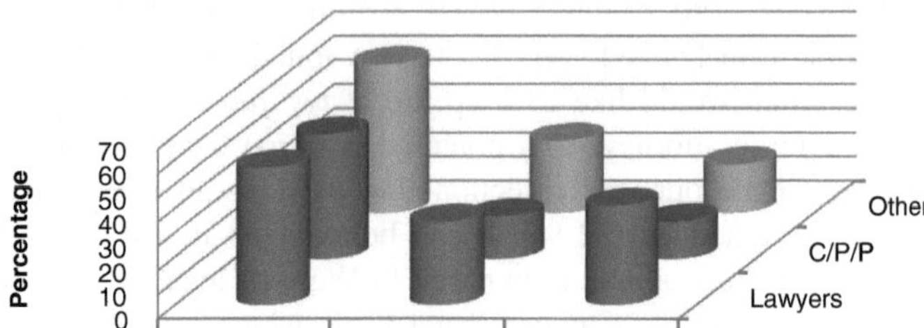

	Materials omitted (X2=2.81)	Photocopying not allowed (X2=15.99*)	Photocopying too expensive (X2=43.12*)
Lawyers	56.6	34.2	40.8
C/P/P	51.4	17.5	15.3
Other	61.3	29.7	19.8

Fig. 8.13 Lawyer's difficulties in accessing case file

additional major difficulties to include "photocopying not allowed" and "photocopying too expensive." These problems currently lie in gray areas of the law and by default fall largely within the discretion of the court officials. However, even with explicit provisions in law, lawyers' rights to fully defend their clients are inadequate, conditional, and under-protected.

Figure 8.14 illustrates the outcomes in response to the questions: what does the court do when a criminal defense lawyer asks to: (1) call for witness to testify; (2) collect new evidence; (3) reappraise existing evidence; and (4) submit new evidence. It is clear that there is no guarantee that the rights supposedly enjoyed by the lawyers in executing their responsibilities as defense counsels are actually realized. Less than 40 % of the lawyers in our survey say they had approval from the court to call witnesses to testify or to collect new evidences. Courts granted approval to lawyers' requests to submit new evidences only about half of the time (both lawyers and "iron triangle" groups are in agreement, 54.5 and 55.7 % in their responses, respectively). When asked to pin-point the sources for the great difficulties in Chinese criminal defense work (see Figure 8.15), respondents are more in agreement with two factors: lack of community of legal professionals (55.5 %-lawyers; 49.2 %-"iron-triangle"; and 41.4 %-other) and insufficient legislation (55.7 %-lawyers; 40.1 %-"iron-triangle"; and 47.7 %-other). Lawyers as a group also identifies that "court provides little support" to the criminal defense work (61.5 % lawyers agreed) as a major problem, which seems to be an assessment disputed by the "iron triangle" group (only 29.9 % "iron triangle" group would agree). There remains an issue of public misunderstanding of criminal defense lawyers' work (i.e., the sentiment that defense lawyers help bad guys avoid punishment) but the extent of such misunderstanding as an obstacle of criminal defense seems to be a less serious factor compared to the others.

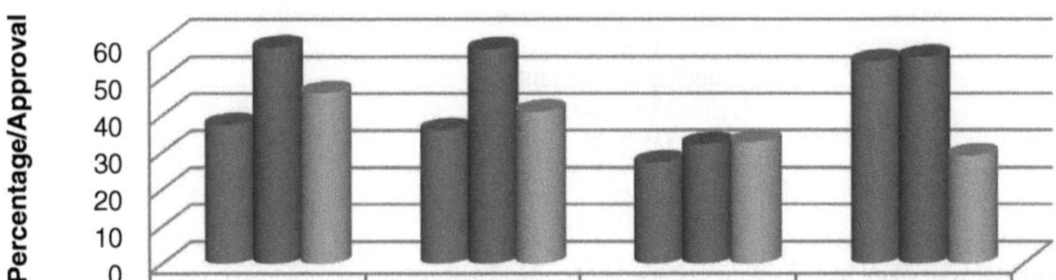

	Call for witness to testify (X2=44.94*)	Collecting new evidence (X2=50.64*)	Reappraisal of evidence (X2=32.62*)	Submit new evidence (X2=86.63*)
Lawyers	37.4	36	27.2	54.5
C/P/P	58.3	57.8	32.1	55.7
Other	46	41	32.7	29

Fig. 8.14 What does the court do when lawyers ask for the followings?

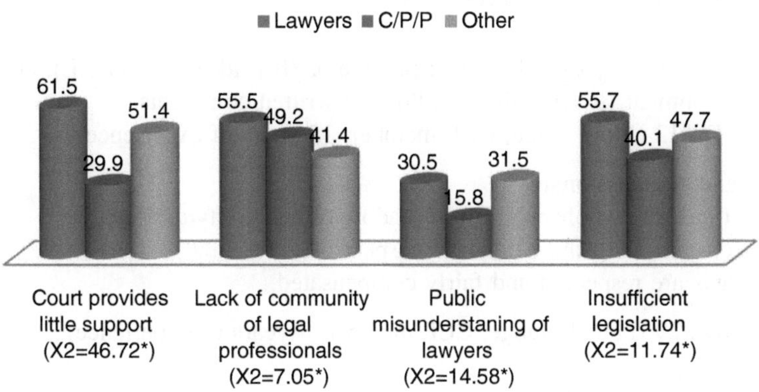

Fig. 8.15 Major correlates for the problems in Chinese criminal defense work

In spite of the legislative struggle to afford greater rights to the lawyers and their clients, the most recently revised Chinese Lawyer's Law (2007) fell short in its actual implementation. Figure 8.16 reveals a consistent pattern of assessment on five major defects in actualizing lawyers' rights across three occupational groups, i.e., rights to review case dossier are unclear or insufficient; no remedies protecting lawyers' rights; right for correspondence with client abolished; lack of defense against procedural unfairness; and lack of rights to represent client at police investigation. Lawyers claim the existence of these problems to the greatest extent, in sharp contrast to the corresponding assessments by the "iron triangle" group. The results reported by the "other" respondents fall in between.

A worthy question may be asked: what are the current states of mind representative of the Chinese legal practitioners and, as agents of law, are they converging upon some common grounds that define the ideal *modus vivendi* and *modus operandi* respective to their professions. Asked with four open-ended questions at the end of our survey of legal practitioners in J Province, respondents

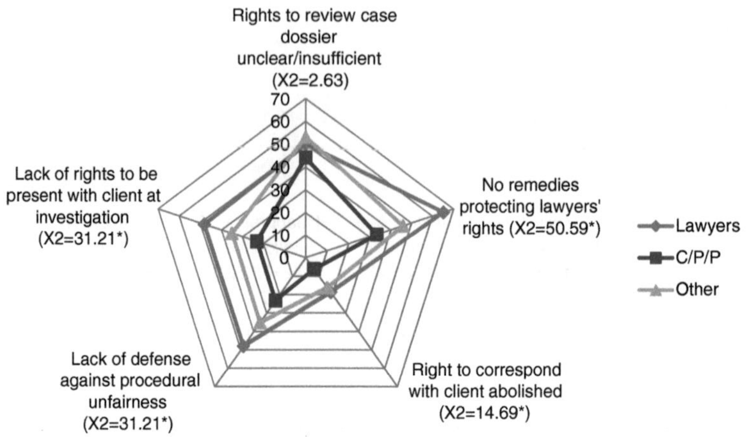

Fig. 8.16 Major defects in the Lawyer's Law

describe their ideal judge (IJ), ideal procurator (IP), ideal lawyer (IL), and ideal court environment (ICE) with the following written comments.[12]

Case ID #12 (Male judge, CCP member, 15 years of experience):

IJ: Fair and compassionate
IP: Don't cast the whole world in a shadow of negativity/darkness
IL: Be considerate to the defendant; respectful of the law
ICE: Judges are respected and fairly compensated.

Case ID #29 (Female judge, CCP member, 4 years of experience):

IJ: Symbol of fairness
IP: Symbol of justice
IL: Professional; modest manner
ICE: Division of labor in fulfilling professional duties.

Case ID #45 (Male procurator, CCP member, 7 years of experience):

IJ: Value neutral
IP: Righteous
IL: Professional
ICE: Balance of power between prosecution and defense.

Case ID #15 (Female procurator, CCP member, 10 years of experience):

IJ: Professional; Does not cave into political pressure
IP: Honest; professional

[12] We intent to offer flavors of responses from a small sample with a mixture of gender, occupational status, CCP affiliation, and years of work experience of respondents. Unfortunately, almost all of the police officers and most of the procurators in our sample offered no additional written comments.

IL: Honest; not a gold-digger
ICE: Fair; allow all parties to speak freely.

Case ID #57 (Male, no party affiliation, lawyer, 3 years of experience)

IJ: Like those in America
IP: Like those in America
IL: Like those in America
ICE: Prosecution and defense are treated equally in a neutral court.

Case ID #120 (Female, CCP member, lawyer, 30 years of experience)

IJ: Upright, professional, and courteous
IP: Same as above
IL: Professional, charismatic, capable of making penetrating arguments
ICE: Designate office space inside court building for visiting lawyers.

Case ID #44 (Male, CCP member, non-legal professional):

IJ: Able to resist undue pressure; can uphold justice and fairness
IP: Follow the road of judicial fairness; let leaders of the Party and government get lost!
IL: Be a true professional; dare to fight for justice and provide the best defense for the client; make honest money
ICE: It is only possible when the large socio-political environment is improved.

Case ID #62 (female, CCP member, non-legal professional):

IJ: Easy to communicate; respect the rights of the defendant and defense attorney
IP: Respect lawyers, polite
IL: Not an anti-social type; not hostile toward judges; be responsible to the defendant
ICE: Not interfered with by the public power; realization of substantive justice via procedural justice.

Although only a small sample of the responses is offered here, we begin to see patterns that are both generic and occupation-specific. Traces of Western inspired rule of law concepts and practices are indeed detected, especially among legal professionals of the younger generation. The most frequently used terms in describing an ideal judge are the words such as "fairness" and "equality." Similarly, some of the most frequently used words to describe an ideal procurator include "justice" and "righteousness", in addition to the use of word of "fairness." In contrast, an ideal lawyer is described in myriad ways bookended by the claims such as "I have never seen a good lawyer" (Case ID #150, male/CCP/judge) to "Those like in America" (Case ID #57, Male/no party affiliation/lawyer). It seems that when commenting on ideal lawyers, judges and procurators are more likely to invoke two words: "responsibility" (i.e., making an effort to provide the best defense for the client) and "professionalism" (i.e., having the ability to provide quality defense work), while lawyers tend to focus on one word only, that is "professionalism." Lastly, the consensus in the descriptions of an ideal courtroom (from all occupational groups) is presented by three key words: "independent", "fair", and "neutral".

8.6 The Visible and Invisible Fences

Unlike general findings reported in Chap. 5, we select a unique set of questions to gauge the perceptions of power and control in Chinese criminal trials by comparing and contrasting the responses from three occupational groups: "lawyers", "iron triangle", and a catch-all "other". We found ample empirical evidences of deep divisions, mistrust, and contentions between the "iron triangle" and a maturing profession of lawyers that is now relatively "unhooked" from the State.[13] As Michelson (2003) correctly pointed out a decade ago, "the plight of (Chinese) lawyers mirrors that of private business entrepreneurs." Both professions continue to depend on "key gatekeepers and decision-makers in government agencies." There appear to be two layers of fences that prevent Chinese criminal defense lawyers from doing what lawyers should and could do (e.g., in a Common Law system). The visible fence is erected in the name of socialist legality with Chinese characteristics that lawyers are structurally inhibited from being effective in providing the best legal defense. This is a concrete, external boundary forced upon all defense lawyers through various provisions included in the Chinese Criminal Procedure Law. It is a manifestation of symbolic power to shape and transform the world by "transforming the words for naming it, by producing new categories of perception and judgment, and by dictating a new vision of social divisions and distributions." (Bourdieu 1987) Data presented in this chapter reaffirms the prevailing existence of the dilemmas facing Chinese criminal defense attorneys today: difficulties in meeting with clients, collecting and submitting new evidences, reappraising existing evidences, accessing case files, and bringing witnesses to court to testify. To make matters worse, these structural deficiencies applicable to the criminal defense lawyers are compounded with a deep culture of distrust, disregard, and disrespect of the individual rights of the criminal defendants/suspects.

The invisible fence, on the other hand, is the outcome of learned experience. It is the *habitus* (Bourdieu 1977) accumulated from practicing law on an uneven playing field that favors only the government apparatus. The boundary of such an invisible fence, however, remains internal and indeterminate. As well stated by Jones (2003, p. 40), "the ultimate form of the Chinese legal system cannot be

[13] "Unhook" is the literal English translation of the Chinese word "**脱钩**" (*tuo gou*), which captures the image of Chinese lawyers' symbolic occupational separation from the judicial apparatus. The legal practice of Chinese lawyers as an occupational group remains under control at local level by the Bureau of Justice and at national level by the Ministry of Justice.

predicted at the present time. It seems likely that it will continue to look like a western system but contain the influence of its own traditions besides in ways that are hard to foresee."

References

Belkin, I. (2011). China's tortuous path toward ending torture in criminal investigations. *Columbia Journal of Asian Law, 24*, 273–302.

Bourdieu, P. (1987). The force of law: Toward a sociology of the juridical field (translated by Richard Terdiman). *Hastings Law Journal,38*, 805–853.

Bourdieu, P. (1977). *Outline of a theory of practice*. Cambridge: Cambridge University Press.

Brown, R. C. (1997). *Understanding Chinese courts and legal process: Law with Chinese characteristics*. Hague: Kluwer Law International.

Chen, J., & Dickson, B. J. (2010). *Allies of the state: China's private entrepreneurs and democratic change*. Cambridge: Harvard University Press.

Congressional-Executive Commission on China. (2010). *Annual report. One-hundred eleventh congress, second session*. Retrieved from http://www.cecc.gov

Dezalay, Y., & Madsen, M. R. (2012). The force of law and lawyers: Pierre Bourdieu and the reflective sociology of law. *Annual Review of Law and Social Science,8*, 433–452.

Efron, B. (1982). *The Jackknife, the bootstrap and other resampling plans*. Philadelphia: Siam Publishing.

Efron, B. (1979). Bootstrap methods: Another look at the jackknife. *Annals of Statistics,7*, 1–26.

Inglehart, R. & Welzel, C. (2009, March/April). Development and democracy: What we know about modernization today. *Foreign Affairs*, 33–41.

Jones, W. C. (2003). Trying to understand the current Chinese legal system. In S. Hsu (Ed.), *Understanding Chinese legal system: Essays in honor of professor Jerome A. Cohen* (pp. 7–45). New York: New York University Press.

Lawyers Committee for Human Rights. (1993). *Criminal justice with Chinese characteristics: China's criminal process and violation of human rights*. New York: Lawyers Committee for Human Rights.

Liu, S., & Halliday, T. C. (2011). Political liberalism and political embeddedness: Understanding politics in the work of Chinese criminal defense lawyers. *Law and Society Review,45*, 831–865.

Lu, H., & Miethe, T. D. (2002). Legal representation and criminal processing in China. *British Journal of Criminology,42*, 267–280.

Lubman, S. (2003). The study of Chinese law in the United States: Reflections on the past and concerns about the future. *Washington University Global Studies Law Review,2*, 1–35.

Michelson, E. (2008). Dear lawyer Bao: Everyday problems, legal advice, and state power in China. *Social Problems,55*, 43–71.

Michelson, E. (2006). The practice of law as an obstacle to justice: Chinese lawyers at work. *Law and Society Review,40*, 1–38.

Michelson, E. (2003). Unhooking from the state: Chinese lawyers in transition (Ph.D. Dissertation, University of Chicago).

Terdiman, R. (1987). Translator's introduction. The force of law: Toward a sociology of the juridical field by Pierre Bourdieu. *The Hastings Law Journal,38*, 805–813.

Zheng, Y. (2009). Can the communist party sustain its rule in China? In K. Lee, J. -H. Kim, & W. T. Woo (Eds.), *Power and sustainability of the Chinese state* (pp. 186–209, Chap. 10). London: Routledge.

Zuo, W. (2007). Empirical study on the operation mechanism of criminal procedure in china (中国刑事诉讼运行机制实证研究). Beijing: Law Press (法律出版社).

Chapter 9
Conclusion: Making Sense of Chinese Criminal Trials

Chinese culture and law have many features. Both have been flexible and adaptive for centuries and, both were radically reshaped in the twentieth century. With a focus on China's attempt to accelerate its legal and criminal justice reform efforts in the past two decades, this study shows in a limited fashion what the effects of some of these innovations have been: they are modest at best. The current Chinese juridical practice is set in a political climate that can be defined as adaptive authoritarianism where elements of the rule of man, rule by law, and rule of law coexist. The field of Chinese criminal justice can be figuratively described as a "fenced-off playground with paternalistic guards." (The Economist 2013)[1] There is a general recognition that China's economic ascendance in recent decades has created a genuine dilemma pitting a liberated (and increasing liberal) grassroots economic spirit against the old, stifling political constraints induced by the government. In particular, researchers have noticed the expanded expectation for the Chinese court to serve not only as impartial and effective adjudicators of private disputes but also as necessary checks on state power (Liebman 2008).

Contemporary Chinese criminal trials conducted at the grassroots level are in limbo. Organizationally, Basic People's Courts in China are inundated with ever increasing volumes of cases without corresponding increases in the number of judges (see Fig. 9.1).[2] Resources (e.g., judges, courtroom spaces, and other budgetary needs) allocated for criminal trials are often a second priority, after the more urgent needs for handling civil and economic cases are met. Criminal cases tried in Basic People's Court mostly involve relatively less serious criminal offenses perpetrated by the most disadvantaged, powerless and neglected social underclass. Isolated individual criminal incidents (compared to highly visible collective incidents which may or may not end in court; see in Chap. 3) have yet to pose immediate threat to social stability. To a great extent, Chinese criminal trials

[1] The quote was originally used to describe the current status of Chinese internet.

[2] The President of the Supreme People's Court pointed out in his 2009 Annual Report (SPC 2010) to the National People's Congress a major problem due to shortage of judges overall, quality of judges in the peripheral regions (central and western), and exploding caseloads in large and medium sized cities. See also Liebman (2007).

N. He, *Chinese Criminal Trials*, DOI: 10.1007/978-1-4614-8205-5_9,

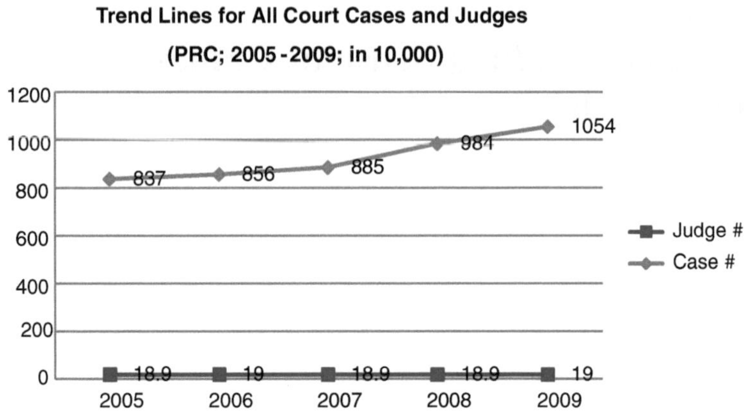

Fig. 9.1 Trend lines for all court cases and judges (PRC; 2005–2009; in 10,000)

have remained as mundane, secondary procedures in an administrative-judicial continuum where the fate of criminal defendants seems to have been sealed at the conclusion of the administrative stage (i.e., the police investigation).

In an investigation-centric legal system (see Chaps 6 and 7), there is little courtroom drama to speak of. In most criminal cases tried at grassroots level, there are limited legal representations for the criminal defendants, very little new evidences presented by the defense and rarely any witnesses who come to testify. As a result, no cross-examination is necessary and no challenges to the prosecution's evidences are expected (or accepted) by the court (see Chap. 8). Chinese criminal trials thus may be characterized as rehearsed plays with dispirited actors. Every player knows or is expected to know the outcome beforehand. Scripts of sentencing recommendations and defense arguments that were prepared prior to the trials are submitted at the end of the trial mostly without change. Sensitive or difficult cases are discussed and decided by court's de facto power center-the Adjudication Committee, before being assigned to trial judges. Final court judgments are reviewed, revised, and approved before they are announced.

Inside the courtrooms, trial judges are often impatient and bored at the same time, pressured by heavy caseload, and weighed down by procedural hypocrisy (see Chap. 7); procurators are frequently absent[3] or seen as arrogant (e.g., Liang 2008),[4] and defense lawyers are sometimes as clueless and helpless as their clients, and their professionalism is questioned or questionable (see Chap. 8). In spite of all these, the forced transparency expected of the court trials and the heightened public expectation on procedural justice have made the Chinese courtroom a needed symbolic center stage where the flame of hope for both procedural and

[3] It is allowable in simplified criminal trials where the defendant has already pleaded guilty to the charge and the estimated sentence is under 3 years of imprisonment.

[4] Liang (2008) describes that procurators sometimes refuse to stand up when the judges are entering the courtroom to showcase their equal or superior occupational status.

substantive justice is expected to be put on display. It is in the spirit of reconciling the harsh realities and the noble expectations that we tie this book with the following final thoughts.

Context always matters. Chinese legality which is used as the common thread in this book remains a contestable concept. The collision between the western impressions of the Chinese socialist legality and the native Chinese interpretations (via public media, political, and academic discourses) has created animosity with wide mood-swings. The typical western impression of Chinese law and legal system is preconditioned on the liberal-democratic rule of law as a taken for granted universal ideal. Some Western scholars have shown strong interest in gauging the status and process of China's legal history and the compatibility of Chinese civilization and legal culture with the western conception of the rule of law. A plethora of insightful studies have been produced, many of which have been cited in the current study. Western politicians and media, however, have a tendency to focus exclusively on the negative incidents of abuse and the neglect of human rights in the Chinese criminal justice system. They did so without paying sufficient attention to the Chinese cultural–historical context or giving credit to the indigenous solutions and progresses made.[5] In response to the external criticisms, the Chinese government takes a defensive (and increasingly defiant) position to claim victim of the external interference of China's domestic affairs on the one hand, and expose the high violent crime rates and discriminatory criminal justice practices of certain western countries on the other. The prevailing Chinese *nationalist sentiment* of learning from the West to defeat the West and the *socialist legality with Chinese characteristics* (see Chap. 1), although keys to unlock the puzzling current criminal justice practices are rarely made relevant or well understood in the communications between the acrimonious parties. This omission is quite unfortunate.

We made an attempt to operationalize Chinese law's rationale, spirit, and authority throughout this book. The first three chapters are intended to bridge the past with the present, to locate the source for the *habitus* (Bourdieu 1977) of the Chinese civilization and to explore its relevance to the evolving Chinese legal system. It is worth repeating that, during much of the time under imperial rule, penal law is to be feared and avoided at all cost. Legalized torture was the norm and the predicament applies to all parties involved in a criminal trial. In fact, criminal trials were conducted so as to prevent trials in the future. This is an intentional outcome consistent with the confines of Confucian orthodoxy where

[5] A recent example is the 2011 Annual Report released by the US Congressional-Executive Commission on China. The Report states that "During the Commission's 2011 reporting year, the Chinese government's failure to uphold legal protections for criminal suspects and defendants, promote transparency of the judicial process, and implement legal reforms highlighted ongoing programs within the criminal justice system." (p. 80) The Report went on to introduce actual cases (with real victims' names used) in each of the seven areas: abuse of police power, pretrial detention and prisons, arrest and trial procedure issues, arbitrary detention, medical parole, and capital punishment.

law is placed lowly in the hierarchy of conduct norms. Rule by law (associated with pain and punishment) placed alongside with rule of man (associated with paternalistic Magistrate) became a *doxa* (Bourdieu 1977), the undisputed and undiscussed habit of mind of the Chinese for thousands of years. The resignation by the Chinese public to the weight of their pacifist tradition bears some responsibility to either the tolerance of despotic rule in Imperial China and a gram of at the current time with the CCP as the surrogate emperor, or the lack of outrage against systematic suppression of individual rights in favor of social order and collective gain.

The western rule of law's introduction to China in late nineteenth century and early twentieth century never really gained momentum before the country was tossed back into decades of warfare and continuous revolutionary struggles. The language of rule of law in a new country easily betrays the spirit of rule of law from its origin. Individualism that characterizes the Western notion of rule of law is a flavor that is missing from the Chinese notion of rule of law based on collectivism. This is true in late Qing as it is likely true in the later decades of the twentieth century. Whenever rule of law reforms are stifled, China gravitates to the familiar tradition of the past regardless of the painful memories. Twice in the same (twentieth) century, rule of law was a mantra touted by reformers with a nationalistic mandate. Either at the beginning of the twentieth century when nation building with collective rights placed over individual rights or at the end of the twentieth century when fighting for the survival of the socialist state amidst the whirlwind of global democracy movement and collapsing former socialist States, rule of law in China was never about enhancing individual rights nor restraining state power. The legal system is necessarily politicized to solidify both state power and sovereignty. In other words, the rule of law in China's modern history is no more than a recitation of the instrumental rule by law mantra heard throughout its long imperial history. Rule of law was promoted in China to repair injured national pride or threatened national sovereignty. The translated rule of law language is to some a part of guided action driven by utilitarian and manipulative reformers. To others, this rule of law promotion is simply the tail that wagged the dog.

Chinese domestic legal scholarship is increasingly eclectic, representing a full spectrum of standpoints, from genuine western admirers at one end to staunch traditionalist at the other. Still, a sizeable segment of the population seems to sit squarely in the middle of all debates. First-hand empirical evidences from the MacArthur pilot study in China reaffirm this observation among legal practitioners. It is no exaggeration that the current socio-political context in China offers a prime opportunity to reconnect with China's ancient legal history and to reassess China's commitment to embrace rule of law as a component of modern legality. So far it has been proven difficult if not impossible to interfuse the non-native, liberal-democratic rule of law principles with the millennial tradition of "Chinese Constitutionality." (de Bary 2000).

The Chinese government continues to instill suspicions against the foreigners' true intentions and treats the western rule of law's promotion in China synonymously as imperialistic impulses. The propaganda's impact is far greater in a

Fig. 9.2 Trust: world value survey-China (2007)

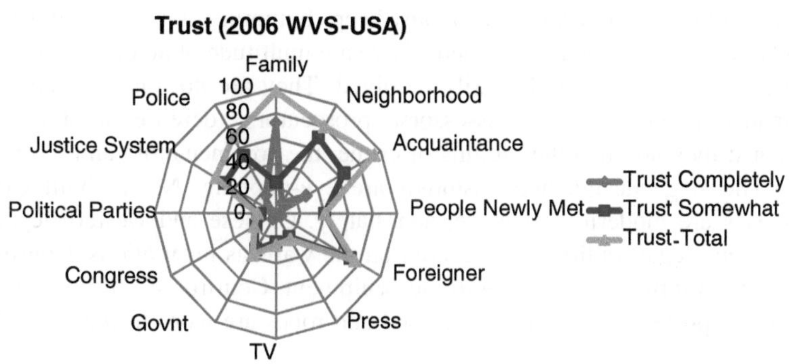

Fig. 9.3 Trust: world value survey-USA (2006)

country like China than elsewhere. The historical humiliations suffered by the Chinese are written into the Preamble of the Constitution. Comparing China with the U.S. with the same set of questions measuring "trust" of various institutions (see Figs. 9.2 and 9.3),[6] one quickly discerns both the similarity of high degree of trust in "family," "neighborhood" and "acquaintance", and the vast differences in the trust toward public institutions such as the branches of the government and media outlets. The Chinese clearly place far greater trust in their public institutions including the police, the justice system, political parties, People's Congress, and central government. This is hardly the impression one would get from the news media and government reports from outside China. Simply stated, the fact that the Chinese rarely trust any foreigners and foreign governments remains both

[6] China participates irregularly in the World Value Survey (WVS). The 2007 WVS-China survey and the 2006 WVS-USA survey are the closest comparison we can have.

unchanged and difficult to change.[7] Most significant of all, this means that the renewed rule of law promotion in China would have to be more adaptation than adoption. In addition, it is also more likely to motivate indigenous solutions that would allow imitations of selective western legal practices, scientific methods, and organizational management know-how without compromising the socialist spirit of law and legal practice.[8] Relating to the study and understanding of Chinese criminal trials, the juxtaposition of the foreign and domestic legal practices can be understood as a lively performance produced for public consumption.

What we are witnessing can be described as a Chinese rule of law dance that is vivid in appearances but dull in substance. The choreographers are at all levels of government-central, provincial, and local. The show's ultimate promoter is the CCP's all-out propaganda machinery including the powerful state-controlled media outlets.[9] Foreign states, NGO parties, and old or new China-hands watch on with cautious optimism at best. Resources needed to sustain the theatrical outfit are abundant as long as the Chinese economy keeps humming along and the needs for the continued appearance are justified. There are multitude of actors and audiences who are voluntarily or involuntarily involved. They are not only the courtroom participants-judges, people's assessors, prosecutors, defense attorneys, and defendants; they are also the victims of crime, the commentators and the general public. The stage design and costumes are eye-popping. Newly built Chinese courthouses are modern, expensive, and stately. Chinese and western legal philosophers and legal traditions are carved on the walls as inspirations. Courtrooms are filled with top-of-the-line electronic equipment. Courtroom setting now looks western and professional. Gavels are used and robes are worn to replace military

[7] Pye's ([1968] 1992) writing on the spirit of Chinese politics touches upon the paradox between a Chinese "superiority complex" (i.e., historical greatness and longevity of Chinese civilization) and a Chinese "inferiority complex" (e.g., scientific development, modern economic, military, and political power). The Chinese lack of sustainable enthusiasm and conviction for westernized reforms and modernity is in sharp contrast to the experience of Japan.

[8] For example, Liebman (2007) cited the explicit warning from Cao Jianming-the Vice-President of Supreme People's Court that the People's Courts need to follow Party leadership and avoid negative influence of Western rule of law theory.

[9] The propaganda operation is increasingly sophisticated. For example, a White Paper on Chinese Judicial Reform (State Council Information Office 2012) is released via Internet with the assistance of the State Internet Information Office. The White Paper manages to avoid making any mention of CCP leadership or directives. It references Chinese traditional legal heritage and uses language such as "learning from the legal advancement in human civilizations" prior to descriptions of western-inspired reform measures such as sentencing guidelines (where American influence is evident), case guidance system (inspired by but distinguishable from the Common Law Case Precedent system), case management system (drawing from modern management theory), simplified trial procedure (which came out of a plea bargaining experiment), judicial transparency and democracy, right to counsel, right against self-incrimination, exclusionary rules, witness protection system, community correction, and etcetera.

style uniforms.[10] Judges demonstrate the artistic side of the (Confucian) scholar-official qualities through calligraphy, painting, and photography works dotting along the hall ways in the workplace (see Chap. 7). Judges and procurators are now required to be trained in conducting empirical research and are expected to publish research articles as part of their annual evaluation and professional development. The cultivation of "spiritual civilization" and "professionalism" among criminal justice officials is used to enhance legitimacy and give essence to the image of a modern socialist rule of law with Chinese characteristics.

The inspiring exterior courthouse design, the soft touches inside the courtrooms and the cultivation of justice officials as true professionals and cultured public servants project hope to the realization of a tripartite alliance of the Chinese traditions of rule of man and rule by law with the reengineered rule of law. The appearance of public participation in delivering justice has also seen improvement. For example, in recent years, some provinces require that the number of people's assessors selected in each jurisdiction should be no less than the number of judges in the corresponding local court. Experimentations of "people's jury system" can be found in some provinces (Cohen 2011).[11] In what was described as "controlled transparency," courts are increasing their openness and at the same time working with the media to generate positive image of the courts (Liebman 2007). The assumptions and consumption of justice in Chinese legal practices are quietly evolving, motivated by pragmatic needs presented by a changing social reality. To be fair, this is hardly a unique Chinese experience. Reflecting on the experience of the U.S., political scientist Robert McCloskey (1960) argued long before that the U.S. Supreme Court has learned to become an adaptive institution that responds nimbly to the "drift in public opinion and the distribution of power in the American republic" (p. 223) and, it did so by operating "near the margins rather than in the center of political controversy." (p. 229).

A Chinese model of legal development and criminal justice practice should be regarded as not only possible but necessary. The scientific development in the Chinese field of law and justice is increasingly evidence-based (He 2014). Dewey's early twentieth century call for pragmatic reforms and experimentations in Chinese education as well as in politics seems to be in full swing a century after. The Chinese culture, law and criminal justice should be viewed as semiotic. Their interactions are likely to transform both quantitatively and qualitatively. The global rule of law enterprise has already influenced China and may be influenced as much by the Chinese experience. The Chinese communitarian strand of rule of law model based on a collective democracy is likely to compliment the western

[10] Unlike the hammer-shaped "gavel" used in the west, an "oblong, square piece of hardwood of about one foot long" was used by Chinese imperial magistrates when conducting trials in ancient time. Chinese call it 惊堂木 or "wood that frightens the hall." (van Gulik [1956] 1997: 315).

[11] The so-called "people's jury system" uses carefully selected local citizens to participate in trials in consultation roles. The group (7–9 people, aged 23–70) may express opinions that are not legally binding. The "innovation" is intended to enhance legitimacy of the court and increase transparency of the trials.

liberal-democratic model. The future challenges are the adaptation of historical Chinese principles and ethical standards to the demands of modern global capitalism and capitalist values. New conversations could benefit from looking at both the degrees and varieties of the rule of law, and both the normative discourses and empirical evidences.

In many aspects, the American legal practices and legal scholarships are highly informative to China. Skolnick's (2012) review of the legacies of the sociology of criminal law and criminal justice in the U.S. offers a stern reminder of an unsettled old debate between the "legal realists" (represented by Yale Law School faculty who laid the foundation for the field of sociology of law in the 1930s) and the "conceptualists" (represented by the Harvard Law School faculty). The legal realists see the judicial decisions as reflecting the political philosophy of the judges, especially in deciding constitutional law cases. The conceptualists, on the other hand, insist that judges apply the black letter laws but do not make them. It was not difficult for Skolnick (2012:9) to reach his own conclusion based on two recent U.S. Supreme Court decisions, i.e., *Arizona v. U.S.* (2012; which concerns Arizona immigration law) and *Natl. Fed. Indep. Bus. V. Sebelius* (2012; which concerns Obama's health care law) that "…the Court uses constitutional law to accomplish social policy ends."

Judicial decision-making, especially at the U.S. Supreme Court level remains at the center of contention for social scientists and legal scholars in the U.S. While such inquiries have inspired interesting writings on the so-called "acceptable hypocrisies and the rule of law" (see Bybee 2010, 2012), the Chinese Supreme People's Court is blunt with its own goals: courts are to enforce the laws according to the strategic visions of the Party-Central in order to "protect economic growth, people's quality of life and social stability." (SPC 2010) The socialist legality with Chinese characteristics is undisguised in that Chinese courts at all levels are expected to follow guiding principles that are promulgated to safeguard (in order) the Party's interest, the People's interest and finally, the Constitution and laws. This is to be achieved through application of "scientific development perspective" (科学发展观) with eclectic local innovations and adaptations. "Science" is now a neutral term that is used to camouflage all ideas that are practical, regardless of their origins. Science is also the code word that launches all pragmatic ideas befitting a revisionist socialist ideology.[12] To the outside world, a distinction is intentionally made by the Chinese government to distinguish between the western liberal-democratic "rule of law" and the "socialist rule of law with Chinese characteristics." The adaptive use of "rule of law" language is already a significant progress from the type of blunt legal nihilism advocated under Mao's leadership. Exercises exemplified in the current study illustrate the utility of Bourdieu's

[12] The deposed former CCP General Secretary Zhao Ziyang commented in an audio-recorded interview before his death that "the primary stage of the socialism is capitalism." The official uses of languages such "socialist market economy" rather than "capitalism" and "socialist rule of law" rather than the common (western) notion of rule of law can be viewed as another example of Bourdieusian "misrecognition.".

sociology of juridical practices with focuses on the study of law in action and the symbolic struggle for power.[13] Although the scope of this study is necessarily modest, we find value and promise in bridging tradition and contemporary development for a better understanding of the rationale, spirit and the authority of Chinese law.

References

Bourdieu, P. (1977). *Outline of a theory of practice*. Cambridge: Cambridge University Press.

Bybee, K. J. (2012). Paying attention to what judges say: New directions in the study of judicial decision making. *The Annual Review of Law and Social Science,8*, 69–84.

Bybee, K. J. (2010). *All judges are political except when they are not: Acceptable hypocrisies and the rule of law*. Palo Alto: Stanford University Press.

Cohen, J. (2011). People's jury system: Is It possible in Mainland China? http://www.usasialaw.org/?p=5226

Congressional-Executive Commission on China. (2011). *Criminal Justice* (pp. 80–93)002E Annual Report, 2011. Washington, D.C

De Bary, W. T. (2000). *Asian values and human rights: A confucian communitarian perspective*. Cambridge: Harvard University Press.

Ewick, P., & Silbey, S. (1998). *The common place of law: Stories from everyday life*. Chicago: University of Chicago Press.

He, N. (2014). The Politics of numbers: Crime statistics in China. In L. Cao, I. Sun, & W. Hebenton (Eds.), *Handbook of Chinese criminology*. New York: Routledge Publishers.

Liang, B. (2008). *The changing Chinese legal system, 1978-present: centralization of power and rationalization of the legal system*. New York: Routledge.

Liebman, B. L. (2007). China's courts: Restricted reform. *Columbia Journal of Asian Law,21*, 2–44.

Liebman, B. L. (2008). China's courts: Restricted reform. *Columbia law school, public law and legal theory working paper group (an extended version of liebman, 2007)*. pp. 8–180.

Lubman, S. (2003). The study of Chinese law in the United States: reflections on the past and concerns about the future. *Global Studies Law Review,2*, 1–35.

McCloskey, R. (1960). *The American supreme court*. Chicago: University of Chicago Press.

Popkin, W. D. (2007). *Evolution of judicial opinion: Institutional and individual styles*. New York: New York University Press.

Pye, L. W. ([1968] 1992). *The Spirit of Chinese Politics*. Cambridge: Harvard University Press.

Skolnick, J. H. (2012). Legacies of legal realism: The sociology of criminal law and criminal justice. *The Annual Review of Law and Social Science,8*, 1–10.

Supreme People's Court. (2010). *Annual report of 2009*. PR China: Beijing.

The Economist (2013). China's internet: A giant cage. Special report on China and the internet. April 6th, 2013. http://www.economist.com/news/special-report/21574628. Access on 4/8/2013.

The State Council Information Office (PRC) (2012). China's Judicial Reform White Paper. http://www.scio.gov.cn/zfbps/ndhf/2012/201210/t1226622.htm. Accessed on 11/19/12.

U.S. Supreme Court (2012). Arizona v. U.S., 567 U.S.

U.S. Supreme Court (2012). National federation of independent business v. Sebelius, 567 U.S.

[13] Likewise, Stanley Lubman (2003) made the study of law in action (rather than texts) a major recommendation to western scholars.

Index

N. He, *Chinese Criminal Trials*, DOI: 10.1007/978-1-4614-8205-5,

MIX
Papier aus verantwortungsvollen Quellen
Paper from responsible sources
FSC® C105338

If you have any concerns about our products,
you can contact us on
ProductSafety@springernature.com

In case Publisher is established outside the EU,
the EU authorized representative is:
Springer Nature Customer Service Center GmbH
Europaplatz 3, 69115 Heidelberg, Germany

Printed by Libri Plureos GmbH
in Hamburg, Germany